BEAUFIGHTER

By the same author

Calshot, 1913-61
The Flying Elephants – 27 Squadron RFC/RAF
Mosquito at War
Hurricane at War
Airmen of World War One
Sunderland at War
Hampden Special
Beaufighter at War
Path Finders at War
Albert Ball, VC
For Valour – The Air VCs
Sopwith Camel – King of Combat
History of the RAF
Guns in the Sky – The AGs
Coastal Command at War
Spitfire
Fighter Command, 1936-68
Age of the Biplane
Air War over Europe, 1939—45
Desert Air Force at War (co-author)
Encyclopaedia of British Military Aircraft
Bomber Group at War
Images of Air War, 1939-45
Bomber Barons
Eugene Esmonde, VC, DSO
Wellington at War
Royal Air Force Handbook, 1939-45
Bristol Blenheim
Fighter Pilots of the RAF, 1939-45
Mosquito Squadrons of the RAF
Men of the Desert Air Force, 1940-43
Gloster Meteor
Men of Coastal Command, 1939-45
Bristol Fighter – King of Two-Seaters
Tales from the Bombers
The Wellington Bomber

Edited:
Bomber Pilot, 1916-18
Fighter Pilot on the Western Front
Wings over the Somme
Fall of an Eagle – Ernst Udet

BEAUFIGHTER

CHAZ BOWYER

WILLIAM KIMBER · LONDON

First published in 1987 by
WILLIAM KIMBER & CO. LIMITED
100 Jermyn Street, London SW1Y 6EE

ISBN 0-7183-0647-3

Photoset in North Wales by
Derek Doyle & Associates Mold, Clwyd
Printed in Great Britain by
Redwood Burn Limited, Trowbridge, Wiltshire.

Contents

'If men could learn from history,
what lessons it might teach us!'

– Samuel Taylor Coleridge, 1772-1834
Biographia Literaria, 18 Dec 1831

List of Illustrations

Acknowledgments

A book of this nature is only possible if the author obtains help and encouragement from very many people. As ever, I have been privileged to have received unstinting aid in so many ways from colleagues, friends, acquaintances, even total strangers during the period of research and compilation. Accordingly, I wish to record here my sincere gratitude to each of the following selfless 'assistants' in particular without whose help this book would not have reached fruition – listed in no significant order of precedence: Squadron Leader R.C.B. Ashworth; N.L.R. Franks; B. Robertson; R.C. Sturtivant; N. Parnell; K. Merrick; D. Vincent; K. Munson; J.B. Cynk; Flight Lieutenant A. Thomas, RAF; G. Pentland; F. Smith; L.G. Frise; R. Mack of the RAF Museum; T.J. Denny; Wing Commander H.J. Garlick, DFC; H.R. Rhodes; F. Pedgeon; L. Barcham, DFC; T. Armstrong, DFC; D. Marrow, DFC; B.F. Hartness; D.J. Innes; E.S. Welch; R.F. Chandler; R. Cartwright; S.J. McLaren; R. Loffill; N. Carr; K.L. Collett; P.T. Malone; Wing Commander C.V. Ogden; J.E.M. Young; E.W. Johnson; R. Aveyard; H.J. Meyer; the late J.C. Bell; Air Vice-Marshal D. Hughes, CB, CBE, DSO, DFC, AFC, MA; J.K. Gardner; Squadron Leader V. Cashmore RAAF; Group Captain R. Haines, OBE, DFC; Group Captain W.D. David, CBE, DFC, AFC; L. Green; the late MRAF Sir Thomas Pike, GCB, CBE, DFC; Air Chief Marshal Sir Christopher Foxley Norris, KCB, DSO, OBE, MA; I. Masson; G. Simister; H. Brotherton; K. Battrick; A. Chantrey; K.G. Thomas, DFC; P.J. Davies; Wing Commander G. McLannahan; P. Geldart; W.G. Hood; D. Gray and J. Richardson of Walkers Studios, Scarborough; Public Record Office, Kew; Imperial War Museum Photographic Library.

Introduction

The Bristol Beaufighter's prime claim to permanent fame in Royal Air Force annals is the simple fact that it was the most heavily-armed fighter of *any* type to see widespread operational service with the RAF from 1940 until the advent of airborne missiles in the late 1950s. Nevertheless, the 'Beau' had several other claims to prominence, particularly in the context of the war years 1940-45, when it was a major pioneer of RAF nightfighter defence of the United Kingdom and other theatres of war; provided Coastal Command with an outstandingly successful strike weapon for the unceasing maritime aerial war; and gave the Middle and Far East air forces a lethal low-level instrument of destruction; apart from demonstrating its ubiquity in a number of other minor roles never envisaged in its original design envelope. Conceived purely for wartime exigency, the Beaufighter was destined to remain in firstline service until 1960; while the gross total of nearly 6000 Beaus produced wholly or partly equipped a total of 77 Squadrons of the RAF, RCAF, RNZAF, RAAF, SAAF, USAAF, and FAA, a host of other flying units, and saw limited use by certain foreign air forces in the post-1945 era.

Despite the French connotation of its universal nickname 'Beau' it was not an aesthetically beautiful design, but a brutish, pugnacious-looking, unmistakable weapon of war. Any graces it possessed merely amounted to beauty in the eye of the beholder – that illogical, inexplicable attraction twixt 'beauty and the beast' so often encountered in human relationships. Indeed, the Beau's lines might readily be compared with the bunch-shouldered, snub-nosed, naked power of a finely-bred boxer canine – a pure fighting machine beloved by its 'owners'. Moreover, its muscle was not restricted to the astonishing weight and variety of armament it was capable of lifting. Beaus were truly tough in every facet, able to absorb frightening physical punishment and still deliver a live crew from any consequent crash-landing; an asset directly responsible for saving the lives of many hundreds of air crews, and which bred a deep confidence between man and machine by no means always engendered by many other wartime aircraft. A utilitarian hybrid in origin, the 'Mighty Beau' carved out a unique niche as one of the few all-time classic fighters ever to bear RAF roundels.

CHAZ BOWYER
Norwich, 1986

CHAPTER ONE

Roots

The chain of events which eventually resulted in the 'birth' of the mighty Beaufighter can be said to have originated in the late 1930s, when the Air Ministry, in close liaison with most British aircraft manufacturers, attempted to modernise the Royal Air Force's firstline equipment after nearly two decades of partial neglect, parsimonious budgeting, outright complacency by blinkered past governments, and – not least important – a very recent international industrial recession of almost catastrophic effect. During the years 1935-37 in particular a host of new aircraft design specifications were issued by the Air Ministry, inviting projects and tenders from the UK aviation industry. A majority of the eventual paper designs submitted in response to those specifications never progressed beyond their drawing boards – indeed, too many were patently impractical and/or simply a waste of effort – but others provided the genesis of several (later) outstanding aircraft for RAF service during World War Two.

High on the Air Ministry's list of priorities was the crucial need for ultra-modern fighter designs of monoplane configuration for aerial defence of the United Kingdom. Closely allied to such a necessity was the desire for substantial advances in aircraft armament for the new fighters in order to finally dispense with the long out-dated, standard two machine guns considered sufficient in RAF fighters for the previous 20 years. In pursuance of the latter requirement, two basic avenues of research and design were instigated. One view was to simply increase the number of standard 0.303-inch calibre Browning machine guns fitted up to eight; the other parallel line of thought was to replace the Brownings with heavier calibre shell guns i.e. cannons of 20mm or larger calibre.

Among many other individual aircraft manufacturers, the Bristol Aeroplane Company (later retitled Bristol Aircraft Ltd) submitted several designs for cannon-armed single-seat fighters to Air Ministry Specifications issued in 1935 and 1937 only to have these rejected. Nevertheless, the experience and research involved in these various projects left the Bristol design team, led by Frank Barnwell, well aware of the future trends required by the RAF and the Air Ministry. By August 1938 the Bristol company was fully engaged with production of its Blenheims and their derivant, the Beaufort torpedo-bomber, but on 2 August the company lost the invaluable services of their chief designer, Barnwell, who was killed in a flying accident. His place as head of the Bristol design team was taken over by Leslie G. Frise. A graduate of Bristol University, who had served with the Royal Naval Air Service (RNAS) at the outbreak of World War I, Frise had originally joined the Bristol company's design team, under Barnwell, in 1915, and was to make major contributions to Bristol aircraft design in subsequent years, including, in 1930, the design of the first Bristol gun turret, and the Frise aileron patented previously in 1921.

Within weeks of taking up his new appointment Frise and his team, along with all other British aviation designers, were shocked by the Munich Crisis with its razor-thin, eleventh-hour avoidance of all-out war with Nazi Germany, and activity within the company increased apace. Among other considerations, Frise and his colleagues recognised the RAF's contemporary lack of any long-range, preferably cannon-armed fighter in the short term prospect. Thus in October 1938, with the Beaufort just beginning to replace the Blenheim IV on Bristol's Filton production lines, Frise and his colleague Roy Fedden (later, Sir Roy) formed a proposal for a 'Beaufort Fighter' design which would utilise the existing Beaufort's wings, tail unit, and landing gear married to a redesigned fuselage to incorporate a battery of four forward- firing 20mm Hispano cannons in its belly, and be powered with Bristol Hercules engines in place of the Beaufort's Taurus powerplants (thereby giving a 50 per cent increase in power). In Frise's own words:

> The birth of the Beaufighter was unusual, and did not follow an Air Ministry Specification, but came about in this way. Just

> before the war we recognised the obvious and *urgent* need for a long-range fighter of decisive striking power. Now the design and construction of the prototype, testing, tooling, and putting into production of a new aircraft is a matter of a few years, however hard we try. Looking round for a solution to this difficulty I got the idea of using as many parts as possible of the Beaufort, and actually, by putting in the larger Hercules engines, and altering part of the body to take cannons and fighting equipment, was able to produce the required fighter in six months.*

On 15 October 1938 the first Beaufort prototype (L4441) made its first flight, and within a few days of that event the first layout of Frise's projected 'Beaufort Fighter' was submitted to the Air Ministry, where it was received with enthusiasm and resulted in prompt instructions for the Bristol team to proceed with four prototypes. Accordingly detail designs commenced at Filton from 16 November 1938 for what was now designated the Bristol Type 156 – the design receiving the name Beaufighter on 2 June 1939. At the start of the detail design Frise and his team projected a gross weight, fitted with Hercules VI engines, to be 16,000lb (7257kg), and estimated that the Hercules powerplants would, with hoped-for Rotol fully-feathering, constant speed airscrews, offer a maximum speed of 360 mph at 15,000 ft. Unfortunately, actual production of Hercules VI engines at the Accrington factory was then insufficient to meet Bristol Beaufighter production needs initially, while the designated Rotol propellers were also in short supply pro tem. Therefore it was decided to install Hercules III engines and De Havilland non- feathering, bracket-type 'props' in the first batch of Beaus, although this meant a revised estimated maximum speed of 335 mph at 13,500 ft (a figure which matched the Hawker Hurricane I).

Looking ahead immediately to further possible developments of the Beaufighter, two projects were suggested on 4 January 1939 for a three-seat bomber version with a dorsal gun turret incorporated (Bristol Type 157), and an 'improved' fighter variant with a much

* Lecture, 25 May 1942

slimmer fuselage – a so-termed 'Sports Model' – designated as Type 158; this latter being later recorded as 'Mk III' and 'Mk IV' Beaufighter, according to the engine installation to be used, whether Hercules or Griffon respectively. Although some progress was made with the design of the Type 158 in early 1940, the project was nullified by the start of the Battle of Britain and the more urgent need to concentrate on production of the original Beau design. On 3 July 1939 the Air Ministry placed a contract with Bristols for 300 Beaufighters – including the four prototypes already under way – and issued AM Specification F.17/39 to cover initial production standards required; there being no previous Specification which entirely met the case of the Beaufighter specifically.

This Specification called for an armament of just four 20mm Hispano cannons, but indicated that in view of the pressure on Hercules engine production at that time to fulfil the heavy bomber programmes, the Beau's engine installation should be readily interchangeable as a complete unit in order to accommodate possible alternative Rolls-Royce Griffon engines. Merely two weeks after the issue of AM Spec.F.17/39 the first Beaufighter prototype, serialled R2502, made its first test flight from Filton airfield on 17 July 1939, with the Bristol company's chief test pilot, Cyril Uwins at the controls. For this initial flight R2502 had been fitted with Hercules I-SM engines (precursors of the Hercules III) and had been flown 'clean' i.e. without any armament or other eventual Service equipment installed. By any standard, that first airborne test of a new prototype fighter design was a remarkable achievement – a mere six months after the first layout design had been drawn up.

The report on the Beaufighter's initial test flight indicated little real defects. The tendency to 'swing' on take-off – destined to be feature of all Beaus to some degree – was noted, with a recommendation for the fin area to be increased slightly; while it was suggested that the elevator control circuit be stiffened. However, with an eye on the future service use, which would include probable heavy landings by night, it was decided to exchange the Beaufort Vickers' main oleo-leg assembly fitted for a longer-stroke Lockheed unit. This modification reduced the

Views of R2052, the first Beaufighter prototype.

fuselage angle on the ground and necessitated cropping three inches off the initially-fitted 13ft airscrew diameters.

The second prototype, R2053, was also initially test-flown in 'clean' condition, but the third prototype, R2054, was fitted out with service operational equipment, which included four cannons with their blast tubes, a bullet-proof windscreen, internal armour plate, oxygen crate, radio mast, and a camera gun mounted on the fuselage top just behind the cockpit canopy. The remaining prototype, R2055, was set aside for armament development trials.

The first two prototypes, R2052 & R2053, were equipped to full standard and were then handed over to the RAF in the first week of April 1940. R2054, with its full service equipment installed, was delivered to the Aeroplane and Armament Experimental Establishment (A&AEE), Boscombe Down in June 1940 for Service trials, where its tested maximum speed was found to be only 309 mph at 15,000 ft, fitted with Hercules III engines (the intended production powerplants for future Beaus). Various suggestions for remedying this lower performance figure by replacing the Hercules IIIs with Hercules VIs or Rolls-Royce Griffons were nullified by unavailability of either type of engine immediately, and it was therefore decided to install Rolls-Royce Merlin XX in 450 of the Beaufighters now on the Filton productions lines – almost half of the 1218 aircraft in total officially contracted by then. The Merlin-engined version was to be designated Beaufighter Mk II, and three airframes, R2058, R2061, and R2062, were set aside as the Mk II 'prototypes' while awaiting availability of Merlin XXs.

The third Mk II prototype, R2062, was later destroyed during an enemy bombing raid on Filton on 25 September 1940, but in the interim R2058, fitted with Merlin XX engines – actually Mk Xs 'converted' to XXs – first flew at Hucknall on 14 June 1940, followed shortly after by R2061. The longer engine nacelles tended to increase each Beau's inherent wish to swing on take-off, resulting in both R2061 and R2062 being fitted with tall, angular fins and rudders – though this modification failed to cure the problem entirely.

Production contracts for Beaufighters were steadily increased in mid-1940, with two for 500 aircraft each being sub-contracted out to new shadow factories at Stockport (Fairey Aviation) and

Beau R2058, the prototype Mk II. Served with 25 Squadron in late 1940. Became Instructional airframe 3344M in Sept 1942.

Beau IIF,T3144 which was transferred to the FAA, 8/9/43.

Weston-super-Mare (Bristol company). These latter 1000 Beaus were to have six 0.303-inch calibre Browning machine guns mounted within wings – two in port wings and four in starboard wings – additional to the standard four 20mm Hispano cannons in the forward fuselage; an increase in muscle which was incorporated in all Beaus on Filton's production lines *after* the first 50 airframes to be completed. This combination of cannons and machine guns made the Beaufighter the most heavily armed fighter used by the RAF during 1939-45 – and for many years postwar for that matter.

Various experiments with alternative forms of armament were projected, although none were to be incorporated in production Beaus for RAF operational use. The fourth Mk I prototype, R2055, for example, was stripped of its intended quartet of 20mm cannons, these being replaced by two 40mm shell guns; a Vickers 'S' on the starboard side of the nose section and a Rolls-Royce 40mm on the port side; this trial eventually resulting in the adoption of the Vickers 'S' gun on Hawker Hurricane Mk IID 'tank-buster' aircraft as used operationally in the North African campaigns. Two others trials of revised armament were made in Beaus R2274 and R2306, both Merlin-engined, which were converted at Filton in March 1941 to replace standard armament, except two 20mm Hispano cannons, with a Boulton Paul BP1 four machine gun turret, as fitted in the ill-fated Boulton Paul Defiant fighter, located immediately aft of the pilot's cockpit – the normal observer's dorsal cupola being faired over. The idea was not adopted for a variety of technical reasons, not least being the fact that the turret obstructed the pilot's parachute exit. In this form the two Beaus were titled as Mk V, albeit being standard production Mk IIs apart from the experimental armament, and both Beaus were tested in firstline conditions by No 29 Squadron in May 1941.

Even before the Beaufighter began reaching RAF operational units, it had been recognised that the design was not the easiest aircraft to fly, having several inherent mini-vices. A majority of such irritations were quickly eliminated by modifications, but the constant attempt to veer off during take-off (particularly) and landing (to a lesser degree), though manageable, remained a permanent factor of Beau operation to some degree throughout the type's career. Moreover, the Beau displayed instability when flying at lower speed levels – such as climbing and letting down for landing – in the longitudinal plane; a facet which increased if flaps were lowered.

The designers made urgent attempts to cure such unstable characteristics in various ways. A production Mk I, R2268, was fitted with a wider-span, twin-tailed empennage but this failed to resolve the problem. Then another Mk I, R2057 and a Mk II, R2270 were modified to give their tailplane 12 degrees of dihedral – a successful ploy which later became a production feature. Both aircraft eventually flew operationally with firstline squadrons (Nos 25 and 604 Squadrons respectively) whose crews commented that the modification now made the aircraft *too* stable for combat manoeuvrability. R2057 was also the vehicle for another experimental installation, having Fairey-Youngman bellows-type dive-brakes fitted above and below the trailing edges of its outer wing panels (inboard of the ailerons); a modification intended for nightfighters initially but eventually to be a boon when the Beaufighter later became converted for torpedo-strike roles.

Finally cleared for RAF squadron service on 26 July 1940, five production Mk Is left Filton next day on delivery to the RAF Maintenance Units (MUs) where they were to receive final equipment, be tested, then issued to firstline units for operational use. Further Beaus were then delivered to the Fighter Interception Unit (FIU), starting with R2055 which reached the FIU on 12 August 1940, followed by R2059 marked 'A-2' on 1 September. While still with the FIU, R2059 had the distinction of flying the first-ever Beaufighter night operational sortie on the night of 4/5 September 1940, was then taken on charge of No 25 Squadron where it was coded ZK-A (later changed to ZK-H), but was lost on 12/13 September 1940. Beaufighter R2077, which had its initial service trials under the aegis of No 23 Squadron, a Blenheim IF unit based at Wittering/Collyweston in mid-1940, was then transferred to No 29 Squadron based at Digby from where, crewed by Wing Commander S.C. Widdows/Pilot Officer Watson, it made the first Beau night operational sortie *in squadron service* between 2355 and 0105 hrs on the night of 17/18 September 1940, albeit an unproductive patrol. The first four Beaufighters to reach firstline operational nightfighter squadrons each went to a different unit but all on the same date, 2 September 1940. These were R2056 to No 25 Squadron at Martlesham Heath; R2070 to No 219 Squadron at Catterick; R2072 to No 29 Squadron at Digby; and R2073 to No 604 Squadron at Middle Wallop/Coltishall. All four squadrons at that period were equipped with the makeshift Blenheim IF 'fighters'. Six days later, on 8 September, Beaus R2071 and R2076 became the first examples to be issued to No 600 Squadron based at Redhill.

The impact of the Mighty Beau on its new owners generated great enthusiasm – and no little awe. As the official unit diarist on No 29 Squadron described:

> The machine appears a very popular aircraft with those who have flown it. It is not much more difficult to fly at night than a Blenheim. The lack of nose in front of the pilot for approach and landing is rather strange, but the machine generally is more pleasant at night than a Blenheim owing to its superior manoeuvrability.

For one crew member of No 604 Squadron, the late C.F. – 'Jimmy' – Rawnsley (later, DSO, DFC, DFM), his first sight of the Beau was awe-inspiring:

> There she stood, sturdy, powerful, fearsome, surrounded by an enthusiastic crowd. Most of us admired from the outside as only those with influence or possessed extreme cunning got inside. Pilots, engineers, fitters, riggers, armourers and signals mechanics were in attendance, and they probed and tinkered and adjusted until they had brought her to a state of good-tempered serviceability. Then they all tiptoed quietly away for, like all young monsters in unfamiliar hands, she showed promise of being temperamental. Even Mick Wheadon, the Flight Sergeant in charge, was said to have been seen walking away backwards from the Presence ...*

By early 1941 actual production of Beaufighters had increased

* *Night Fighter* by R.C. Wright/C.F. Rawnsley; Collins, 1957

steadily. On 7 December 1940 the 100th Beau had rolled off the Filton production lines, to be followed by the 200th on 10 May 1941, including the first production Mk II (R2270) on 22 March 1941. Elsewhere other production Beaus began to flow from the Fairey and Weston-super-Mare workshops in February 1941. With the virtual cessation of German night raids on the UK in the spring of 1941 came the opportunity to seriously consider other forms of operational uses for the standard Beaufighter. Initial priority was given to a request from Coastal Command for 'long-range fighters' (*sic*) – an urgent need highlighted by the German occupation of Norway and the consquent threat to Allied shipping in the North Sea, and the possible resumption of attacks along the eastern coast of Britain by Norwegian-based Luftwaffe units. In response to that request, the Bristol design team modified a Mk I Beau, R2152, by removing all wing machine guns, providing a hinged table and necessary instruments for navigators, and replacing the camera gun on the top fuselage, just behind the pilot's cockpit, with a DF loop. The point of removing the wing guns was to install 50-gallon fuel tanks in their place, although initially these additional tanks had to be fitted inside the forward fuselage, between the cannons, until proper production-designed wing tanks became available. In this modified form the Beau was designated as Mk Ic (C for Coastal) and first deliveries went to No 252 Squadron, a unit of Coastal Command which had been reformed at Bircham Newton on 21 November 1940 under the command of Squadron Leader R.G. Yaxley, MC (later, Wing Commander, MC, DFC), then moved to Chivenor ten days later and began receiving Beau Mk Ics in December.

Declared fully operational by the end of March 1941, No 252 Squadron's crews commenced sorties on 6 April from their latest base, Aldergrove, and on 16 April claimed their first aerial victim when Flight Lieutenant Riley shot a Focke Wulf Fw 200 into the sea. In that same month German forces invaded Greece, resulting in another urgent request for Beaufighters to be despatched to the Mediterranean theatre. In response, 13 Beaus of 252 Squadron flew to Malta during the first week of May to be based on Luqa for operations commencing on 8 May. A proportion of the squadron's personnel, left behind at Nutts Corner, were then 'disbanded' on 15

T3177, a Mk II fitted experimentally with RR Griffon engines in 1941. Note installation of early AI radar.

R2274, a Mk V fitted with a BP1 four-gun dorsal turret. Service- tested on 29 Squadron, it later served with 406 Squadron RCAF, and was eventually SOC on 25/2/43.

June 1941 as 252 Squadron, but became the nucleus of No 143 Squadron which was reformed at Aldergrove on the same day, commanded by Squadron Leader G.G. Stockdale, as the second Coastal Command unit to be equipped with Beaufighter Ics. Remaining virtually an operational training unit for non-squadron air crews destined for overseas service, and flying a mix of Beaufighters and Blenheim IVs, No 143 Squadron finally became operational in its own right by October 1941, by when it was based at Sumburgh.

Even as Beaufighters steadily flowed to the squadrons in both Fighter and Coastal Commands, a variety of projected developments and/or experimental modifications were being applied to basic production-standard Beau Is and IIs at Filton. Much attention was given to providing higher power engines, including successful flights with Hercules VI power plants in Beau R2130; a projected 'high altitude' variant having Hercules VIII engines with two- stage blowers, though this came to nothing in the event; and Beau II, T3177 which went to Rolls-Royce as a testbed for that firm's Griffon IIB in-line engines. Most energy was put into improving the radial engined variants because of the contemporary heavy demand for Rolls-Royce Merlin engines for Lancasters, Spitfires and Hurricanes *et al* which inevitably incurred a shortage of such in-line engines for Beau IIs.

It might be added that the Beau Mk II was in any case not particularly liked by a majority of operational pilots, although such deprecation really depended on the pilot's previous experiences with other types of twin-engined aircraft. One skipper who disagreed with that general condemnation of the Merlin-Beau was Peter Geldart, who had first 'converted' on Beauforts – 'a hopelessly underpowered aeroplane, incapable of maintaining straight and level flight on one engine'. At No 54 OTU, Geldart's first Beau experience was in a Mk II:

> I found the Mk IIF fighter, with two Rolls-Royce Merlin XX 1280hp engines, a real pleasure to fly. It was the first operational aeroplane over which I felt I had complete mastery. It was docile to handle, fore and aft control was very delicate, and there was always a tendency to over-correct if one was ham-fisted ... I

> think what really sold me on the Beau was the excellent, unlimited forward vision – one felt like a Chinese idol sitting right out in front of everything and yet, paradoxically, everything in front of you.*

The next major Mark of Beaufighter to emerge was the Mk VI, which was basically a Mk I with Hercules VI engines instead of Hercules IIIs or XIs, and now rated for best performance at higher altitude than the standard Mk I. Although the Mk VI retained almost all Mk I features, certain modifications in the light of experience were to be incorporated in later production Mk VIs, the most apparent being a 12-degrees' dihedral tailplane to improve longitudinal stability. Other improvements were soon to include provision of external bomb carriers under wings and, eventually, fuselage, and the much-improved AI Mk VII centimetric radar which used a nose dish-scanner in a radome in place of the former arrow-head style of aerial. Ultimately AI Mk VIII radar installations became available and were installed in some Mk VIFs.

Primarily the Beau Mk VI was produced for two major roles; fighter (day and/or night) designated Mk VIF, and coastal strike titled Mk VIc, thereby determining which modifications might be incorporated while still under production at factories. After the first Mk VIcs had been received with Coastal Command, however, reports from operational crews voiced dissatisfaction with the low-level performance of their Beaus. As a result the Mark's Hercules VI engines were modified by cropping their impellers and locking the blowers in 'M' gear, thereby converting the Hercules VI to Hercules XVII for best 'urge' at 500 feet (or lower) altitude – the more usual operating height for Coastal Beau crews in their anti-shipping roles.

This 'conversion' of the standard Mk VI also changed the Beau's designation to Mk X when the changes achieved full production standards, but also heralded a number of other improving modifications to satisfy fresh operational roles for the Beaufighter. The first significant such alteration resulted from an Air Staff request before the end of 1941 for the Bristol firm to produce a

* See *Beaufighter at War* by C. Bowyer; Ian Allan, 1976.

V8526, a Mk VIF fitted with Hercules VI engines. Later served with Nos 96 and 153 Squadrons, then SOC on 29/3/45.

R2058, the Mk II prototype, fitted experimentally with extended fin and rudder.

R2268, a Mk I fitted with twin-tail empennage experimentally, Filton, 1940. Eventually SOC on 6/2/45.

T3032, a Mk II used for initial testing of long dorsal fin.

X7610, fitted for nightfighting, transferred to the USAAF on 10/10/41.

Beau TFX,RD767, with AI Mk VIII 'thimble' nose housing, which was later converted to TT.10 standard.

successor to the Beaufort as a torpedo-bomber. Frise's design team therefore proposed a version of the Beaufighter, carrying an 18-inch standard British torpedo externally as a modification to the Mk VIc in March 1942, and on 13 April received the official 'go-ahead' to make a trial installation, but to cater for carriage of either the British 18- inch or the American 22.5-inch torpedoes.

Beau X8065 was selected as the trials aircraft, arriving at Filton from its Weston-super-Mare factory on 17 April. Trials of the completed installation were carried out at Filton by 8 May, and X8065 was then flown to the Torpedo Development Unit (TDU) at Gosport for actual torpedo trials. Tragically, the aircraft crashed at Gosport on 16 June due to an engine failure, killing its pilot Wing Commander Shaw, but by then the trials had indicated that the installation was successful. Accordingly, a further 16 Beaufighter torpedo aircraft were requested urgently with a view to equipping fully No 254 Squadron, based at Dyce under the command of ex-Cranwell Wing Commander R.H. McConnell, DFC. This unit had been flying Blenheims under the control of Coastal Command since January 1940, and commenced conversion to Beaus in June 1942, although the prolonged working-up training prevented full operational activities until the following November. Once in service the torpedo-carrying Beaufighter soon acquired the common nickname of 'Torbeau'. Thereafter 'converted' Mk VIcs having the torpedo gear were referred to as TF Mk Xs, but identical production aircraft *without* the torpedo installation became titled Mk XIcs.

A further addition to the Beaufighter's already outstanding battery of weaponry came with the introduction of a single, hand-operated Vickers Gas-Operated (VGO) 0.303-inch calibre machine gun – usually referred to as the 'K' gun – for the observer's rear cupola, ostensibly for tail defence but usually regarded as simply a 'scare gun' by the crews; a fitting on most Mk Xs which became a retrospective installation on existing Mk VIcs. A far more significant addition to the Beau's armoury was the three-inch rocket projectile (RP) for anti-shipping strikes. In September 1942 Beau VIc EL329 had a trial fitment of eight RP fitted, four under each wing. These lethal missiles were designed to accept interchangeable war heads i.e. 25lb Semi-Armour Piercing or

LAST OF THE LINE. SR919, the ultimate production Beau, later converted to TT.10 standard.

Armour Piercing (SAP or AP), or 60lb High Explosive (HE), which could be easily screwed into the rocket motor body. Anticipated problems with blast effects on the underwing surfaces were initially responsible for additional 'blast plating' being fitted under the wings, but experience soon proved such an additional encumbrance as unnecessary. Thereafter the three-inch RP became a standard anti-shipping weapon by Coastal crews until the end of the war.

As mentioned previously, Beaus were also modified to be able to carry a 250lb HE bomb under each wing if needed, and this accumulating warload foisted upon the Beau was necessarily compensated by strengthening the nacelle and main undercarriage. The overall increase in sheer weight – a Mk X with a full warload was now topping well over 25,000lb at take-off – quite obviously affected handling characteristics, and yet another modification was added to Mk Xs which later became a production feature i.e. a long dorsal fin and slightly enlarged elevators. This form of dorsal fin had originally been fitted and tested on Beau II, T3032 among the various early attempts to cure the Beau's inherent tendency to swing, particularly on take-off.

One projected final wartime version of the Beaufighter was to have been the Mk XII, fitted with Hercules 27 engines and able to carry a 1000lb HE bomb under each wing. Although this project was later cancelled – due to a lack of Bendix carburettors for its engines – the much-strengthened wing mooted was utilised for production of the final series of Mk Xs enabling these to lift heavier bomb loads. In the interim some Beau squadrons, during the weeks immediately preceding the Allied invasion of Normandy on 6 June 1944, added bomb carriers under fuselages capable of holding two 500lb HE bombs in addition to the underwing pair of 250-pounders – yet another overt example of the brute strength of Beaufighter construction and power. When bombs were not carried these fuselage carriers were often used for attaching extra fuel drop-pod tanks to extend the aircraft's range and endurance.

Production of Beaufighters in Britain ultimately closed on 21 September 1945, at the Weston-super-Mare factory, by which date a gross total of 5564 Beaus had been built in England, while a further 365 had been manufactured in Australia exclusively for RAAF use. In the contemporary mode of aircraft production during wartime, a majority of Beaus had been built by licensees or other contractors than the original Bristol firm at Filton, as under;

Old Mixon, Weston-super-Mare	3336
Bristol Company, Filton	1468
Fairey Aviation, Stockport	500
Department of Aircraft Production, Australia	365
Rootes Securities, Blythe Bridge	260
	5929

Of these totals, the Marks most produced, i.e. as *originally* built/ordered, were Mk Xs (2205 aircraft) and Mk VIs (1852), though it is emphasised that various original Marks were later to be converted to other titular versions. A modest lease of life for the Beau came in November 1947 when a target-towing conversion variant, designated TT.10, was approved, and Beau NT913, the prototype TT.10, was first flown in May 1948 in its new guise. Such a role for the Beau had first been mooted as early as 1942, but had been shelved pending the cessation of hostilities. In all, 35 Mk TT.10s were 'produced' at Filton and delivered to the RAF in 1948-50, and these were to give useful service for some ten years before the ultimate RAF Beau sortie – by a TT.10, RD761 at Seletar in May 1960 – brought an end to the RAF's use of Beaufighters in firstline units. Remaining Beaus were mainly scrapped thereafter, although one or two lingered as instructional airframes in technical training schools for embryo fitters and mechanics to learn the art of 'metal-bashing'; an ignominious fate for an aircraft which had given the RAF almost exactly 20 years of faithful service.

CHAPTER TWO

Night Hawks

Much of the original conception of the Beaufighter had been simply to provide the RAF with an aircraft capable of filling an overt 'gap' in its firstline strength in the late 1930s i.e. a long-range, preferably cannon-armed fighter with a 'modern' performance at least on a par with any contemporary fighter on the European scene then. Even so, the concept was for a *day* fighter – the equal necessity for a distinct *night* fighter design, for metropolitan aerial defence against hostile bombers, had still not been fully grasped by the contemporary Air Ministry hierarchy.

The omission of such a *day* fighter design was intended, by the Air Ministry, to be filled by a radically-designed, twin-engined single-seat fighter to be produced by Westland; the P.9, later named Whirlwind, built to meet AM Specification F.37/35, and which incorporated an armament of four 20mm cannons grouped together in its slender nose section. The first Whirlwind prototype, L6844, made its first test-flight from Yeovil on 11 October 1938, proving to be faster than any existing RAF fighter (including the Spitfire) at low and medium altitudes.

Production orders for a total of 400 Whirlwinds were placed before the outbreak of war with Germany, with initial deliveries due by September 1939. However, production problems, exacerbated by initial teething troubles, delayed the delivery schedule, resulting in the actual first deliveries to RAF units only commencing in July 1940, with merely eight Whirlwinds being received on RAF charge by October that year, and operational sorties beginning in December.

In the event only 114 Whirlwinds were produced, and merely two squadrons, Nos 137 and 263, fully equipped with the type; these being employed on low-level strike operations during 1941-42 before being phased out altogether. The demise of the Whirlwind –

despite its being a superb pure flying machine – can fairly be blamed on its dependence on the Rolls-Royce Peregrine engines around which it had been designed; power plants not fully developed in time and having low production priority in 1939-40.

By the time the first few Whirlwinds had reached the RAF in mid-1940, the Air Ministry and the RAF were already giving high (and hasty) priority to the need for an effective *night* fighter for UK defence – a role for which the Whirlwind was totally unsuitable. Thus, at that moment in time the only 'nightfighters' available in RAF service were barely modified versions of standard day fighters, such as the ill-starred Boulton Paul Defiant and the Blenheim IF. The latter aircraft – in itself already a standard day bomber 'converted' to fighter by bolting a four-gun pack under its belly – was selected as the main pioneer vehicle for the new Airborne Interception (AI) radar – codenamed Radio Direction Finding (RDF) initially – on the recommendation of the AOC-in-C, Fighter Command, Sir Hugh Dowding that a twin-engined, multi-crew aircraft would be more suitable than any single-seat fighter. The choice of the Blenheim IF to carry the early AI equipment was partly due to the space available within its fuselage to accommodate the bulky AI 'black boxes' – these amounting to some 600lb in gross weight at first – although it was soon recognised that the Blenheim I design was hardly ideal for night AI operations. Blenheim IFs, fitted with early AI paraphernalia, were first received by No 25 Squadron on 31 July 1939, and by 3 September this squadron had 15 such Blenheims on strength – the world's first operational radar-equipped fighters.

Throughout the remaining months of 1939 until early 1941 the AI-Blenheim air crews struggled manfully to make AI-interception by night a practical purpose, despite a host of technical problems which might well have destroyed the morale and enthusiasm of lesser men. The AI-operator had his hands full attempting to cope with recalcitrant sets which abhorred even mildly damp atmospheres, occasionally emitted smoke, or simply refused to function. Even when the 'black boxes' co-operated these were never precise or even reliable, and failed to indicate any incoming raider if it flew below 7000 feet altitude. Inevitably, the Blenheim crews spent more than a year of accumulating frustration with no tangible results for their indefatigable labours – then it happened! On the night of 22/23 July 1940 a Fighter Interception Unit (FIU) crew, Flying Officer G. Ashfield/Pilot Officer G.E. Morris/ Sergeant R.H. Leyland, using Mk IV AI radar, were skilfully 'talked' onto an incoming Dornier Do17 from 2/KG3 and shot it down into the Channel. The 'Magic Mirrors' worked! This isolated victory was, nevertheless, merely one bright spot in an otherwise gloomy vista, until by September more individual AI-Blenheim successes followed slowly.

An illustration of the odds against such combat victories came on the night of 14/15 November 1940 when the Luftwaffe despatched more than 400 bombers to devastate the cathedral city of Coventry. Of the 129 individual RAF fighter interception sorties flown that night, 39 were by Blenheim crews of which only two actually fired their guns but none achieved a victory. Just five nights later, however, another AI-kill was registered – by a Beaufighter. Beau R2098, NG-H of 604 Squadron, crewed by Flight Lieutenant J. Cunningham/Sergeant J.R. Phillipson shot down a Junkers Ju88* – the first Beau *AI-assisted* kill; though not the first Beaufighter (*non*-AI) victory, which had been credited to Beau R2097 of 219 Squadron, a Dornier Do17, on 25 October, the RAF crew being Sergeants Hodgkinson/Benn. John Cunningham was later to become Group Captain, CBE, DSO, DFC and a top-scoring nightfighter pilot.

With its marginal performance range – for a so-termed fighter – and other disadvantages, the makeshift Blenheim IF 'nightfighter' was clearly in need of replacement; the Beaufighter thus appeared at a most appropriate time to 'take over the reins' of the UK's meagre night defence. Even so the Beau crews had also had their share of frustrating, non-productive patrolling over Britain during 1940, not being fitted with the earlier Marks of AI sets. By the autumn of 1940 the Beau units began receiving AI Mk IV equipment, identifiable externally by characteristic 'arrow-head' aerials in the nose and on wing leading edges, which though by no means 100 per cent reliable as yet were soon to prove highly effective when, from January 1941, these were 'linked' up with

* The unit records called it, incorrectly, a Heinkel. WO J R Phillipson, DFC was to be killed on active service on 5/1/43.

Ground Controlled Interception (GCI) 'married' to Plan Position Indicators (PPI). These latter innovations enabled ground controllers to plot both fighter and 'bogey' (enemy aircraft) simultaneously on their targets with a good degree of accuracy.

To the various problems for Beau crews during those early months of attempted AI-assisted night interceptions was added a not uncommon risk of being misidentified as an enemy aircraft by the various forms of UK defences. To the ill-informed, or over-eager, observer the Beau bore a distinct resemblance to the Luftwaffe's Junkers Ju88 – dismal aircraft recognition thereby resulting in Beaus being damaged and even shot down by 'friendly' guns. One of the first such tragedies occurred on 13 November 1940 when Beau R2071 from 219 Squadron was brought down by UK anti-aircraft gunners, killing both crew members. Then, on successive nights, Beaus X7550 and R2240 from 29 Squadron received damage from the air gunners of Wellington bombers as the Beaus approached to identify the bombers. These were but the first of a succession of Beaufighters destined to be attacked and/or damaged or destroyed by Allied aircraft throughout the years 1941-45, and not only over Britain.

The night victories gained by the Beau crews during November 1940 to February 1941 were insignificant in relation to the number of Luftwaffe bombers arriving over Britain each night. It was a period of experimentation, improvisation, determination – and no little frustration – for the small band of Beaufighter crews as they struggled with learning the precise tactics and technicalities of operating airborne radar in the raven blackness of the night skies. Probably the most important facet to be learned and constantly practised was the necessary – indeed, vital – teamwork between pilot and crew in each aircraft. In the most successful Beau crews this partnership reached almost telepathic standards, where a pilot could virtually anticipate his radar set operator's next remarks and instructions simply by a tone or nuance of voice. Such an understanding was achieved only by dint of prolonged, patient practice over many months of otherwise fruitless airborne patrols during the winter of 1940-41 by the Beau crews, but by spring 1941 that patience began to pay handsomely in the context of results.

Even so the most competent air crews could have been of little avail without a matching expertise of the GCI ground controllers who guided and pinpointed the targets and – not least important to many crews – brought the Beaus safely back to base eventually. Pure navigation in the blackness of night, particularly after a series of sharp changes of course during any pursuit, was always likely to deteriorate to a point where a Beau crew were literally 'lost', needing expert advice on how to regain their own base airfield on the conclusion of any patrol. Thus the whole intricate night defence system depended on a foundation of interlinked co-operation and trust between ground and air crews.

The long winter's comparative lack of success for the Beau crews of crews of Nos 25, 29, 219, 600 and 604 Squadrons came to a sudden upsurge in victories starting in March 1941, in which month UK nightfighters (of *all* types) claimed 22 enemy aircraft shot down; a total which would be doubled in April, and quadrupled in May. In those three months most of the RAF's leading nightfighter pilots of the whole war were to claim their initial successes. By March two pilots in particular had already achieved four victories apiece flying the ponderous Blenheim IFs prior to converting to Beaufighters, these being John Cunningham of 604 Squadron and the New Zealander, Michael J. Herrick of 25 Squadron.* Other Beau pilots soon to join the nightfighter 'ace' lists during March-July 1941 included Tom Pike, commander of 219 Squadron, later Marshal of the Royal Air Force Sir Thomas, GCB, CBE, DFC; Roderick Chisholm (219), later Air Commodore CBE, DSO DFC; John Topham (219 Squadron), later Air Commodore, DSO, OBE, DFC; Edward Crew (604); Keith Geddes (604); Guy Gibson (29), later Wing Commander, VC, DSO, DFC; and a man destined to become the RAF's most-decorated fighter pilot, John – 'Bob' – Braham of 29 Squadron, later Wing Commander, DSO, DFC, AFC, CD. Leading scorers for this period were the crews of 604 Squadron who claimed at least 60 enemy aircraft destroyed or damaged by the end of June. The 'star' of 604 was John Cunningham who, with his usual set operator 'Jimmy' Rawnsley, claimed eight victories in the month of April alone, adding further successes in May including one Heinkel He111 in

* Squadron Leader M.J. Herrick, DFC & Bar was killed in a Mosquito on 16 June 1944 by Leutnant Robert Spreckels of JG1.

Beau IF,T4638, 'F-Freddie' of 604 Squadron.

(*Left* Sqn Ldr M.J. Herrick, DFC, a New Zealander who served with 25 Squadron, eventually killed in action on 16/6/44. (*Right*) Group Captain John Cunningham, CBE, DSO, DFC.

604 Squadron crews outside their Mess, the Pheasant Hotel, 1942, including (from rt) 'Jimmy' Rawnsley, 'Bob' Wright, John Cunningham, Michael Constable Maxwell.

V8324,RO-B of 29 Squadron, late 1942 and named 'Bambi'. Later served with 51 OTU in 1944.

X7673, 'E' of 29 Squadron and flown on occasion by Guy Gibson, which later served with 89 Squadron.

MM856,NG-C of 604 Squadron, which served later on 54 OTU, 1944.

(Above) X7583,WM-E of 68 Squadron. Served with 51 OTU in 1944, and SOC on 21/4/45.

(*Left*) Group Capt Hon 'Max' Aitken, DSO, DFC, OC 68 Squadron from February 1941 until January 1943.

flames which victory was witnessed by no less a personage than HM King George VI who was visiting the squadron's base on that occasion.

By July 1941, although occasional successes were still being claimed by Beau crews, the Luftwaffe's night offensive against Britain had waned considerably due to Hitler's final decision to launch *Operation Barbarossa* – the massive invasion of Russia from eastern Europe – with a consequent reallocation of his air forces, leaving only four *Gruppen* of the 44 originally employed to attack Britain to maintain a slender offensive by night. This diminishing attack led the commander of Fighter Command, Sholto Douglas, to declare later: 'We were confident that if the enemy had not chosen that moment to pull out, we should soon have been inflicting such casualties on his night-bombers that the continuance of his night-offensive on a similar scale would have been impossible.'*

It was, at best, an over-optimistic opinion of the actual capabilities of Fighter Command's nightfighter defences at that period. On 11 May 1941 Douglas's nightfighter strength comprised a total of 16 squadrons, plus the FIU at Ford. Of these only six had Beaufighters, as follows:

Squadron	*Base*	*Commander*
25	Wittering	Sqn Ldr H.P. Pleasance, DFC
29	West Malling	Wg Cdr S.C. Widdows
219	Tangmere	Wg Cdr T.G. Pike, DFC
600	Colerne	Sqn Ldr G.H. Stainforth, AFC
604	Middle Wallop	Sqn Ldr M.F. Anderson

The sixth unit was No 68 Squadron at High Ercall, commanded by Wing Commander Hon 'Max' Aitken, DFC, which had been reformed at Catterick on 7 January 1941 with a mixture of Blenheims and Beaufighters and was still in the process of converting fully to Beaus, albeit already declared 'operational'. The remaining ten squadrons, although intended for re-equipment with AI-Beaufighters as soon as possible, were for the time being still flying a motley array of Hurricanes, Defiants, and Havocs. Even

* Quoted in *The Defence of the United Kingdom* by B. Collier: HMSO, 1957.

allowing for rapid re-equipment with Beaus, and the shortly available superlative De Havilland Mosquito, RAF nightfighter strength in the spring of 1941 was far from being capable of implementing Sholto Douglas's over-confident claim for *many* months to come.

On 10 May 1941 a new unit joined Fighter Command's strength when No 406 ('Lynx') Squadron RCAF was officially formed at Acklington under the command of Wing Commander D.G. Morris, DFC, RAF*. It was the first RCAF nightfighter squadron to be formed outside Canada and for its first few weeks flew a mix of Blenheim Is and IVs, gradually converting to Beaufighters in June-July and working up to full operational fitness. Its first recorded operational sorties were flown by two Blenheims on 17 June, without incident, but on the night of 1/2 September 1941 Beau II R2336, crewed by Flying Officer R.C. Fumerton/Sergeant L.P.S. Bing, destroyed a Ju88 over Bedlington; the squadron's – and the RCAF's – first nightfighter victory. It should be added that *officially* the squadron as a unit was yet to be designated operational, and the sorties mentioned here were flown by some *crews* considered fit for operations *per se.* Fumerton, later, Wing Commander, DFC and nicknamed 'Moose', was to run up a tally of at least 12 enemy aircraft destroyed in the Middle East while serving with No 89 Squadron, then returned to the UK to command his old unit, 406 Squadron RCAF from August 1943 to July 1944.

Before the end of 1941 a total of five more Beaufighter squadrons were either 'born' or converted fully to Beaus within the aegis of Fighter Command. In July No 255 Squadron, a nightfighter unit flying Hurricanes and Defiants from Hibaldstow under the command of Wing Commander J.S. Bartlett, DFC, began slowly converting to Beaufighter IIs and was stood down from operations on 23 August to accomplish this exchange. Declared operational again from 26 September, the unit failed to score a Beau victory until 14 January 1942 by which date it had become based at Coltishall, Norfolk and was now commanded by Wing Commander D.P.D.G. Kelly.

While 255's crews were struggling to master the characteristics of

* On 8 May 1962, Morris, by then Air Marshal Sir Douglas, KCB, CBE, DSO, DFC, became AOC-in-C, RAF Fighter Command.

(*Above*) Beau VIF,X7842, WM-P of 68 Squadron, named *Birmingham Civil Defence* sporting two swastika victory symbols. At left, Flg Off Raybould. This Beau crashed on take-off and burned on 5/9/42.

(*Right*) Wg Cdr D.G. Morris, DFC as OC No.406 ('Lynx') Squadron, RCAF at Scorton, 2/7/42.

Crews of 406 Squadron RCAF at Acklington, 15/9/41. From left; Flt Lt F.W. Hillock; Sgt E. Vickers; Flg Off H.J. Findlay; Sgt M. Vineberg; Flt Lt D. Carr-Harris.

R2402, a Mk IIF of 255 Squadron at Coltishall, Sept 1941, which later served with 410 Squadron RCAF.

their new Beaus in August 1941, three more units became 'Beau-men'. No 141 Squadron, a nightfighting Defiant unit based at Ayr and commanded by Wing Commander G.F.W. Heycock, re-equipped with Beau IFs and recommenced operations during August 1941, though without successes until February 1942. At Exeter No 307 (Polish) Squadron, commanded by Squadron Leader Jerzy Antonowicz, started exchanging its Defiants for Beau IIs in August – its first Beau arriving on 14 August – and resumed night operations from 15 October, claiming five successful interceptions in the following month.

The third Beau unit of August was No 409 ('Nighthawk') Squadron RCAF, formed originally at Digby on 7 June 1941 but based at Coleby Grange by late July. In August the unit began converting from Defiants to Beau IIs and during the working-up period lost its commander, Wing Commander N.B. Petersen, in a flying accident on 2 September. Petersen's appointment was taken over by Wing Commander Paul Y. Davoud, DFC with effect from 5 September who duly claimed the squadron's first-ever night victory, a Dornier, on 1 November, with Sergeant T. Carpenter, RAF as his navigator on that occasion. Davoud's combat report read:

> I increased speed and turned to port and obtained a visual at 6000 feet, silhouetted against the clouds in bright moonlight. I throttled back and lost height until slightly above and 400 yards to rear of enemy aircraft who dived for cloud cover. I closed to approximately 200 yards, identified bandit as a Dornier 217, and fired a short burst observing hits on starboard mainplane. The Dornier returned fire and having closed to about 200 yards I fired two long bursts, seeing the second burst hit his starboard engine. Just before the Dornier entered cloud a big explosion blew his right engine and wing off. I pulled up to avoid a collision and the Dornier fell burning straight into the sea. I then returned to base, landing at 2255 hours.

The last Beau unit to join Fighter Command in 1941 was No 456 Squadron RAAF, which was first formed at Valley on 30 June 1941, to fly Defiant nightfighters. In command was Wing

Commander Charles G.C. Olive, DFC, an Australian-born pilot who had joined the RAF pre-1939 and emerged from the Battle of Britain as a six-victory 'ace' after service with No 65 Squadron RAF. Apart from Olive, however, the initial personnel of 456 Squadron were wholly RAF i.e. non-Australian, and it was not until the end of the year before sufficient Australian crews, air and ground, had been posted in to the squadron and begun to give a distinct 'Aussie' character to the unit. Officially declared operational on Defiants from 5 September 1941, it immediately began converting to Beaufighter IIs in that month.

Being in a 'backwoods area', 456's crews saw no real action until the night 10/11 January 1942 when, despite still not being officially declared operationally 'fit' on Beaus, the squadron despatched one Beau, crewed by Squadron Leader J.S. Hamilton/Pilot Officer D.L. Norris-Smith (both RAF officers),* to intercept some raiders near Liverpool and, after losing several contacts, this crew eventually chased a Do217 for some seven minutes then shot it down with two bursts of cannon fire.

For the next six months 456 Squadron literally saw no direct action against the Luftwaffe, and the crews – air and ground – had to endure a grinding monotony of fruitless 'Readiness' states, uneventful patrols, and a steadily declining state of morale in general. On 27 March 1942 Wing Commander Olive was taken ill and command of the unit passed to Wing Commander E.C. Wolfe, DFC, an Englishman who had previously commanded No 141 Squadron RAF. By May the crews were flying convoy escort patrols by *day*, and one such patrol on 18 May produced a victory at long last when Pilot Officer D.B. Wills, RAF (later Flight Lieutenant, DFC) destroyed a Ju88. It fell to Wing Commander Wolfe to register the unit's next confirmed 'kill' on the night of 30 July. His combat report is quoted here to exemplify the techniques involved in flying a 'controlled' nightfighter at that time. After obtaining three separate contacts (blips on his radar screen) without completing any interception, Wolfe received a fourth which

* Later, Wing Commander J.S. Hamilton, DFC, AFC and Squadron Leader D.L. Norris-Smith, an Englishman and an Australian respectively, though both serving in the RAF.

Beau VIF of 307 (Polish) Squadron bringing General Sikorski to the unit base, Exeter in Sept 1942.

Wg Cdr (later Grp Capt) Paul Davoud, DSO, DFC, commander of 409 ('Nighthawk') Squadron RCAF at Coleby Grange, Nov 1942, with his dog 'Beau' and the German propeller blade used as the squadron's scoreboard.

> ... appeared ahead slightly to starboard and slightly above Beaufighter which was now flying at 8000 feet. Beaufighter followed and enemy aircraft jinked making rate one, 50-degree turns. Closing in I obtained a visual at 2000 feet range, identified the enemy aircraft as an He111, the exhausts on each side of the engines being very apparent. I closed in at an indicated air speed of 270-280 on enemy aircraft now descending slightly to port, and fired a two-second burst with a slight port deflection at 250 yards, followed by a second burst of one-second at 150 yards range.
>
> No return fire resulted, the upper gunner having been shot through the head, the pilot's controls lost, and the port engine put out of action during the first burst delivered. The He111 now skidded off to port, jettisoning its bomb load of incendiaries, and I broke away to starboard, closing in again to fire a two-second burst from 50 yards with no deflection, and breaking away violently to avoid a collision. From this burst bright flashes and falling fragments from the fuselage resulted. A large dark object passed beneath the Beaufighter slightly to port. This is now presumed to be the port engine as this engine has not yet been found in wreckage. The enemy aircraft was well on fire by this time. Both aircraft were now losing height and I closed in to fire a final burst of one second at 150 yards' range with slight port deflection, breaking off this last attack at a height of 4000 feet, then climbed to starboard and levelled out. I saw the He111 burning in fuselage and port wing and continuing to lose height rapidly. It turned slowly towards Pwhelli (*sic*) ... and when over the beach at approximately 2000 feet dived vertically, exploding and burning on the beach.*

The first six months of 1942 were to see a further six units become equipped with Beaufighters for night defence of the United Kingdom. The first of these, No 153 Squadron, had been reformed at Ballyhalbert on 14 October 1941 as an off-shoot from 256 Squadron, to fly Defiant nightfighters, but in January 1942 the squadron began exchanging its Defiants for Beau IFs. Another

* Quoted in *Air War Against Germany & Italy*, 1939-43 by J. Herington; AWM, 1954.

Defiant unit, No 125 Squadron, which had reformed at Colerne on 16 June 1941, became non-operational in January 1942 in order to re-equip with Beau IIs, with a new commander, Wing Commander D.V. Ivins. The conversion was spread over several months, during which the unit continued operations with both Defiants and Beaus.

The third Beau unit was also the third RCAF nightfighter unit to be formed 'overseas', No. 410 ('Cougar') Squadron RCAF, which had originally formed on 30 June 1941 at Ayr with Defiants. By April 1942 the 'Cougars' were based at Drem, commanded by Wing Commander C.M. Lipton, in which month they began receiving Beau IIs. Further moves of base to Ayr on 15 June, and Scorton on 1 September, followed, with the successor to Wing Commander Lipton, Wing Commander F.W. Hillock taking up his appointment with effect from 19 August. During these moves the unit's 'A' Flight was detached to various other airfields including Drem, from where on the night of 6/7 September 1942 Beau II, T3428, crewed by Pilot Officer R.R. Ferguson/Pilot Officer D. Creed claimed a Ju88 as 'damaged' over Whitby – the squadron's first combat claim. By the beginning of November 1942, however, the Beaus began being replaced by Mosquito FB VIs, and the squadron returned its last Beau to store on 26 January 1943. By then, No 153 Squadron had already left the UK, posted *en bloc* to Maison Blanche in North Africa in December 1942, from where it recommenced operations on 25 December.

No 96 Squadron, a veteran nightfighter unit which had flown Hurricanes and Defiants since its reformation in December 1940, was based at Wrexham by May 1942 when it first began receiving Beau IIs as its latest equipment. Becoming operational on these by July, commanded then by Wing Commander R.J. Burns, 96 Squadron found little 'trade' for the following year and by June 1943 had started converting to Mosquito NF XIIs for future intruder operations over the Continent. Another well-experienced nightfighter unit, No 256 Squadron – which had provided the nucleus for formation of 153 Squadron – was based at Squires Gate, near Blackpool in May 1942 when it began replacing its well-worn Defiants with Beau IFs. Commanded by Wing Commander J.S. Adams, 256 was declared operational again on its new warhorses on 23 July by which month it had moved base to Woodvale. A virtual absence of the Luftwaffe over the UK left its crews little to do operationally, apart from a lone Do217 destroyed off Worthing on 28 April 1943, and conversion to Mosquito XIIs began in May.

Finally in 1942 No 488 Squadron RNZAF was 'reborn' at Church Fenton on 25 June 1942 equipped with Beaufighter IIs. In command was Wing Commander R.M. Trousdale, DFC,* already credited with eight combat victories – five of these by night – while his Flight commanders, Squadron Leaders P.W. Rabone, DFC† and J.R. Gard'ner were also well experienced fighter pilots. Despite many difficulties, including an initial lack of trained ground staff, the squadron's crews patiently worked up to operational standards over several months before moving base to Ayr in September 1942, from where the first albeit uneventful operational sorties were flown at the beginning of October. For the final months of the year the Beau crews were occupied in routine coastal patrols, without any clashes with German aircraft, and then received improved AI-equipped Beau VIs. In February 1943 Wing Commander Trousdale was succeeded in command by Wing Commander J. Nesbitt-Dufort, DSO, a former Flight commander, but on 30 June 1943 the squadron received its first Mosquito XII, the forerunner of a complete change of aircraft.

By early 1943 some Beaufighter squadrons had commenced forms of intruder operations over France and the Low Countries, seeking prey such as trains and airfields, and especially any airborne Luftwaffe aircraft. It was also a year in which most Beau units had already, or were about to exchange their aircraft for the ubiquitous Mosquito for all former operational roles. The changeover to an offensive role (intruding or *Ranger* sorties) was a logical decision since Luftwaffe raiders were rarely to be found over Britain by late 1942. Nevertheless, the occasional enemy bomber was encountered and was not always a simple target. One such raider was intercepted and destroyed by Beau V8255 of 141 Squadron on the night of 8/9 September 1942 – but with tragic result for the Beau's skipper.

Crewed by Warrant Officer R.C. Hamer and Flight Sergeant

* Killed in aircraft accident, 16 June 1947
† Killed on operations 24 July 1944

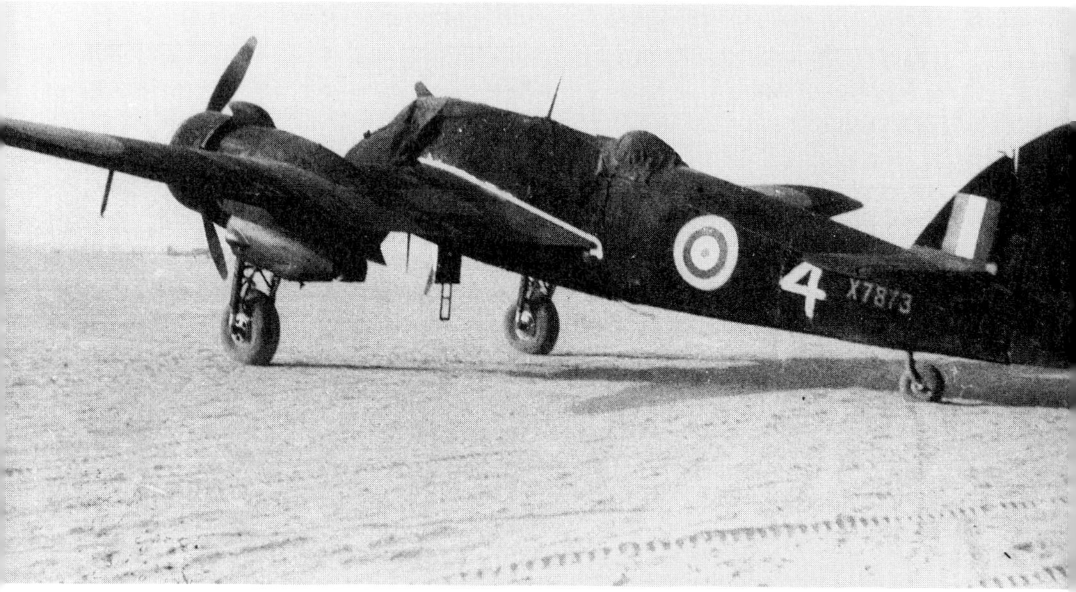

BLACK BEAUTY. X7873 of 456 Squadron RAAF at RAF Valley originally, and later served with 46 and 227 Squadrons in the Mediterranean theatre. It crashed at Ta Kali, Malta on 14/12/42.

Beau VI,V8443,JT-B of 256 Squadron, Woodvale in early 1943. Later served in the Middle East and finally SOC on 29/3/45.

Walsh, the Beau set out from Tangmere and at 0140 hrs the crew was able to obtain a visual contact with a Heinkel He111, which 'materialised' 100 feet above the Beau south-east of St Alban's Head. Throttling back, Hamer closed to 300 feet range and gave the Heinkel one burst without apparent effect. Closing to 200 feet, Hamer gave it a second, longer burst and strikes were seen all over the bomber, mainly in its starboard wing, and the starboard engine and wing erupted in flames. Aboard the doomed Heinkel its dorsal gunner stuck to his gun, firing several bursts but not hitting the Beau. Hamer dropped back to 300 feet and gave the Heinkel a final 12-second burst, exhausting his cannon ammunition. The Heinkel's starboard wing, all aflame, suddenly flew off, hitting the Beaufighter and slewing it to its starboard. The Heinkel's doughty gunner seized his last chance, pouring a long burst into his tormentor and scored a hit on the Beau's starboard engine which burst into flames.

Walsh, in the rear, had seen 'flashes' (*sic*) around his pilot's cockpit and felt sure Hamer had been hit, but when he asked Hamer over the R/T whether he was all right, his only reply was 'You bastard!', after which Hamer attacked the Heinkel yet again, with his wing machine guns silencing the German's return fire. The Heinkel then fell in a streaming fireball into the sea.

The Beau's starboard engine was still ablaze, so Walsh asked Hamer if they should take to their parachutes. Hamer's voice, in a tone quite obviously unnatural, came back saying, 'Hang on a bit. We may cope.' Hamer then shut the flaming engine's throttles right back and, at 6000 feet, headed back to Tangmere on the port engine's power. Telling Walsh to remain in the rear fuselage, Hamer insisted on doing all R/T transmissions to the ground controller, but was steadily losing height until he was down to 2000 feet.

As the northern coast of the Isle of Wight came into view the port engine juddered to a stop. Only then did Hamer order Walsh to bale out and the navigator dropped safely onto the beach near Newtown. Meanwhile the crippled Beaufighter fell away into an uncontrollable dive, and the ground radio operator heard Hamer say, 'Afraid I'm finished. I'll have to go over now'; then the Beau dived into the earth near Lymington, totally wrecking itself and killing the pilot.

Walsh, in his report, emphasised that in his view Hamer might have survived had he allowed both men to bale out while still over the sea, but that Hamer had deliberately decided to regain the land before permitting his navigator to take to his parachute. Only a few weeks previous Hamer had been a godfather at Walsh's child's christening. And Hamer was well aware that Walsh was a *non*-swimmer ...

Hamer's decision to give his navigator a good chance of survival, despite the fact that his own wounds would prevent the pilot following suit, led to 141 Squadron's commander forwarding a recommendation that Hamer should be awarded a posthumous Victoria Cross. This recommendation was turned down by the sector commander. Shortly after, a new CO for 141 Squadron, Wing Commander 'Bob' Braham, DSO, DFC, rewrote that recommendation and forwarded it again with a covering letter requesting reconsideration. This was also rejected.

With the apparent near-cessation of Luftwaffe night raiding over Britain, several Beau units were released from home defence duties and posted to North Africa to assist the final stages of the Allies' advance westwards and eventual victory in that theatre of war. In November 1942 Nos 255 and 600 Squadrons flew out to Maison Blanche, Algiers; in May 1943 No 219 Squadron left Catterick to stage through to Bône; while 256 Squadron, after converting to Mosquito XIIs beginning in May 1943, sent a detachment to Malta soon after, with the rest of the squadron joining this detachment by October.

Of the Beau units remaining in Britain, most changed from Beaus to Mosquitos by the end of 1943. In October 1942, No 25 Squadron received its first Mosquito on the 21st, and finally phased out its Beaufighters by February 1943; while 410 Squadron RCAF also began conversion to Mosquito NF IIs from November 1942, completing this process in January 1943. No 456 Squadron RAAF received its first three Mosquitos on 30 December 1942 and within a month had disposed of its Beaus. No 307 (Polish) Squadron finally relinquished its Beaus in December 1942, having been steadily converting to Mosquito NF IIs since the previous September; while by June 1943 three more squadrons, Nos 29, 96, and 488, had either started conversion or were already operating on

Mosquitos, with 29 Squadron flying its first 'Mozzie' sorties on 15 June, and 488 receiving its first Mosquito two weeks later.

By 1 September 1943 the remaining Beaufighter squadrons of Fighter Command based in Britain were:

Squadron	*Base*	*Commander*
68	Coltishall	Wg Cdr A.P. Dottridge, DFC
125	Exeter	Wg Cdr R.F.H. Clerke
141	Wittering	Wg Cdr J.R.D. Braham, DSO, DFC
406 RCAF	Valley	Wg Cdr R.C. Fumerton, DFC
409 RCAF	Acklington	Wg Cdr J.W. Reid
604	Scorton	Wg Cdr M.H. Maxwell, DFC

The opportunities for direct engagements with the enemy were few and far between for all Beau units at this period, but Nos 68 and 141 Squadrons were at least able to undertake night *Ranger* intrusion sorties over Europe, usually attacking the French railway system or other 'opportunity' objectives, with very rare but satisfying clashes with lone German aircraft caught unawares. For 141 Squadron operational action took a fresh direction when, on the night of 14/15 June 1943, six of its Beaus, led by the CO, Bob Braham, set out from Coltishall – where it had first flown to top up fuel before the actual operation – and carried out its first *Serrate* sorties. Their tactics were to infiltrate the main bomber stream attacking Oberhausen that night and by using their *Serrate* and AI radar – the *Serrate* device enabled the Beaus to home on to radar signals emitted by German nightfighters – hunt and hopefully destroy any German *Nachtjäger* which approached the heavy bombers. Braham and his navigator, Flight Lieutenant 'Sticks' Gregory,succeeded in destroying a Messerschmitt Bf110 over the Zuider Zee, and all six Beaus returned safely.

No 141 Squadron continued its *Serrate* sorties with rising success over the following weeks, claiming 23 German nightfighters destroyed – nine of these by Braham alone – including three Bf110s from the crack Luftwaffe nightfighter unit 4./NJG1 on the night of the famous Peenemünde attack by Bomber Command on 17/18 August 1943. These types of operations placed a heavy strain on 141's crews, having to accompany virtually every main bomber attack night by night, with all the hazards of flak, searchlights, nightfighter attack – and in addition occasionally being fired on by gunners in the bombers they were trying to protect – during about two hours actually over enemy-occupied territory.

Beau losses were, fortunately, relatively light, but this might have been due, at least in part, to the limited operational range of *Serrate* sorties which did not involve deep penetration into German skies where the bulk of the Reich's huge defence system was mainly concentrated. Objectively, it was soon realised that the Beaufighter was not the ideal vehicle for *Serrate* operations – it could be out-run and out-manoeuvred by any experienced Luftwaffe fighter – and it was decided to exchange Beaus for Mosquitos in the role.

Accordingly, 141 Squadron began full conversion to Mosquito NF IIs by November 1943, and then was transferred to the aegis of No 100 Group with effect from 3 December 1943. The squadron's operational 'balance sheet' for its *Serrate* period showed a total of 179 completed sorties, during which 13 enemy aircraft had been destroyed and five others claimed as at least badly hit, while the Beau losses amounted to three aircraft and their crews lost.

No 68 Squadron, which had exchanged its Beau IFs for Mk VIFs in early 1943, continued a largely fruitless routine of night defence and occasional coastal patrols throughout the rest of that year, but after claiming two Messerschmitt Bf410 raiders in the autumn 'blotted its copybook' on 12 December when Beau V8619 was vectored onto and shot down a Mosquito near Stowmarket. A form of 'poetic justice' followed six months later, on 28 May 1944, when Beau V8594 of 68 Squadron was itself a victim of a 'friendly' fighter! By June 1944 the squadron was based at Castle Camps, commanded by Wing Commander D. Hayley-Bell, DFC, and in July gave up its Beaufighters in exchange for Mosquito XVIIs. The other extant Beau squadrons had already made similar changes. No 125 Squadron began conversion to Mosquito XVIIs in February 1944; 604 Squadron has re-equipped with Mosquito XIIIs by March; 409 Squadron had completed its exchange of Beaus for Mosquito XIIIs by the start of April; while its fellow-Canadian unit, 406 Squadron followed suit in April with Mk XII 'Mozzies'.

It was the close of almost four years of firstline night operations by Beaufighters with Fighter Command, during which period – having benefited greatly from the pioneering efforts of its Blenheim predecessors – the Beau had quickly proved to be a major vehicle for frustrating the Luftwaffe's attempts to bomb Britain by night.

CHAPTER THREE

Coastal Warriors

The RAF's lack of a specifically-designed long-range fighter in first-line service during 1939-40 – as described in Chapter II 'Night Hawks' – not only diminished Fighter Command's potential offensive capability, but soon became an overt gap in the operational ranks of other Commands, especially after the Axis invasions and occupations of such countries as Norway and Greece in the early months of 1940. For the UK-based squadrons of Coastal Command then the prospect of carrying out offensive sorties across the North Sea to Norwegian targets was somewhat problematical. Concerned primarily with protection of merchant ship convoy supply routes in the Western Approaches – for which the Command had temporarily increased its numerical strength by borrowing squadrons from Bomber Command – its only form of strike aircraft were a handful of Beaufort torpedo-bombers equipping just two units, Nos 22 and 42 Squadrons, during 1940. The Command's remaining types of aircraft – Sunderlands, Ansons, Blenheim IVs, Whitleys, *et al* – were either incapable of long-range sorties to Norway and/or were not suitably armed to risk in aerial clashes with Luftwaffe firstline fighters.

Accordingly, the Bristol firm decided to modify a standard Beaufighter Mk I, R2152, by removing its wing gun installations for eventual replacement by additional fuel tanks, then incorporated a working table and necessary extra instruments for the observer/navigator in the mid-fuselage. Once proven satisfactory in this modified form, designated Mk Ic (C for Coastal), a batch of 80 such Beaus was built with all speed, and the first to reach an operational unit of Coastal Command went to No 252 Squadron, based at Chivenor from 1 December 1940. After some three months of working-up to operational fitness, 252 moved base to Aldergrove on 4 April and flew its first Beau operational sorties on 6 April 1941.

In that same month the unit was joined at Chivenor by No 272 Squadron, a Blenheim IVF unit previously based at Sumburgh, commanded by Squadron Leader A.W. Fletcher, DFC. At Chivenor 272 Squadron exchanged its Blenheims for Beaufighters but in May the squadron left the UK en route to Abu Sueir, Egypt for operations in the eastern Mediterranean zones. No 252 Squadron received orders on 25 April to detach 15 aircraft to Malta and these set off from St Eval on 1 May, though one aborted and returned, while another forcelanded in Portugal and was interned. The 13 Beaus which reached Luqa then flew various missions over Sicily and Crete, losing two on operations and four others destroyed on Luqa by enemy air raids.

The squadron's personnel still in Northern Ireland – seven Beaus and nine air crews, plus ground crews, commanded by Flight Lieutenant G.G. Stockdale – continued sorties over the Irish Sea but on 14 June were 'absorbed' into 143 Squadron which reformed at Aldergrove next day. 143 Squadron remained non-operational until the following October but then commenced operations from a new base, Sumburgh under the command of Squadron Leader G.V. Carey, escorting convoys. This activity only lasted until December when the unit's Beaus were taken over by 235 Squadron at Dyce, leaving 143's crews to soldier on with well-worn Blenheims until being virtually reduced to cadre status by February 1942. In May 1942, however, fresh Beaufighters began arriving and Beau operations recommenced in August, commanded by Wing Commander E.W. Thornewill.

No 235 Squadron, a Blenheim IV unit which had been transferred from Fighter to Coastal Command in February 1940, had first received a few Beaufighter Is in December 1940 but continued to fly both Blenheims and Beaus for a further year before becoming fully equipped with Beaus in December 1941. By then the squadron was based at Dyce, commanded by Wing Commander Hugh J. Garlick, DFC, who has described his – and the squadron's – early weeks:*

> After conversion on Blenheims, and about ten hours on Beaus, I was appointed CO of 235 Squadron based at Dyce in October

* Correspondence with author

1941. 235 was then equipped with Blenheims but had two Beaus on which the air crews were slowly gaining a little flying time. As the squadron was still operational and maintaining regular reconnaissance patrols along the Norwegian coast, the rate of experience on Beaus was very slow. After a few weeks I had a 'phone call from the AOC, 18 Group. 'Would *I* operate Beaufighters from Sumburgh at *night* bearing in mind there was a 600ft hill at one end of the runway, a 900ft hill at the other, and the cross-runway was only 700 yards?' I replied Yes. 'OK. Tomorrow at first light fly all your Blenheims to Sumburgh, hand them over to 143 Squadron and take over their Beaufighters, and get them to Dyce and have your squadron operational as soon as possible.' Our flight from Sumburgh to Dyce, the immediate check on our aircraft, our signal saying it would take six weeks to get the aircraft operational – the Air Ministry 'experts' who were on the doorstep next morning disagreed, saying it would take *eight* weeks – the frantic flying programme, the night I flew three circuits and landings (without light) *before* Flying Control could be woken up, put on the lights, and *then* gave me permission to take off ... all are part of a book in themselves!

Another call from the AOC in late December, and on Christmas Eve we flew to Sumburgh for our first op. This was to be long-range fighter cover for the Army and Navy in the first combined operation of its type, the Vaagso raid. Christmas Eve was very sober as we were due to operate next day. A 24-hours' postponement brought an equally sober Christmas Day made worse by the fact that the turkey we had brought with us was stolen. On Boxing Day the job was 'on' and the narrative reads:

1st Sortie – 4 aircraft
1. W/Cdr Garlick/F/O Payne
2. F/Lt Wigmore/F/Sgt Crow
3. S/Ldr McConnell/Sgt Burnside
4. P/O Hughes/Sgt Myhill

Set course in formation 0859 – arrived Vaagso 1015 (just light) and took over patrol – 1030 sighted one Ju88 which made off – 1050 chased away a second Ju88 – 1055 chased off one Me109 –

relief due 1145 but not sighted – 1203 vectored onto two low flying aircraft which turned out to be Me109s – a hot ten minutes for all concerned – Bill Hughes seen to dive in but not believed shot down* – relieved 1210 – Wigmore chased two more Me109s on return journey – landed 1330.

2nd sorties – 3 aircraft
1. S/Ldr Cook/F/Sgt Ludlow
2. P/0 Chandler/Sgt Whitfield
3. P/0 Austen/Sgt Hornsby

Set course 1200 – arrived Vaagso 1345 – patrolled unit 1445 without incident (dusk) – landed 1600.

We had at least justified our claim that one could operate Beaufighters at night from Sumburgh, and kept enemy aircraft away from our naval and military forces despite our inexperience on the type. I was the most experienced with some 23 hours total flying time on Beaus – the least experienced had only eight and a half hours!

In 1941 two more Coastal Command units converted to Beaufighter Ics, these being Nos 248 and 236 Squadrons. No 248 Squadron had been flying operations in Coastal Command since February 1940, and by July 1941 was based at Bircham Newton, commanded by Wing Commander S.G. Wise, DFC, flying Blenheim IVFs primarily on convoy escort and general reconnaissance sorties over the North Sea and off the Dutch coast. With the change of equipment the unit continued in these roles, but on 22 August despatched its first designated 'anti-shipping' strike against some enemy R-boats. By October the squadron was mainly operating from bases in Cornwall – Portreath, Carew Cheriton, and St Eval – patrolling over the Scillies. The second unit, 236 Squadron, had also come under the control of Coastal Command in February 1940, and was also operating on Blenheim IVFs in mid-1941, based at Carew Cheriton, led by its commander Squadron Leader A.M. Glover, when it began changing equipment to Beau Ics in August. At that time 236's crews were engaged in night

* Pilot Officer W.H. Hughes and Sergeant C.F. Myhill were presumed killed.

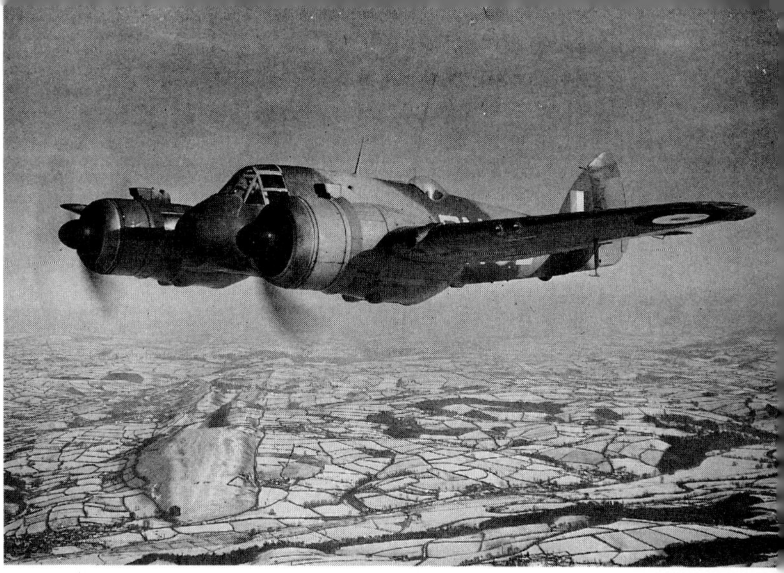

Beau I,R2192, PN-B of 252 Squadron, Coastal Command in 1941. Later served with 29 Squadron, and eventually SOC on 10/8/45.

Mk VIc,JL447, 'G' of 248 Squadron during the winter 1942-43.

NT950, 'T-Tommy', of 236 Squadron, 1944, displaying 'D-Day' striped livery.

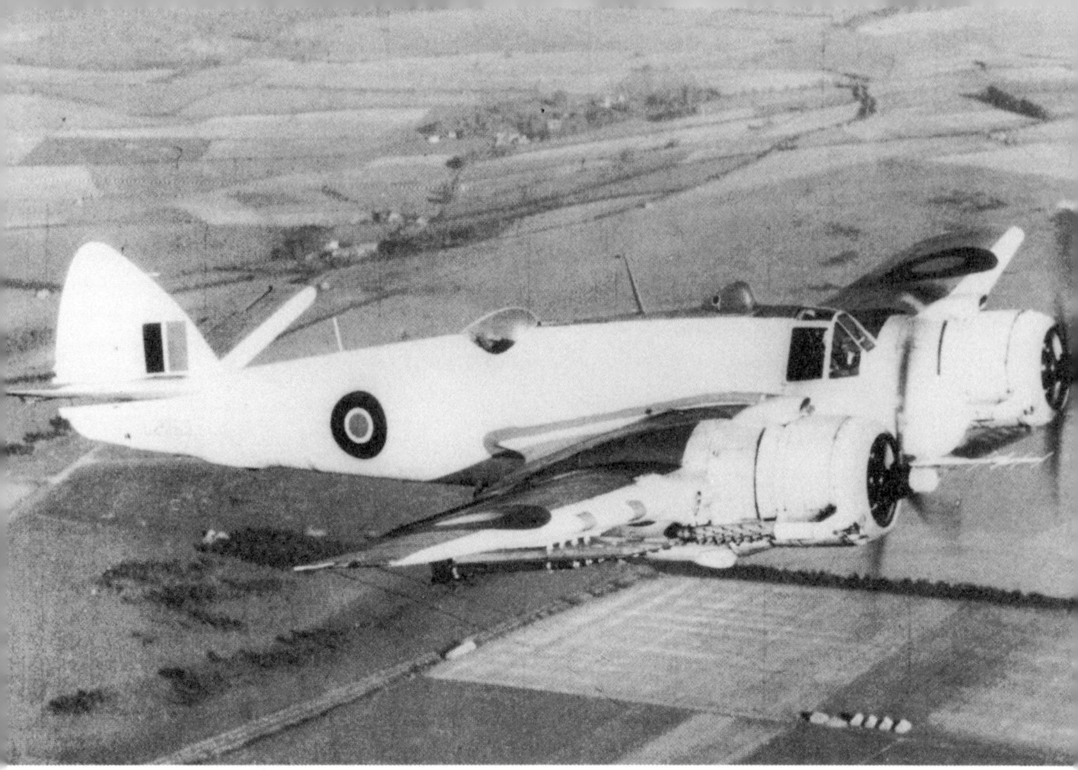

LZ293 which also served as MB-T with 236 Squadron but crashed on 11/8/44.

Beau Ic,T4800,ND-C of 236 Squadron in which Flt Lt K. Gatward flew his famous 'tricolores' sortie over Paris on 12/6/42. It eventually crashed into the sea at the mouth of the Humber on 6/2/43.

intruder raids on German airfields in the Brest peninsula, and the Beaus were slowly mixed in with Blenheims from November, until the ultimate Blenheim sorties flown on 1 January 1942.

Moving north to Sumburgh in the new year, 236 Squadron was stood down from operations by February 1942 in order to supply most of its experienced Beau crews to the Middle East theatre – the remainder being posted to No 2 OTU at Catfoss – but on 9 February 1942 was officially posted to Wattisham and 'reconstituted' with fresh personnel and new Beau Ics to resume its operations in March, primarily in an anti-shipping strike role. On 15 March one such operation saw the squadron lose Beau T4878, followed by two more aircraaft losses four days later, including T4890.

In June 236 Squadron's Beaus received widespread publicity via a singular exploit by one of its crews when, on 12th Flight Lieutenant A.K. Gatward/Sergeant G. Fern* flying Beau T4800, ND-C, took off from Thorney Island and flew to Paris, where Fern dropped two French *tricolores* over the Champs Élysées, then rounded out the sortie by blasting the German Kriegsmarine HQ building with cannon-fire.† The crew were awarded a DFC and DFM respectively for this feat, and a few weeks later Gatward completed his second tour of operations, but was to return for a third tour later, flying Beaus with No 404 Squadron RCAF. In that month 236's Beaus started being fitted with wing bomb carriers to add two 250lb HE bombs to their warload. By 6 July 1942 the unit was based at Oulton, though it should be remarked that – as with all existing Coastal Beau squadrons – 236 was to often operate detachments as far afield as Wick and Thorney Island, Predannack and Leuchars during most of the year.

Two more squadrons in Coastal Command were to become Beau units during 1942. At Dyce No 254 Squadron, commanded by Wing Commander R.H. McConnell, DFC – a unit which had been operational with the Command since January 1940 – commenced conversion to Beaufighters in June with a projected role as a torpedo-strike unit. In the event the squadron did not commence

* Later Group Captain, DSO, DFC and Squadron Leader, DFM respectively

† For personal account of this sortie by Gatward see *Men of Coastal Command, 1939-45* by C. Bowyer; Wm Kimber, 1985

such operations until November. The other unit to convert to Beaus that year was No 404 ('Buffalo') Squadron RCAF. Formed originally at Thorney Island on 15 April 1941, the 'Buffaloes' were based at Dyce from 24 September 1942 where the unit began replacing its Blenheims by Beaus and by the end of September had 15 Beaus on squadron strength. While its crews underwent 'conversion' to Beaus the squadron continued operating a few Blenheims until January 1943 when the unit was declared fully operational with their new aircraft.

Commanded then by Wing Commander G.G. Truscott, 404 Squadron moved base south to Chivenor on 22 January to come under the aegis of No 19 Group, tasked with long-range fighter escorts for Coastal Command's anti-submarine aircraft over the Bay of Biscay. Despite the eager crews' anticipation of plentiful engagements with the Luftwaffe henceforth, however, the following two months brought 'little excitement' (*sic*) apart from an isolated clash with a gaggle of seven Ju88s in March, one of which left bearing apparent damage.

In September 1942 the Air Ministry finalised an agreement that the Beaufighter was to be adopted as Coastal Command's principal strike aircraft, and had compiled a programme for the establishment of a force of ten Beaufighter squadrons within the Command by April 1943. Of these, five squadrons were to be 'Torbeau' (torpedo-strike) units, and the remainder either straight fighters or anti-flak aircraft. This original intention was to be able to form three Beaufighter Strike Wings, each comprising three squadrons – one 'Torbeau' and two fighter/anti-flak – with the tenth squadron to be held in reserve for contingency measures in the event of any enemy break-out by heavy ships.

The three Wings were meant to be based at North Coates, Leuchars, and Wick. The concept was for each Wing to be, in effect, 'self-supportive' i.e. one squadron would first provide a smothering attack on flak opposition, followed *immediately* by the second fighter-bomber Beau wave, then in could come the 'Torbeaus' to apply a *coup de grâce* to shipping targets. Where target-range permitted, an aerial fighter escort of two or three squadrons, mainly Spitfires initially, would provide an air 'umbrella' against Luftwaffe fighter interference in the Beaus'

Wg Cdr (later Grp Capt) A.K. Gatward, DSO, DFC in cockpit of a 404 Squadron RCAF Beaufighter as the unit commander.

TORBEAU. TFX RD438, QM-H of 254 Squadron.

FLYING BUFFALO. 'G-George' of 404 ('Buffalo') Squadron RCAF about to leave for an anti-shipping sortie, loaded with AP-headed RP.

(*Left*) Flg Off Ivor Johnsson in the cockpit of his 404 Squadron RCAF Beau *'Morning Glory'* at Tain, 29/7/43. (*Right*) Wg Cdr Neil Wheeler, DSO, DFC, OC 236 Squadron. Later ACM Sir Neil, GCB, CBE, DSO, DFC, AFC.

activities. Despite the declared urgency in establishing these three Wings, the contemporary overall priorities for reinforcing the RAF in the Mediterranean and in India were to delay ultimate establishment until late 1943.

Nevertheless, the first Strike Wing was brought together at North Coates in November 1942, comprised of Nos 236 Squadron, commanded by Wing Commander H.D. Fraser, OBE, and 254 Squadron, led by Wing Commander R.E.X. Mack, DFC, with a third squadron, 143 commanded by Wing Commander W.D.V. Bennett, DFC, AFC, joining the Wing and already based at North Coates since August 1942. On 20 November came the first attempt at a 'combined' strike against a reported enemy ship convoy off the Dutch coast. For this operation Nos 236 and 254 Squadrons were to be led by Fraser, with a promised fighter escort top cover. In the event contact with the escort was never made, and the Beaufighters lost three aircraft, including Wing Commander Fraser, to the flak, with many others either crashing on return or otherwise badly damaged. The strike had been a costly failure – merely one German tug vessel had been sunk – and badly co-ordinated.

Fraser's command of 236 Squadron passed to Wing Commander Neil Wheeler, DFC (later, ACM Sir Neil, GCB, CBE, DSO, DFC, AFC, FRAeS), but the North Coates Wing was promptly withdrawn from operations in order to receive a thorough training in the new tactics necessary for such complex strikes in cohesion. Only the more experienced crews undertook individual sorties spasmodically during the next four months, while all three Beau squadrons were subjected to an intense flying programme to hone formation-keeping, ultra-low level flying over the sea, navigation and timing, apart from improving accuracy in the matters of cannon, bomb and torpedo practice.

The second Beau Strike Wing was intended to be based at Wick, to comprise of Nos 144 and 404 Squadrons. No 144 Squadron in early 1943 was based at Leuchars flying Hampden torpedo-bombers, but began re-equipping with Beaufighter VIcs in January, then recommenced operations in March as a 'Torbeau' unit. No 404 ('Buffalo') Squadron RCAF was still based at Chivenor during those months, operating over the South-West Approaches as long-range fighters primarily, but on 2 April it moved to Tain in Scotland, then became based at Wick from 20 April. On 27 April 404's Beaus provided advance cover for four 'Torbeaus' of 144 Squadron for a strike on a German convoy. Despite fierce flak opposition, which hit two Beaus heavily, wounding one pilot of 404, the attack saw 144's torpedo-men hit one vessel with three 'fish',* and all Beaus returned to base.

The continuing demands for Beaufighter crews (and squadrons) to reinforce the Middle East campaigns nullified completion of the Wick Strike Wing for many months, exacerbated by the move of 144 Squadron from Scotland to North Africa in June 1943. This diversion of a steady supply of Beaus to Coastal Command also delayed the formation of the projected Leuchars Wing until late 1943; its intended units, Nos 455 Squadron RAAF and 489 Squadron RNZAF continuing to fly their Hampden torpedo-bombers from Scottish bases until November-December.

In April 1943 the first Strike Wing at North Coates finally resumed operations when, on 18 April, 21 Beaus drawn from 143,236, and 254 Squadrons led by Neil Wheeler set out in the early afternoon and, after rendezvousing with their fighter escorts from Coltishall – Spitfires and Mustangs from Nos 118,167, and 613 Squadrons, led by Wing Commander H.P. 'Cowboy' Blatchford, DFC – attacked a German merchant convoy off Texel an hour later and sank the largest ship, *Hoegh Carrier*, apart from severely damaging several other vessels. The actual onslaught lasted no more than four minutes, and all aircraft returned safely to base; a tribute to the skills of each Beau crew and the result of the carefully practised tactics mainly instigated by Neil Wheeler.†

By April 236 Squadron's Beaus had been modified to carry a new weapon, three-inch rocket projectiles (RP) under their wings, and 143 Squadron had also begun to adapt their Beaus for RP fitment; the rockets thereby replacing wing machine guns and bombs as future anti-flak weaponry for 'first-wave' Beaus on combined Wing strikes. One pilot of 236 Squadron, Flying Officer M. Bateman flying Beau T5258, 'B', proved the effectiveness of RP as an anti-shipping weapon on 1 June when he attacked and sank the German U-boat *U-418* with RP some 130 miles west of Brittany.

* Common RAF nickname for torpedoes.
† For fuller details, see *The Strike Wings* by R. Nesbit; Kimber, 1984

Beau VIs of 144 Squadron preparing for take-off.

143 Squadron Beaus attacking an enemy convoy on 22/6/43.

Thereafter the Strike Wing Beaus' use of RP in attacking enemy shipping was to become a regular ploy.

The success of the North Coates Wing on 18 April set the pattern for future tactics. As described by Norman Carr, a pilot with 143 Squadron from late 1943:

> The method of operation was a sea-level trip to the target area, then up to about 3000 feet and close ranks on sighting, attack in quick succession in the following order – anti-flak aircraft with cannons and machine guns; rockets if carried or further cannons and mg; finally torpedoes. The secret of success was in good position and accurate timing, so that each attack was followed *immediately* by the next. With practice and experience the time taken in actually attacking was, I suppose, remarkably short, but the concentration of fire in such a brief period must have been quite dreadful at the receiving end.

One man who could testify to the 'dreadful' effect of such a concentrated attack was Hans Joachim Meyer, a gunner on a *Vorpostenboote* – a converted trawler packed with anti-aircraft guns, usually termed flak-ships by the RAF, used mainly to escort merchant ships in convoy:

> On one such engagement in September 1943, we were escorting four cargo ships along the Dutch coast, heading for Emden, when our look-out warned of some approaching enemy aircraft. Every crew man dropped whatever he was doing and leapt to his appointed battle place; in my case to a twin-20mm cannon mounting in the forward part of the deck. Within minutes a wave of two-engined fighters came at us with cannons and machine guns blazing at mast-height. I commenced firing but immediately found myself in the midst of a hail of shells exploding and ricochetting on and off the deck and superstructure. The noise was ear-splitting, with smoke and fumes everywhere – a frightening experience.
>
> I stuck to my guns during the first onslaught – more by automatic obedience to my duty than common sense – but when this was immediately followed by another wave of Tommies

NE543, UB-E (later, UB-N) of 455 Squadron RAAF at the moment of firing a salvo of eight RP.

Training Beaus from 2(C) OTU, Catfoss, 17/3/43.

Loading three-inch RP with AP 'shot' heads onto their wing rails on a 404 Squadron RCAF Beau, 1944.

236 Squadron Beaus loaded for game, late 1944.

firing rockets, I let go my guns and fell flat on the deck with my hands over my ears – and praying ... An awful bang only inches away from me must have been a rocket missile direct hit on my gun emplacement because when I dared to open my eyes I saw the gun mounting was wrecked, while my No 2 gunner was lying yards away, dead, with an awful stomach wound.

The whole attack could only have lasted a few minutes – then all was quiet again. My head was throbbing with the after-effects of the noise and sheer fear, but I was lucky to be still alive. The deck was a shambles of twisted metal, shattered wood and glass, with the bodies of eight of my comrades lying among the debris. The most frightening part of such attacks was the suddenness – we never really had time to steel ourselves for defence before the Tommies were upon us, strafing and slaughtering; experiences I can never forget.

The successful strike on 18 April was repeated on 29 April when Neil Wheeler led the Wing against some enemy shipping off Terschelling and the Beaus sank three ships, though lost a Beau of 143 Squadron to the flak-gunners. Two days later, however, 31 Beaus set out to find the German cruiser *Nürnberg* off south-east Norway but, without their usual fighter escorts, were swamped by a force of German fighters and lost five Beaufighters in the ensuing maul. Forced to jettison all bombs and torpedoes, the Beaus were still no match for the Focke Wulf Fw190s and Messerschmitt Bf109Fs when it came to pure dogfighting combat manoeuvrability.

Dismayed by these losses but undeterred, the Wing's crews struck again on 17 May, sinking three ships for no Beau losses, then on 13 June all three squadrons participated in a strike against a convoy off Den Helder and in the teeth of a fierce hail of flak sank two vessels but lost one Beau from 143 Squadron, skippered by Squadron Leader P.J.E. Ritchie, DFC. Nine days later the Wing mounted its first strike using RP against an enemy convoy when 34 Beaus struck at a gaggle of ships off Vlieland – with depressing outcome. Two 'Torbeaus' of 254 Squadron were shot into the sea by flak, while three others suffered such severe damage that they were forced to crashland on return. Damage to the enemy vessels was relatively light. Within 72 hours a further loss was that of 143

Squadron's leader, Wing Commander W.D.V. Bennett, whose Beau failed to return from a recce patrol; his place on the unit being then taken over by Wing Commander R.N. Lambert, DFC.

In August 1943 the whole question of retaining the Strike Wings *per se* became the subject of a high-level policy meeting at Air Ministry on August 20; a conference initially requested by the AOC-in-C, Coastal Command, Air Marshal Sir John Slessor who had originated the Strike Wing concept but was by then having to cope with a variety of operational requirements for his Command, including the top priority offensive against U-boats in the Bay of Biscay which called for long-range fighters to help guard the submarine-hunter Leigh Light Wellingtons and Sunderlands from Luftwaffe fighter interference. At the meeting the pros and cons for continuing the Strike Wing plan were debated, backed by statistical evidence of results, costs, and implications in the context of the need for such facets as almost constant necessity for Fighter Command to provide aerial cover escorts. It was stated that in the year ending May 1943 strike squadrons overall had sunk only 21 ships, whereas Bomber Command's mine-laying aircraft could claim a total of 79 enemy vessels. On the other hand, intelligence confirmed that apart from specific sinkings of enemy shipping, the strike squadrons' offensive had created a large reduction in merchant ship traffic along the Dutch coastal zone; while it was also known that Luftwaffe fighter defences had been increased in the Low Countries to counter such attacks, thereby reducing fighter strength in other vital areas of German defences.

The outcome of this meeting was a decision to retain the Strike Wing planning for three such Wings ultimately (as originally conceived by Slessor). Even so, Slessor was still dogged by the steady drain of newly-trained Beaufighter air crews to the Middle East battle areas, delaying his ability to create all three Wings. No 144 Squadron had been withdrawn from his command in June 1943 for operations in the Mediterranean and did not return to Coastal Command again until August when it became based at Tain, later Wick, for the remainder of the year, commanded by Wing Commander David O.F. Lumsden DFC.

The third (Leuchars) Strike Wing finally came into existence at the close of 1943, comprised of two squadrons, Nos 455 RAAF and

Beaus strafing an enemy destroyer with RP and cannon shells.

Beau TFX with full load on RP and torpedo crutches under its belly.

CLOSE WORK. Beaus of 144 Squadron strafing a moored ship in a Norwegian fiord with RP.

SOUND AND FURY. The German *Sperrbrecher* 'Magdeburg' about to die off Royan on 13/8/44, being attacked by Beaus from 236 and 404 Squadrons.

Wg Cdr J. Davenport, DSO, DFC, OC 455 Squadron (centre) with his Flight commanders Sqn Ldr A.L. Wiggins (L) and Sqn Ldr Colin Milsom, DFC. Leuchars, 1944.

Death of a flak-ship in the Skagerrak on 15/10/44 as Beaus of 404 Squadron RCAF attack with RP and cannons.

489 RNZAF. The latter unit, which had spent the previous two years as a Hampden torpedo-bomber squadron, began converting to Beaufighter TFXs at Leuchars in November 1943, commanded by Wing Commander J.S. Dinsdale, DSO, DFC, and was declared operational again from 8 January 1944. No 455 Squadron RAAF, also based at Leuchars flying Hampden TBs, changed its aircraft for Beau TFXs in December 1943 in which month it received a fresh CO, Wing Commander J.N. Davenport, DSO, DFC. The Leuchars Wing – more usually titled the Anzac Wing for obvious reasons – went into action on 14 January, and was to continue operating from Leuchars until the start of April when the squadrons were moved south to Langham as part of the massive preparations for the forthcoming Allied invasion of France in June 1944.

As the renamed Langham Wing, the Anzac squadrons flew their first strike operation on 6 May, attacking a 12-ship convoy off the Dutch coast and sinking one for the loss of one Beau. Eight days later 12 RP-armed Beaus of 455 Squadron led six 'Torbeaus' and six anti-flak Beaus from Langham to seek out a reported convoy off the Dutch coast. Rendezvousing with its Mustang escorts, the Beau force pressed through limited visibility weather conditions and located the objective off Ameland – four merchant ships heavily guarded by no less than 16 flak-ships and minesweepers. A 489 'Torbeau' sank its torpedo into one 3000-ton vessel, leaving it ablaze, while the 1800-ton *Vesta* was hit and left sinking. Not to be outdone 455's RP-Beaus promptly sank a minesweeper, *M-435*, and several other escorts were at least badly damaged. The intense flak encountered shot Beau 'B' of 489 Squadron into the sea and damaged at least six other Beaus badly, causing some eventual 'hairy' landings back at base.

On the night of 5/6 June 1944 the long-anticipated Allied invasion of France commenced – the greatest invasion force ever assembled in the history of human warfare. On that date Coastal Command's Beau squadrons were located as follow:

Sqn	*Base*	*C.O.*
143	Manston	Wg Cdr E.H. McHardy, DSO, DFC
144	Davidstow Moor	Wg Cdr D.O.F. Lumsden, DFC

Sqn	*Base*	*C.O.*
235	Portreath	Wg Cdr J.V. Yonge
236	North Coates	Wg Cdr P.D.F. Mitchell
254	North Coates	Wg Cdr R.E. Burns, DFC
404	Davidstow Moor	Wg Cdr A.K. Gatward, DSO, DFC
455	Langham	Wg Cdr J.N. Davenport, DSO, DFC
489	Langham	Wg Cdr J.S. Dinsdale, DSO, DFC

Of these, No 235 Squadron, though still retaining some of its Beaus, was in the process of converting to Mosquito VIs in June 1944, flying its first Mosquito sortie on 16 June, and relinquishing its last Beaus in July. The other Beau units had been alerted for action on D-Day, with various units sending detachments of Beaus to southern airfields, e.g. 455 Squadron, which sent six Beaus fully loaded with two 500lb and two 250lb bombs apiece from Langham to Manston in the early hours of 6 June, there to stand by at instant 'readiness' throughout the day. As with most other units of Coastal Command, the Beau squadrons' prime role during the initial stages of the invasion was to attack any German surface craft attempting to interfere with the cross-Channel Allied shipping, in particular German E-boats or other fast, armed naval vessels.

Covering the Western Approaches to the Channel in this context were Nos 144, 404, and 235 Squadrons, and on receiving reports of three heavy destroyers of the *Seetier* class setting out from Gironde with the apparent intention of sailing into the Channel, 404 Squadron despatched 14 Beaus in company with aircraft from 144 and 235 Squadrons in mid-evening to attack this trio. The 404 contingent was led by Flight Lieutenant (later, Squadron Leader) Syd Shulemson, DSO who first spotted the destroyers off Belle Ile and promptly led his men down out of the sun, achieving complete surprise. Over the next two days, helped by the Royal Navy, the Beaus wrecked all three destroyers.

At the eastern end of the Channel the attendant Beau units saw little action during the first few days of the Allied invasion, apart from a variety of individual attacks on occasionally-met E-boats, trawlers, and other small ships; these sorties being maintained by day and by night. One exception to such spasmodic success occurred on 15 June when the North Coates and Langham Wings combined for a mass strike on a German convoy reported near Schiermonnikoog. A total of 42 Beaus, escorted by Polish-manned Mustangs from 316 Squadron, originally set out, and eventually located the convoy – the 8000-ton merchantman *Amerskerke* and a 4000-ton E-boat depot ship, protected by 10 M-Class minesweepers and seven R-boats* – off Ameland. Through a hail of flak the Beaus proceeded to sink both major vessels, blew up one minesweeper, badly damaged four other M-Class ships, and registered hits on the remainder. No Beau was lost though several staggered back to bases displaying horrendous scars of battle. This outstanding success had been led by Wing Commander 'Tony' Gadd, the North Coates' Wing Commander Flying, and he received a DFC for his superb leadership, as did his navigator, Flying Officer Duncan Marrow, shortly after.

By August 1944 the Allied invasion forces were sufficiently established in Normandy for the Coastal Beaufighter squadrons to resume their more usual forms of operations, with a re-allocation to other airfields in some cases. No 404 Squadron shifted its base to Strubby on 1 July as part of No 154 (GR) Wing, although in August a detachment returned south to participate in anti-shipping strikes in the Bay of Biscay, and on 7 August Wing Commander 'Ken' Gatward actually landed at Cherbourg – and claimed that this was the first Coastal Command aircraft landing in Europe since D-Day. For three weeks 404's crews flew a total of 141 sorties against enemy shipping, losing three crews in these operations, then on 3 September became based at Banff, commanded now by Wing Commander E.W. Pierce who succeeded Gatward on 24 August.

This latest move brought the 'Buffaloes' back to familiar hunting grounds off Norway, and on 14 September a typical strike was mounted against six ships off Kristiansund, resulting in one ship sunk and others burning. Flak opposition was especially heavy, claiming one Beau forced to ditch and damaging other Beaus severely; one Beau skippered by Squadron Leader Schoales flying the whole return flight to Banff with only one functioning engine, while another Beau piloted by Flying Officer A. Menaul received a

* *Räumboote* i.e. small minesweepers. The RAF title E-boat was applied to German *Schnellboote* – literally, speed-boats.

Dallachy Strike Wing – Nos 144, 455, RAAF and 489 RNZAF Squadrons – seen here at Langham on 5/5/45 prior to a strike on shipping at Kiel.

Wg Cdr Tony Gadd, DFC (rt) with his usual navigator Duncan Marrow, DFC.

direct hit as it was about to attack, wounding Menaul in his arm, shoulder, chest and face. Pressing home his attack regardless of his wounds, Menaul was then given first aid by his navigator Flying Officer J. Tomes and helped by Tomes to guide the crippled aircraft back to a safe landing at base. Both men were awarded immediate DFCs. On 22 October the 'Buffaloes' were on the move again, this time to Dallachy – their fourth shift since May and 14th move of base since original formation.

Joining 404 Squadron at Banff by October 1944 came No 143 Squadron from North Coates, still commanded by the New Zealander 'Sam' McHardy, but in that month 143 began exchanging its Beaus for Mosquito VIs, and in December welcomed a new CO, Wing Commander 'J.M. Maurice', DSO, DFC – the wartime pseudonym for the Frenchman Wing Commander Max Guedj, DSO, DFC, a veteran of Coastal Command strike operations who had previously served on 248 Squadron. A third unit to move to Banff, in September 1944, was 144 Squadron, from Strubby, commanded by Wing Commander A. Gadd, DFC, which continued to fly Beaufighters.

Meanwhile the Anzac Wing at Langham – Nos 455 RAAF and 489 RNZAF – moved base to Dallachy on 20 October, where they were joined two days later by 404 Squadron and 144 Squadron. The four Beau units now formed the Dallachy Wing, leaving Banff Wing as an all-Mosquito Strike Wing. For its first few weeks of existence the Dallachy Wing flew few sorties due to bad weather conditions, but on 8 November the Wing sank three merchant vessels off Midtgulen, and sank ten more vessels of various types by the end of the month.

On 9 December 404 Squadron crews destroyed one merchant vessel by riddling it with 30 RP strikes, but one of the squadron's crews, Flying Officer A.K. Cooper/Warrant Officer C.F. Smith, flying only their second operational sortie, pressed home their attack so low that the Beau's wing hit the main mast, ripped away, and the Beau spun into the sea, exploding and killing both men.

The Dallachy Wing's most usual targets at this period – ships of all types sailing along the Norwegian coast – were seldom easy to find and attack, the ships' captains having long learned to hug the rocky coastline and seek shelter moored close to the sheer cliff-faces of the myriad fiords and other inlets which abounded. Such 'sheltered' vessels meant that the Beaufighter crews needed split-second reactions for any actual attack, having to concentrate not only on the target during firing but particularly on avoiding collision with the rock 'walls' dangerously close by. As one Beau pilot described his experiences:

> One needed to approach any ship moored alongside a cliff ideally from the land side and then pass out over the mouth of the fiord towards the open sea if surprise was to be maintained. This method often meant skipping over a bloody steep mini-mountain first, instantly dive into the fiord, line up and fire within seconds, then bank like hell to avoid spreading oneself all over the cliff sides. We usually made such attacks – when possible – in very close single file, which often meant having to fly through a hail of rock splinters and ricochetting cannon shells and bullets fired by the Beau immediately in front. I had two windscreens smashed by 'friendly' cannon shells bouncing off the cliffs as I passed across my target. Another danger was from the fire of the Beau right behind you during any attack. If its skipper was a sprog on operations of this kind he was liable to start firing too soon – which gave me very loose bowels on occasion ...

In January 1944 No 144 Squadron relinquished its torpedo role and reverted to cannons and machine guns for future sorties, thereby leaving 489 Squadron as the sole torpedo-Beau unit of the Dallachy Wing. Operations during January saw the Wing claim only nine vessels sunk, but on 9 February came a strike which was to cost the Wing dear and would thereafter be referred to in unit diaries as 'Black Friday'. In the early afternoon a combined force of Beaus from 144, 404, and 489 Squadrons escorted by Mustangs from 65 Squadron and a pair of ASR Warwicks of 279 Squadron set out for Ford Fiord to attack a reported Narvik-class destroyer, apparently guarded by flak-ships. The operation was led on this occasion by Wing Commander Colin Milson, DSO, DFC who had succeeded Jack Davenport in command of 455 Squadron on 23 October 1944. On reaching the target area Milson attempted to attack from the land side but the position of the prime objective, the destroyer,

DE-BRIEFING. 455 Squadron crews on return from Esbjaerg on 27/6/44/ At table, seated behind the Intelligence Officer, is Wg Cdr Jack Davenport.

HOW THEY CAME HOME. Beau NE812 of 455 Squadron (Flg Off Ian Masson/Flt Sgt Knight) at Langham on return from Borkum, 14/5/44 with flak-damaged hydraulics.

moored close to a cliff, obviated such an approach and Milson finally led his Beaus in from seaward, heading in to the narrow, twisting fiord between towering rock faces and into the teeth of concentrated, awesome flak from shore batteries ranged on each side in addition to the fire from the destroyer's protective flak-ships. Added to this 'valley of death' came a gaggle of Focke Wulf Fw 190s of *Jagdgeschwader 5*, based at Herdla, near Bergen as the Beaus made their attacks.

Within mere minutes a total of nine Beaus had been shot down – six of these from 404 Squadron alone – plus a Mustang; the latter a victim of the German fighters while the Beaus had been mainly victims of the flak. In 'balance', five Fw 190s were shot down, including the 69-victory 'ace', Leutnant Rudi Linz, commander of 12./JG5. Back at Dallachy later many of the Beaus who managed to regain base did so with aircraft severely damaged but crashlanded. It had been the most costly strike to date for the Strike Wings.

No 404 Squadron was to suffer further casualties over the following weeks – four Beaus and their crews during the first three weeks of March – but on 22 March the squadron was notified that it was to convert to Mosquitos and two days later half the squadron moved to Banff for that purpose, followed by the other half of the unit by 3 April. Then on 22 April the 'Buffaloes' restarted operations with Mosquitos. The remaining Beau units continued their near-daily offensive up and down the Norwegian coast during the closing weeks of the European war, with mounting success. On 26 February three 'Torbeaus' from 489 Squadron blew up the German vessel *Alsterufer*, and eventually 489 Squadron flew its ultimate war sorties on 3 May 1945. By then 455 Squadron had also flown its last strike operation, on 26 April, in Norwegian waters, then moved base to Thornaby on 3 May to attack shipping fleeing from the Baltic; damaging the tanker *Taifun* near Kiel that day. No 489 Squadron, commanded by Wing Commander D.H. Hammond, DSO, DFC, since February 1945, later moved to Banff in June ostensibly to convert to Mosquitos, but was disbanded there on 1 August. No 455 Squadron flew its last war sorties on 21 May – an anti-submarine recce searching for U-boats yet to surrender – and four days later was also disbanded, at Dallachy. On that same date, 25 May 1945, the remaining Beaufighter unit, 144 Squadron, followed suit by being officially disbanded at Dallachy, having despatched its final war sorties on 15 May.

The Beaufighters' contribution to Coastal Command's unceasing offensive had been a prodigious and costly record of undiluted courage, determination, and skill. Almost invariably needing to press home every attack into the very muzzles of a host of anti-aircraft flak guns, and prey to any marauding Luftwaffe fighters, which possessed much superior combat agility in any air-to-air engagement, the Beau crews had never faltered in attempting to fulfil their duty, despite a loss rate *proportionally* on a par with the grievous losses of Bomber Command. Their operational tactics had been evolved in the hardest school – sheer 'on the job' experience – but their overall achievements had without question dealt a crippling blow to Germany's merchant shipping life-lines. Moreover, the Beau crews' war had, in the main, been one almost unknown and unpublicised during the fateful years, 1942-45.

CHAPTER FOUR

Desert Eagles

The introduction of the Beaufighter to RAF Middle East Command in early 1941 can be compared directly with the type's initial issue to Coastal Command, in that it provided each Command with its first true long-range offensive fighter. Although that arrival in the Mediterranean theatre of operations was originally a somewhat hasty measure attempting to supplement the meagre Allied air strength in the ill-starred Greek campaign, it was to be in North Africa that the Beaufighter found its real vocation. Here its range, all-round performance, and devastating battery of armament quickly proved to be a feared scourge of Axis ground forces – in essence a long-arm artillery on the wing which might appear at any time, any place, by day or night, cutting a swathe of destruction. Over the following four years in North Africa, Italy, and other eastern Mediterranean zones Beaufighters were to undertake diverse forms of firstline operations as deck-level strafers, night fighters, torpedo-strike ship killers, day bombers, photo-recce 'eyes', apart from other no less vital roles.

The first Beaufighters to arrive in the Mediterranean theatre – as far as can be ascertained from contemporary but incomplete records – would appear to have been the detachment of 15 Beaus from No 252 Squadron which left the United Kingdom en route to Malta on 1 May 1941; one of which aborted and returned to St Eval, while a second Beau, T3229, was forced to land in neutral Portugal and was interned. The remaining 13 Beaus eventually reached Luqa, Malta, safely.

There was, however, an earlier reference to a Beaufighter in North Africa. On 16 April 1941 an Italian fighter pilot, Sergente Luigi Gorrini of 85° *Squadriglia*, 18° *Gruppo*, 3° *Stormo*, claimed to have shot down a lone Beaufighter over Benghazi, its crew of two taking to their parachutes. Whether his victim was misidentified is unresolved. The unit records of 252 Squadron for the period May-November 1941 were lost in the main, with only fragmentary references now available, but it can be established that of the 13 Beaus which began operations from Luqa over Sicily and Crete, four were destroyed on the ground by enemy air raids, while two others failed to return from sorties.

By June 1941, the surviving Beaus and crews of 252 Squadron had moved from Malta to Edku where they were 'merged' into No 272 Squadron until December. On 22 December Squadron Leader A.G. Wincott was appointed in command of No 252 Squadron which became a full squadron in its own right again in January 1942, tasked with 'naval co-operation' duties i.e. convoy escort sorties between Malta and Egypt primarily.

No 272 Squadron, which had converted to Beaufighters at Chivenor in May 1941, left the UK in that month and arrived at Abu Sueir, Egypt on 31 May 1941, via Malta, and on 1 June the unit CO, Squadron Leader A.W. Fletcher DFC, flew the first sortie from Egypt, escorting a convoy evacuating troops from Crete. Two days later the squadron strafed some oil installations at Beirut as the start of operations in the Syrian campaign. By mid-July the squadron was based in Egypt again, at Edku, and on 24 July its crews there made the first combat claims for enemy aircraft when Flight Lieutenant Campbell shot down two Junkers Ju87s from a force attacking an Allied convoy. Four days later further claims came when Flying Officer Clarke shot down an Italian Z.501 flying boat, while Squadron Leader Fletcher destroyed six Italian aircraft on the ground. On 30 July Squadron Leader Fletcher added three more Italian SM79s destroyed on the ground to his personal tally. By late August the squadron was brought up to full strength at Edku – having its various detachments returned to the 'fold' – and on 27th Sergeant Green claimed another enemy aircraft shot down. Though continuing to be based at Edku, 272 Squadron continued detachments of a few Beaus to Malta during the late summer; while in October the unit received a new CO, Wing Commander Robert Yaxley MC, who had led the original detachment of 252 Squadron to Malta and was awarded a DFC on 17 October.

On 18 November 1941 the Allied armies in North Africa launched *Operation Crusader* – the largest Commonwealth offensive

(Top left) Beau BT-D of 252 Squadron, 1942.

(*Centre left*) 272 Squadron Beau – well sanded and oil-bespattered – at Edku, 1941.

(*Below*) 'F-Freddie' of 272 Squadron taxies out, Edku, 1941.

ever mounted to date – and on that first day Allied aircraft ranged far and wide, attacking grounded Axis aircraft primarily. For the Beau crews of 272 Squadron it was a day of mass destruction. Shortly after noon Pilot Officers Crawford and Lee, with Sergeant Ross shot down two Junkers Ju52s, while at 1415 hours six Beaus strafed Tmimi airfield just as five Ju52s were taking off. All five were destroyed, then a Henschel Hs126, followed by four SM79s burned out on the ground. Flying Officer Bartlett rounded out the sortie by shooting down a Fieseler Fi156 *Storch*. Next day brought more intense action when six Beaus returned to Tmimi in the early morning and proceeded to destroy at least seven Bf109s and Ju87s on the ground.

On the third day of *Crusader* 272's Beaus again struck at Tmimi, when in the early afternoon eight Beaus claimed five aircraft shot down, with a further 15 aircraft destroyed on the ground. On the 21st, for the fourth day in succession, 272 returned to Tmimi at 10.00 hours, then two hours later were over Martuba airfield where five Luftwaffe aircraft were destroyed on the ground. All these successful strafes and combats had inflicted no losses on 272 Squadron, but on 23 November, when four Beaus strafed Barce airfield destroying four SM79s on the 'deck', Pilot Officer Lee became a victim of the flak defences. In the event, Lee and his observer returned to the squadron two days later, none the worse for their escapade. On 26 November six Beaus carried out a 'noon' strafe of Jedabia airfield, destroying five Italian aircraft but losing one Beau (Sergeants Price/Southern) to the flak.

December 1941 saw 272 and the 'reconstituted' 252 Squadrons continue their strafing operations daily. On the 2nd five Beaus from 272 strafed Barce airfield, wrecking seven Fiat BR20s on the ground but losing Beau T4665 in the process. Four days later four Beaus from 272 returned to a familiar target, Tmimi airfield, but lost Pilot Officer Snow – almost certainly the victim of Oberleutnant Rödel of II/JG27 who claimed a Beau shot down near Tobruk. Later in the same morning four more Beaus attacked the same airfield, damaging five Ju87s on the ground, but Flight Lieutenant Campbell's Beau was hit by flak and forced to land some 40 miles south of the objective. A fellow Beau skipper, Pilot

Officer Hammond, landed nearby and helped Campbell effect repairs whereupon Campbell managed to take off again, only to crashland later. Hammond duly landed alongside once more, picked up Campbell and his observer, then took off and destroyed the crashed Beau with cannon fire before returning to base.

Another desert 'pick-up' incident occurred on 19 December when the Beaus of 272 were out seeking targets of opportunity and Pilot Officer Crawford's aircraft was hit by ground fire and crashlanded some 35 miles south-west of Barce. Flight Lieutenant Bartlett duly landed and picked up the stricken Beau's crew – only to be fired on by two enemy tanks and a pair of armoured vehicles! Though Bartlett's Beau received several hits he managed to take off and fly back to base.*

On 22 December 272 Squadron lost one Beau (Pilot Officer Orr/Sergeant Jackson) over the Agedabia area, while next day five Beaus from 272 were attacking Agheila when they were 'bounced' by Oberleutnant Gerhard Homuth of I/JG27 who shot down two Beaus in quick succession, skippered by Flying Officers Baker and Lee respectively. Operations were maintained throughout the Christmas 'holiday' period, resulting in the loss of Beau T4720 of 252 Squadron on Christmas Day. By then, although *Operation Crusader* had a few more days to run, aerial activity by the opposing air forces had been reduced on an overall scale; due partly to needs for replenishment of fresh crews and aircraft and, on the Allied side, to the transfer of some units, aircraft and crews to the Far East theatre of operations now that Japan had entered hostilities.

Throughout the bitter fighting of 1941 No 272 Squadron and its 'lodgers' (*sic*) of 252 Squadron had been the only firstline Beaufighter force available in the North African struggles, but fresh Beau units were soon to arrive in the zone during 1942. In January No 252 Squadron finally assumed full squadron operational status, still commanded by Squadron Leader Wincott, and among its pilots was Pilot Officer H.H.K. Gunnis who, on the 18th, accounted for three Ju88s, although in the same engagement Beau T4833 (Pilot Officer Beet) failed to return. Gunnis would later

* Tragically, Bartlett was killed on 1 January 1942 when his tent caught fire at Edku.

claim a total of at least seven enemy aircraft destroyed and was awarded a DFC.

A third Beaufighter unit, No 89 Squadron, had begun arriving in Egypt in November 1941 from Colerne where it had been reformed on 25 September destined for a nightfighter defence role in the Middle East. Commanded by Wing Commander George Stainforth, AFC, of Schneider Trophy fame, 89 Squadron was eventually fully assembled at Abu Sueir by December and began training for its prime role of night defence of the Suez Canal areas, and flying its initial night patrols from 3 January 1942. 89 Squadron's aircraft were fitted with airborne radar for their task – the first AI-equipped examples to join the Middle East RAF. For 252 Squadron, January 1942 proved to be a slow start to operations, with only four days on which the unit carried out routine convoy escort patrols, but two Beaus were lost, T4649 and T4833 on the 8th and 18th respectively.

Another *ostensible* Beaufighter unit in Egypt in 1941 had been No 46 Squadron. In May of that year the squadron, commanded by Squadron Leader A.C. Rabagliati, DFC, had sailed for Egypt but arrived there minus its air crews and Hurricane aircraft, these having been transferred to 126 Squadron on Malta. Thus, 46 Squadron became virtually a maintenance unit at Abu Sueir until May 1942 when it acquired some AI-Beaus of an 89 Squadron detachment at Edku and was allotted a night defence role protecting the Alexandria naval base and the general Nile Delta area, being commanded now by Squadron Leader J.A.A. Read. By early 1942 several other units in the Middle East had been issued with a few Beaufighters as part of their mixed aircraft equipment; two Beaus went to No 69 Squadron at Luqa, Malta in January 1942, while No 2 Photo-Reconnaissance Unit (PRU) in Egypt also received a Beau which was stripped of all armament and re-equipped for camera sorties.

Two more Beaufighter units came under the aegis of RAF Middle East during 1942. No 227 Squadron, which had begun to reform in England as an intended Beau nightfighter unit for service in North Africa, received no aircraft of its own initially, and only came into being as a full Beau squadron when, on 20 August 1942, a detachment from 235 Squadron operating temporarily from

(*Above*) Nightfighter Beau, believed from 89 Squadron, Egypt 1942.

(*Right*) Wing Commander George H. Stainforth, AFC, OC 89 Squadron, 1941.

Luqa, Malta was retitled 227 Squadron, commanded by Wing Commander D.R. Shore, DFC. Able to commence operations *per se* immediately, on the same date the 'new' squadron put up 13 Beaus to escort nine Beauforts of 39 Squadron in an attack on one of Rommel's convoys. Two of 227's Beaus failed to return.

For the following few months 227's Beaus continued to provide protection escorts to anti-shipping units striking at German and Italian convoys attempting to reinforce and resupply Rommel's Afrika Korps but at a steady rate of casualties. By November 1942 the squadron began adding pure aerial offensive sweeps, by day and by night, to its operational roles, and in December its crews claimed at least 20 enemy aircraft destroyed or damaged, apart from setting fire to three enemy vessels. In that month another Beau unit arrived at Maison Blanche, Algiers, No 153 Squadron, commanded by Wing Commander W.G. Moseby, DFC, which commenced operations on 25 December. In January 1943 the squadron opened its victory tally – a Focke Wulf Fw200 shot down by Flying Officer Williamson in Beau V8631 on the 13th – and claimed at least 12 enemy aircraft destroyed during the month, all in night defence sorties protecting the Algiers-Bone areas.

In February 1943, however, No 227 Squadron was withdrawn from operations and its crews dispersed to other units. This disbandment only lasted for a brief period because on 3 March a 'new' 227 Squadron was reconstituted at Edku from crews withdrawn from Nos 252 and 272 Squadrons and operations recommenced on 21 April under the command of Wing Commander R.M. Mackenzie, DFC, AFC. In the interim two more Beaufighter units were to become added to firstline operations, Nos 603 and 108 Squadrons. No 603 Squadron, after a frustrating period of non-operational duties, became operational again at Edku with effect from 1 February 1943, commanded by Wing Commander H.A. Chater, and an influx of air crews – many from 272 Squadron – began joining the squadron.

By the beginning of March full re-equipment with Beaus was completed with most crews converted onto the type, and the unit's initial role was to escort naval convoys along the North African coast; a task occasionally 'enlivened' (*sic*) when the notoriously trigger-happy Royal Navy gunners chose to shoot at their own aerial protectors! No 108 Squadron, which in its previous existence had been a distinguished Wellington bomber unit in North Africa, was reformed at Shandur, Egypt on 10 March 1943 as a Beaufighter nightfighter unit, commanded by Wing Commander J.A.A. Read, DFC, tasked with night defence of the Suez Canal and Nile Delta areas. A part of its initial establishment included a detached Flight of No 89 Squadron based then on Malta, and one of the latter's Beau crews, Flight Lieutenant Verity/Warrant Officer Farquharson, claimed 108's first fighter victory on 17 April by destroying a Heinkel He111 off Trapani.

While these various Beau squadrons gradually joined the Middle East Allied air forces, the brunt of daily operations throughout 1942 fell upon the original units, Nos 252 and 272 Squadrons, with No 89 Squadron now available for night defence of the Egyptian headquarters' zones *et al.* In effect, the two day squadrons had split roles. Though committed mainly to aiding the Allied armies in North Africa by ground-strafing operations and keeping a protective eye over Allied shipping off the coast, they were also frequently required to provide small detachments to Malta to assist the RAF's unceasing attacks on Axis shipping convoys plying between Italy and North Africa – Rommel's supply lifelines, which were increasingly to be supplemented by large formations of Luftwaffe transport aircraft carrying reinforcement troops and vital materials. In common with all Allied squadrons involved in the desert campaigns, the Beaufighter units therefore led virtually a nomad form of living, becoming accustomed to operating at times from forward landing grounds far removed from the unit 'base' airfields, and undertaking such moves often at mere hours' notice. As Jim Gardner, a pre-war RAF 'regular' armourer summed up:

> Life on a forward airstrip was simply work. Everything boiled down to one priority – keep the aircraft flying no matter what it took. We always suffered shortages – food, water, spares, etc – but improvisation was the order of the day. Though every tradesman had his distinct responsibilities, there were no demarcation lines on jobs – everyone pitched in. Life revolved around the 'kites' and the job we were all there to do. Parades, bullshit, 'proper' uniform, 'proper' channels, etc were left to the

gabardine-clothed penguins back in Cairo – out in the bundoo such items were disregarded.

No 89's radar-equipped Beaus took little time in securing success, when on the night of 2/3 March 1942 Squadron Leader D.S. Pain in Beau X7671 and Flying Officer R.C. 'Moose' Fumerton each destroyed a Heinkel He111 over the Alexandria area – the first radar-controlled night 'kills' over the Delta zone. Fumerton, later Wing Commander, DFC, was a Canadian who by July 1944 – when he returned to Canada – scored a total of at least 14 victories, mostly with 89 Squadron.

By March 89 Squadron already had detachments of Beaus at Malta and Edku, and the latter had a particularly successful night on 28/29 April when its Beaus intercepted a mixed force of 25 Ju88s of I/KLG1 and He111s over Alexandria. Of these, Squadron Leader J.A.A. Read destroyed two He111s, while Flight Lieutenant R.M. Mackenzie* claimed a third as 'probably' destroyed. Two nights later 89's crews scored again, with Flying Officer V.C. Lovell destroying a Ju88 and Flight Lieutenant H. Edwards damaging a second Junkers. As stated previously, a detachment of 89 Squadron at Edku became the foundation of a second Beau nightfighter unit, No 46 Squadron, by May 1942, and on the night of 16 May claimed its first victim.

By day the Beau crews of 252 and 272 Squadrons saw virtual non-stop operations throughout most of 1942. An early example of their prowess was on 11 March when Beaus from 252 Squadron helping to cover an Allied convoy bound for Tobruk claimed six enemy aircraft which tried to bomb the ships. Pilot Officer Gunnis alone shot down a Ju88 and two He111s while Flying Officer A.D. Frecker (later, Squadron Leader DFC) claimed a pair of He111s and Pilot Officer Smith destroyed a Ju88. Though nominally a fighter, the Beaufighter was nevertheless not intended specifically for the cut and thrust of any normal aerial combat with opposing fighters, lacking the necessary agility in manoeuvrability for such engagements. This 'defect' seldom deterred Beau crews, however, if

* Later Squadron Leader, DSO, DFC, AFC who served with Nos 89 and 46 Sqns, then commanded 227 Squadron. A New Zealander from Tai Tepu, who had joined the RAF in 1937.

Beau 'R',46 Squadron which crashlanded at Edku when its starboard wheel failed to lock 'Down', March 1943.

Wg Cdr R.C. 'Moose' Fumerton, DFC of 89 and 406 Squadrons.

a clash with Italian and/or German fighters was possible, and no few Beau pilots became relatively high-scoring aces during the Middle East campaigns, both by day and at night.

As an instance of the Beau's ability to mix it if needed, on 14 April four Beaus of 272 Squadron were among the various Allied aircraft which set out from Bu Amud to attack an Axis convoy heading for Tripoli. This convoy was heavily protected by some 30 Ju88, Bf109s and Bf110s, but one Beau pilot, Squadron Leader W. Riley, destroyed two Bf110s and severely damaged a Ju88. Riley, an ex-Battle of Britain pilot, was later to be killed in an air collision on 15 July, having been awarded a DFC.

By May 1942 the Luftwaffe had begun despatching large formations of transport aircraft from Crete to North Africa with reinforcement troops and equipment, and on 12 May five Beaus from 252 Squadron were among 14 RAF fighters despatched to intercept one such reported force. The latter, comprised of 13 Junkers Ju52s loaded in each case with 20 troops, escorted by a Bf110, were engaged head-on some 50 miles from the African coast and in the ensuing mêlée the RAF pilots claimed nine Ju52s and the Bf110 destroyed, with two other Ju52s forced to land on the beachline with wounded aboard. Of these claims, five Ju52s went down under the guns of the Beaus, the successful pilots being Squadron Leader Wincott, Pilot Officer Gunnis and Flight Sergeant Ivey. One Beau (Sergeants Cripps/Bateman) was lost, being shot into the sea in flames by a gunner of one Ju52, Unteroffizier Graf von Polier.

On the morning of 26 May Rommel commenced an all-out offensive against the Gazala-Bir Hacheim line as the start of some six weeks of bitter fighting on land and in the air which was to force the Allied armies to retreat all the way back to El Alamein before the onslaught finally ground to a halt. Once this offensive was under way, the Allied air forces became primarily concerned with direct support for the retreating armies, maintaining almost round-the-clock ground-strafing attacks on Axis troops and vehicles, though such sorties often meant being at a disadvantage whenever the German and Italian air forces appeared on the scene.

Despite this high priority in operations, an equally vital task of protecting the various Allied convoys attempting to resupply and succour the heavily besieged bastion of Malta had to be continued. One such convoy had reached an area between Crete and North Africa – usually referred to as 'Bomb Alley', owing to it being well within range of Axis bombers – on 14 June, and among the various 'shifts' of Allied units trying to cover the convoy were nine Beaus from 252 and 272 Squadrons in the afternoon. In various clashes with Bf109s from JGs 27 and 53, five Beaus were shot down, though one crew, Pilot Officer Rogers/Sergeant Woolven of 272 Squadron, was later retrieved from the sea by a destroyer. Next day two more Beaus of 272 were lost while escorting a force of Beauforts attempting to carry out a torpedo strike against elements of the Italian fleet.

In February 1942 No 272 Squadron had received a new 'boss' for its 'A' Flight, Squadron Leader C.V. Ogden who, in the following month became the squadron CO. Ogden, fresh from the UK, had previously created something of a sensation on being posted to the Catfoss OTU for 'conversion' to Beaus. A quiet, almost meditative man at first acquaintance, Ogden had been 'taken in hand' by one young instructor at Catfoss who patiently explained the general principles necessary for flying a twin-engined aircraft. Ogden listened impassively, then with the instructor's OK to 'try a few circuits to get the hang of it', calmly took off in a Beau, zoomed at an alarming angle to 5000 feet, then put the Beau through a series of aerobatic manoeuvres never witnessed before at Catfoss, ending with a powered dive culminating in a perfect loop! On landing, Ogden listened calmly to an outburst from his instructor, then quietly pointed out that he had until recently been a test pilot with Bristol's – testing Beaufighters! On arrival on 272 Squadron, Ogden quickly began leading his Beaus on operations, and commented:*

> I personally think the Beaufighter did its best work on ground-strafing missions. Various types of target were attacked, but I always felt that the best results were obtained on road-strafes. Our usual technique was to send out two sections, fly about 15 miles out to sea, then turn west parallel to the coast until opposite the target area and then turn in. Having

* Correspondence with author, 1975

ROYAL VISIT. 272 Squadron crews being inspected at Edku, May 1942 by HRH Duke of Gloucester. From L: Plt Offs Deppe (Belgian); Hodgson (Canadian); Pete Cobley (English); Delcour (Belgian); HRH; Wg Cdr C.V. Ogden.

Junkers Ju52 being destroyed on the ground by 252 Squadron Beau on 12/10/42, between Sidi Barrani and Mersa Matruh.

approached well below any radar cover, we preserved an element of surprise. As we approached the road one section would turn right and the other went left. With No 2 about a mile behind the leader, we would then fly down the road at zero feet and fly straight at vehicles on the road. A quick burst at 100 to 50 yards, pull up over the roof of it and down on the road again, ready for the next. Any vehicle missed by the leader would be finished off by his No.2, and if we ran into a convoy there were plenty of pickings for a No.2. Only on two occasions did aircraft actually scrape the road with their airscrew tips, but in each case the Beau returned safely.

Ogden, who remained commander of 272 until September 1942 when he was succeeded by Wing Commander J.M. White, was promoted to Wing Commander and awarded a DFC later.

Ogden also described an 'unofficial' form of additional armament fitted to some of 272's Beaus during his period of command:

Another task allocated to our Beaus during the desert battles was attacking small supply boats (F-boats) which were used in large numbers to carry supplies to enemy advance formations along the coast road. They were usually in convoys of six to eight, and always had fighter protection. This was an unpopular target with Beau crews as the boats always had a single-engined fighter cover, while the boats themselves were heavily armed, each having one 88mm heavy flak and four light anti-aircraft guns. For these attacks I had our Beaus fitted with two rearward-firing Lewis guns, one in each engine nacelle, plus an additional free Lewis gun for the navigator. All three guns were loaded entirely with incendiary bullets; the idea being that when enemy fighters came in to attack we filled the sky behind us with a good pyrotechnic display which caused the enemy fighters to hesitate just long enough for us to make our own attack. Then down on the water and away. We were quite successful in these attacks, and in 1942 over 100 boats were credited as sunk by 272 and 252 Squadrons.

Probably the most dangerous type of ground-strafing sorties were those directed against Luftwaffe airfields, where a combination of fierce ground flak opposition and standing patrols of German fighters could be deadly. On 27 June, for example, four Beaus of 272 Squadron strafed the Derna airfield, riddling six Ju52s on the ground, but lost one Beau (Pilot Officer Wood/Sergeant Naylor) to Feldwebel Heyne of I/NJG2. Next day, over the same target, Pilot Officer Gunnis of 252 Squadron destroyed two Ju52s on the airfield but was wounded badly in the legs by groundfire. His observer, Sergeant E.W. Waller, applied tourniquets to Gunnis' legs, then took over control and flew the Beau back to base – a feat which brought him a well-deserved DFM award shortly after.

On 2 July Beaus from 252 strafed the landing strips LG16, LG17, and LG18 at Fuka and claimed three Bf109s on the ground. As the Beaus then fled out to sea two Bf109s of I/JG27 and some Italian fighters scrambled in pursuit. One Beau was shot into the sea by Leutnant Hans-Arnold Stahlschmidt while a second was shot down by an Italian fighter. A third Beau managed to regain base but looked 'like a colander' ... 252 exacted a modicum of revenge for these losses by returning to Fuka next day and strafing all these LGs, destroying or at least severely damaging eleven Bf109s and an Italian SM79 bomber. That night the radar-Beaus of 89 Squadron proved equally successful by shooting down four Ju88s, plus two other Luftwaffe bombers claimed as damaged. One of these pilots was Sergeant A.M.O. Pring (later, Pilot Officer, DFM) destined to achieve fame and death in India in the following year (See Chapter V, 'Whispering Death').

By the end of July 1942 aerial action over the desert had – relatively speaking – slackened to a degree, although the nightfighter Beaus of 46 and 89 Squadrons continued to add to their scoreboards; 46 Squadron crews destroying four enemy bombers on two nights, 28 July and 31 July. Ubiquitous as ever, 252 Squadron detached six Beaus to Malta on 9 August in anticipation of an incoming Allied supply convoy, while a second detachment from the squadron moved temporarily to Cyprus. By late August, however, all had returned to the main base at Edku to resume normal operations.

Meantime the Beau nightfighters continued to claim victims. On the night of 23/24 August Squadron Leader Pain of 89 Squadron destroyed a Ju88 from II/KLG1, while Pilot Officer White of 46

LATE ARRIVALS. Beau T5045,BT-G of 252 Squadron, crewed by Sqn Ldr A.D. Frecker, DFC/ Flg Off T. Armstrong, DFC, with a fitter Flt Sgt 'Paddy' Clark as 'passenger', was hit by flak over Tamet airfield on 6/12/42, and crashlanded some 30 miles away from target. After 16 days of trekking across the desert all three were safely retrieved by a British armoured car patrol. Photos show crashed Beau (67) and its crew, from left Frecker, Armstrong (holding unofficial squadron badge), and Clark.

Squadron was directed onto a presumed 'Heinkel 111' and shot the aircraft down – only to be told later that his 'Heinkel' had been a USAAF B-25! Fortunately a subsequent court of inquiry absolved White and his ground controller from blame – a case of *c'est la guerre* ...

On the last day of August 1942 Rommel launched a triple-armed offensive all along the Allied front – which proved to be the Afrika Korps' final such offensive of the North African campaigns – and aerial action immediately escalated among the Commonwealth squadrons. The Beaus of 272 and 252 Squadrons were out in the morning seeking targets, with 272 crews destroying two Ju52s, but with 252 Squadron losing two Beaus during ground- strafing sweeps along the Gambut-Bardia section of the long north coast road.

Throughout September the Beaus maintained their daily and nightly operations to good effect, claiming more victories steadily though not without casualties. The nightfighters of 46 and 89 Squadrons were particularly active during the month, such as the night of 4 September when 46's crews claimed three victories to add to a Ju88 destroyed the previous night. 46 claimed two more victims on the night 7/8 September, then on 27/28th added an He111 destroyed.

That same night, however, brought tragedy to 89 Squadron when its commanding officer, Wing Commander George Stainforth and his observer Pilot Officer Lawson, flying Beau X7700, were both killed. The Beau's engines had failed and both men baled out too low for their parachutes to deploy fully. Command of 89 then passed to Wing Commander J.A. Leathart, DSO, a veteran ex-Battle of Britain ace who eventually retired from the RAF in October 1962 as Air Commodore, CB, DSO. In the same month Nos 252 and 272 Squadrons also received new COs; 252 being commanded now by Wing Commander P.H. Bragg with effect from 16 September, and Wing Commander J.M. White taking over the reins of 272 from Wing Commander Ogden.

Actual command of a day Beau squadron at this period was, to say the least, something of an administrative and technical problem, in that the Beau units were rarely altogether on one airfield. For much of September No 252 Squadron had kept one detachment based on Malta, while on 30th it also detached six Beaus to Palestine; the remaining aircraft and personnel being still at the official unit base, Edku. Nevertheless, the Edku-based Beaus reached a peak of intensity in ground-attacks during October 1942; destroying six enemy aircraft and burning four ships into the bargain.

In the evening of 23 October 1942 the crucial battle of El Alamein commenced, preceded by a thunderous Allied artillery barrage of an intensity reminiscent of those fired along the Western Front in France during 1916-18. In the initial stages of the ground offensive the success or failure of the Allied 'push' was very much in the balance, and much of the Allied air forces' operations was aimed at preventing Rommel's forces achieving strong concentrations.

Such priorities did not preclude the long-range Beaus from other types of offensive action, and on 25 October 252 Squadron despatched seven Beaus to attack an enemy convoy reported heading for Tobruk, the ships being escorted by a destroyer and three enemy aircraft. Four Beaus promptly destroyed the three aerial escorts – two Ju88s and a Dornier Do24 flying boat – while the other trio strafed the ships. Later in the day eight Beaus of 272 encountered a mass of 35 Ju52s with six escorting Bf110s north of Tobruk and immediately attacked. Eventually four Ju52s and a Bf110 were known to have been destroyed, but the squadron commander, Wing Commander White and his navigator Flight Sergeant Francis died in collision with one of the Ju52s. White's command was taken over by one of 272's Flight commanders, Squadron Leader Anthony Watson, DFC. An ex-Blenheim pilot who had gained his DFC during the Raschid Ali revolt operations in Iraq in May 1941, Watson was later to be awarded a DSO, be credited with at least eleven enemy aircraft destroyed in air-to-air combat, apart from numerous surface 'scores', and appointed OC 227 Squadron in December 1942, but was lost on operations shortly after taking up that appointment.

On 6 November 1942 No 272 Squadron left en bloc to fly to Ta Kali, Malta in order to join the island's increasing offensive against Axis convoys crossing the Mediterranean, where the unit received a fresh CO, Wing Commander John Kenneth Buchanan, DFC –

Crews of 252 Squadron, Edku, November 1942. 4th from left, Wg Cdr P.H. Bragg, OC Squadron.

Malta Meeting. Wg Cdr J.K. Buchanan, DSO, DFC (centre figure), with other Malta-based pilots, including Wg Cdr M.M. Stephens, DSO, DFC (white suit), 1943. Behind them Buchanan's Beaufighter and the Spitfire flown by Wg Cdr P.P. Hanks, DFC.

'Buck' – a long-experienced bomber pilot in Blenheims in the Middle East with some 230 operational sorties already entered in his log books. Buchanan's first meeting with his crews proved deceptive to those who had never met him before. Immaculately attired, with a quiet 'Oxford' accent, he did not impress the toughened veteran Beau men of 272 as a suitable fighting leader. Buchanan's opening comment: 'I've only flown a Beaufighter once in my life, but I'll do my best to learn quickly', merely added to the crews' hasty opinion. On 21 November Buchanan tacked on to a squadron sortie – and shot down a Heinkel He115 in flames with one brief burst. Next day he destroyed a Cant Z506b, then coolly shot chunks off a giant Junkers Ju90 before his cannons jammed ('Very thoughtless of them' came his calm drawl over the R/T), then shot down four more enemy aircraft within the following week. 272's crews promptly revised their intial doubts about this 'foppish-mannered dandy' (*sic*). Awarded a DSO in January 1943 to add to his DFC & Bar, Buchanan eventually emerged as one of the greatest Beaufighter pilots in the Middle East zone, but when later commanding No 227 Squadron was forced to ditch his flak-damaged Beau in the sea on 16 February 1944 and died from exposure and thirst in his dinghy.*

The nightfighter Beaus of 46 Squadron also commenced a gradual move of base from Egypt to Malta, commencing on 15 November when three Beaus left Egypt. All three failed to arrived on Malta, being claimed as shot down near Bizerta by the Germans. Two days later ten more of 46's Beaus were despatched to Malta, leaving five Beaus to operate from Gambut which rejoined their unit on Malta on 25 November. By then the combined efforts of 46 and 89 Squadrons night operations over Egypt had produced a total of 41 enemy bombers destroyed, a tally 89 Squadron was to increase over the following weeks.

During these moves another Beau nightfighter unit arrived in North Africa when 17 Beaus of No. 600 Squadron arrived at Blida, Algeria on 18 November from the UK (via Gibraltar). Commanded by Wing Commander J.R. Watson, the 'Gallant 600' (their usual soubriquet) was a well-seasoned nightfighting squadron with a

* For further details of Buchanan's career see *Men of the Desert Air Force* by C. Bowyer: Wm Kimber, 1984

Wg Cdr C.P. 'Paddy' Green, DSO, DFC, OC 600 Squadron watches his navigator Flg Off Reg Gillies, DFC paint on their latest victory symbol.

Sqn Ldr F.D. Hughes, DFC of 600 Squadron, later AVM, CB, CBE, DSO, DFC, AFC, MA.

high proportion of experienced air and ground crews; the latter complement of 'Erks' finally rejoining their unit at Blida on 27 November after a sea voyage. On receipt of their radar equipment – flown in by some B-17 Fortresses – the unit commenced operations, and one crew, Flying Officer Hilken/Pilot Officer Mason, opened the squadron's Middle East 'account' on 29 November by destroying a Cant Z506b during an afternoon recce of Cagliari harbour in Sardinia. On 7 December 600 Squadron moved base to Maison Blanche where, on 26 December, a new CO took over command in the shape of Wing Commander C.P. – 'Paddy' – Green, DFC who brought with him his regular navigator Pilot Officer Reg Gillies. In the same month (19th) the unit's 'B' Flight also received a new 'boss' with the arrival of Squadron Leader Desmond Hughes, DFC* with his normal navigator Pilot Officer Laurie Dixon. A further move of base took place in the following month, to Setif, and on the night of 23 January Desmond Hughes and Dixon shot down two Ju88s in less than half an hour.

On 6 December 1942, No 252 Squadron mounted a ground-strafing sortie which cost the loss of two aircraft. Wing Commander Bragg/Flying Officer Nichols were shot down, killing Nichols while Bragg became a prisoner of war; and Squadron Leader A.D. Frecker, DFC, and his navigator Flying Officer T. Armstrong (later Flight Lieutenant, DFC) in Beau T5045, 'G', received four direct hits from a 40mm gun and were forced to belly-land in the desert. The latter crew took several days trekking back to Allied territory before being picked up by a British armoured car patrol. Bragg's place as squadron commander was taken over on 11 December by Wing Commander P.B.B. Ogilvie, DSO, DFC. 252 had also been the 'host' unit for an experiment in Beau armament in November-December 1942 when Beau X7704 was fitted with two 40mm cannons in place of all normal armament. In the event this novel arrangement proved unsuccessful.

During December 252 Squadron remained based at Edku, but ten Beaus had been detached on 2 December to Berka 2 airfield, just outside Benghazi. Beginning on 4 January 1943, however, the

* Later Air Vice-Marshal, CB, CBE, DSO, DFC, AFC, MA.

whole unit came together at Berka, completing this move by 20 January. By then the overall pace of operations had perceptibly slowed; throughout December the unit had lost four Beaus on strafing sorties, but had only claimed one enemy aircraft shot down and a coastal vessel sunk.

In the very early hours of 8 November 1942 the whole of the North African struggle took a new direction, when combined Allied forces initiated *Operation Torch* – a triple-landings' invasion at Algiers, Casablanca, and Oran, with the objective of ultimately linking up with the advancing Eighth Army further east in a pincer-movement which would trap all Axis forces on African soil. This operation had been the prime reason for the internal re-allocation of certain Beau units to Malta and the transfer of additional Beau units, such as 600 Squadron, from the UK.

A second Beau unit, No 255 Squadron, was also brought from England for nightfighting duties protecting the Tunisian ports, arriving on 15 November and based initially at Maison Blanche commanded by Wing Commander D.P.D.G. Kelly. 255 Squadron's first confirmed successes came after moving to Souk-el-Arba in early December when, on the night of 5/6 December two crews – Flying Officer G. Humes/Flight Sergeant Sayers and Flying Officer M.J. Gloster/Pilot Officer Oswald – destroyed five Heinkel He111s between them on simultaneous patrols. On the following night Squadron Leader J.H. Player, DFC/ Flight Lieutenant A. Lammer of 255 shot down three more enemy bombers while another 255 crew Flying Officer C. Cox/Flight Sergeant Croft, added a fourth. On the same night an 89 Squadron crew, Sergeant P.E. Kingsnorth/Warrant Officer R.N. Turnbull, claimed the destruction of two other bombers in the area – an 89 Squadron detachment having joined 255 of 5 December.*

While the nightfighting Beaus were having a particularly busy, and successful, run of combat activities, their day-fighter counterpart squadrons were equally industrious, particularly the Malta-based Nos. 227 and 272 Squadrons, soon to be joined by 46 Squadron. These units flew daily – and occasionally by night – scouring the skies for enemy aircraft, especially transport

* For full details of these and other night combats by Beaus, see *Fighters over Tunisia* by Shores/Ring/Hess; N. Spearman, 1975.

Beau VIF,MM924, YD-L of 255 Squadron at Foggia, 1943.

Sqn Ldr A.D. Frecker/Flg Off T. Armstrong of 252 Squadron strafing an enemy train south of Sidi Barrani on 9/10/42.

formations, and interspersing such offensive sweeps with destructive ground-strafes of enemy airfields; an instance of the latter occurring on 10 November when nine Beaus of 272 Squadron swept low across El Aouina airfield, destroying ten and damaging a further 16 grounded aircraft, although one Beau (Pilot Officers A. Smith/Diaper) was hit by flak seriously enough to force the Beau to crashland on a beach two miles from the target.

In the period 12-14 November the two units (227 and 272) claimed no less than 15 enemy aircraft destroyed and six others probably destroyed during daytime air engagements but lost three Beaus and their crews; while on the 14th seven of 272's Beaus returned to El Aouina and strafed six aircraft on the ground, then in further actions added seven others destroyed. From these actions two Beaus failed to return, though the crew, Squadron Leader A. Watson, DFC, and his navigator, survived their forced landing and walked back to Allied lines to rejoin their unit later.

The hazards, and indeed exhilaration, of zero-height ground-strafing enemy airfields or other targets are graphically described in the reminiscences of the late Sergeant John 'Dinger' Bell:*

> As a relative newcomer to the business of Beaufighter ground attacks in late 1942, I found such operations both thrilling and terrifying. At OTU I'd been firmly warned against *all* forms of low flying, and therefore had had no real experience as such before joining my Beau squadron for ops. My first sortie, only two days after joining, was a strafe of an enemy landing ground known to be in use by the Luftwaffe. There were four of us detailed, led by my Flight commander, and we set out just about sunrise hoping to gain surprise. We flew slightly out to sea off the African coastline for most of the outward leg, keeping right down over the water to stay below enemy radar, then at a wing-waggle from the leader – we had maintained R/T silence all the way out – we wheeled to port and crossed inland, turned again, and flew along the long, black, single coast road with eyes wide open in case any road convoys were about. My nav soon reported, 'Target due in two minutes, Dinger' and I prepared myself for

* Correspondence with author, 1975

the actual strafe, my right thumb poised over the cannon firing tit on the control spectacle. My next sight was smoke and empty shell cases streaming back from the leader's Beau – we'd arrived!

Ahead of me were several German aircraft on a bare piece of desert with the usual scattering of pup tents etc further on. I automatically lined my sight on the nearest couple of kites and fired, even though I must have been about 6-700 yards range at first. A line of sand-bursts began running ahead of me as my shells tracked towards my own targets, then hit the nearest aircraft which immediately exploded violently.

Seconds later I was flying through the muck and smoke of that explosion which reached way over my cockpit, and I actually ducked in fright! Scared or not I kept my thumb down on the gun button and saw my shells plough through several small tents, then splash a lorry parked nearby, and suddenly I was across the airfield and out over bare desert again. It all happened so damned quick that it felt unreal.

Coming to my senses I looked around for the other Beaus and was relieved to find all three not too far away, beginning to close up again on the leader. My nav reported that we'd definitely set fire to at least four aircraft apart from any other items. I asked him if he was OK to which he replied yes, but needed a change of underwear – I knew how he felt! We both checked around as far as possible for any damage to the Beau, but found none. According to my nav there'd been no flak defence fire so we must have achieved total surprise.

My time on Beaus was pretty short – just seven ops – then I was hospitalised after a crash-landing and never returned to the same unit. This crash came after my seventh sortie which proved rather memorable for me personally. Five Beaus set out that morning for a general sweep of the coast road looking for enemy transport mainly but briefed to fire at any concentration of troops or vehicles – so-called 'opportunity targets'. By then I was beginning to feel fairly experienced at this deck-level stuff, so had no real worries about the sortie. One Beau aborted after about half an hour – presumably engine troubles – but the other three and myself pressed on.

We finally came upon a line of three-ton trucks, about seven in all, belting along the coast road, and went down to a height virtually level with the trucks' roofs, flying in a line astern single file so that each man could fire at anything the Beau in front of him missed. I was No 4 in this file, the tail-ender, and therefore had slightly more time in hand before choosing my targets. It also meant I would be flying through anything thrown up from the convoy, incidentally! The leader and his No 2 must have hit something because a cloud of smoke and dust erupted ahead, then No 3 put his shells right inside the back of one truck which exploded right in front of me. Startled by this I failed to fire, but felt chunks of something hard hitting our Beau – then a body of a man rose directly ahead and disappeared overhead! The sight of that poor devil shocked me badly and I began shuddering – nervous reaction.

Clearing the convoy – still without firing a shot – I regained control of my nerves and gradually calmed down. Checking with Reg, my nav, as always, he reported that he was OK but was sure we'd been hit somewhere 'underneath' because there was a 'bloody great hole in my floor'. He then made some facetious remark about 'having to walk home'. I checked all my instruments but all seemed well, so I began the return trip.

On reaching base I let down for a normal landing, but as the wheels touched the whole undercart folded up and I crashed in a belly-landing which threw me forward bashing my head. Once the noise and dust settled down, Reg helped me out and got me well away from the Beau in case it fired. Apart from some dizziness, I felt OK so didn't bother seeing the medic, and debriefed as usual – having my leg well pulled about 'conserving ammunition' ... I was off ops next day, but the following morning when I was due for my eighth trip I woke up with a splitting headache and felt generally ropey. Since I was obviously unfit to fly I saw the squadron quack who examined me pretty thoroughly then told me he was sending me back to the nearest proper hospital – with a suspected skull fracture! To cut a long story short he proved to be correct, so I was off ops for nearly six months and was then posted to a communications unit as a general chauffeur for staff officers at a Group HQ.

The Tunisian campaign, and indeed the whole of the North African struggles, finally ceased on 13 May 1943 when Generale Messe surrendered all Axis forces remaining on African soil, and General Alexander was able to inform Winston Churchill, 'We are masters of the North African shores.' Those first ten weeks of 1943, particularly in the Tunisian zones, had been hard-fought by the opposing air services, with the Beaufighter day and night squadrons well to the fore. In such a period of unceasing operational action for the Beau crews it would need a separate volume to render full accounts of each action, but certain operations deserve particular mention if only as examples of the Beaus' crews' prowess.

The nightfighter units especially found plentiful 'trade' throughout those early weeks of 1943. Between 1 January and 13 May, Nos 46, 89, 108, 153, 255, and 600 Squadrons had claimed a gross total of 113 enemy aircraft destroyed or probably shot down,* for the losses of five Beaus and their crews – all by night. Nominally, the leading scorers were the men of 600 Squadron at that stage who included several particularly successful partnerships; one of which – Flight Sergeant A.B. Downing/Sergeant J. Lyons (later Flying Officer DFC, DFM and Pilot Officer DFM respectively) – claimed five Ju52s during a single patrol on 1 May.

By early May 1943 Middle East Beaufighter strength and location were as follow:

Squadron	*Base*	*CO*
46	Edku	Wg Cdr G.A. Reid
89	Castel Benito	Wg Cdr J.A. Leathart, DSO
108	Bersis	Wg Cdr J.A.A. Read, DFC
153	Maison Blanche	Wg Cdr W.G. Moseby, DFC
227	Edku	Wg Cdr R.M. Mackenzie, DFC, AFC
252	Magrun	Wg Cdr D.O. Butler
255	La Sebala	Wg Cdr J.H. Player, DFC
272	Ta Kali	Wg Cdr J.K. Buchanan, DSO, DFC
600	Souk el Khemis	Wg Cdr C.P. Green, DSO, DFC
603	Misurata West	Wg Cdr H.A. Chater

* A *minimum* figure, confirmed by postwar evidence.

† *Official* base airfields, though several units maintained small detachments at other landing grounds.

No 39 Squadron crew and ground staff at Alghero, Sardinia, 1944.

Within weeks yet another unit was added when No 39 Squadron, a former Beaufort torpedo-strike unit based at Protville from 1 June 1943, began receiving Beaufighter TFXs in exchange for its Beauforts; the first six TFXs arriving on 18 June. Conversion training for the air crews was undertaken immediately and by 1 July the squadron was in a position to recommence operations, having 12 Beaus and 16 trained crews by that date; the squadron being commanded by Wing Commander N.B. Harvey with effect from 12 June. Accordingly, 39 Squadron flew its first Beaufighter TFX operation on 11 July – a torpedo attack against a 4000-ton merchant vessel off the coast of Italy. Six Beaus, led by Squadron Leader S. Muller-Rowland,* eventually crippled the vessel and

* Killed on operations from UK, October 1944

Beau Xs of 39 Squadron on a sortie from Alghero.

damaged one of its escort destroyers, but lost one Beau to some Bf109s during the return flight.

In July 1943 a detachment of Beaufighters of No 256 Squadron arrived from the UK, to become based at Luqa, Malta. 256 was then a nightfighter squadron based at Ford, commanded by Wing Commander G.R. Park, DFC, and its Malta detachment commenced operations in that role, destroying 12 enemy aircraft at night by 18 July. By October 1943 the detachment was joined by the UK-based element on Malta. Three more Beau units were to supplement overall Beaufighter strength in June 1943, these being Nos 47, 144, and 219 Squadrons.

No 47 Squadron, a former Beaufort torpedo-bomber unit based

Wg Cdr A.D. McNeill Boyd, DFC.

at Misurata in June, commanded by Wing Commander A.M. Taylor, DFC moved to Protville in that month for re-equipment with Beau TFXs. Here it was joined by No 144 Squadron from Tain, Scotland, commanded by Wing Commander J. McLaughlin, which already flew TFXs and was ready for operations on arrival. 144 was to remain in the Middle East only briefly, however, and by August had returned to the UK to rejoin Coastal Command's strike force.

For night defence the third unit to arrive was No 219 Squadron, commanded by Wing Commander A.D. McNeill Boyd, DFC, which flew from Catterick to Bône in June and was declared operational again on 30 June. On that date the squadron claimed three German bombers shot down as the beginning of its Middle East sojourn – two of these by the squadron commander. All these additional Beau squadrons were to reinforce preparations already in hand for an imminent Allied invasion of Sicily – and ultimately Italy – whereby the night Beaus were to defend Allied-occupied ports where invasion forces and materials were being assembled; while the Beau TFX units undertook *Rover* operations, sweeping the eastern Mediterranean hunting for enemy shipping. This invasion – code-named *Operation Husky* – commenced in the early hours of 10 July 1943.

For the first two days aerial opposition to the Allied invasion was minimal but by the second night the Luftwaffe began increasing its attempts to bomb the invaders' beachheads. RAF nightfighters destroyed six enemy bombers that night but were soon to exact a heavy toll of such raiders. On the night of 14/15 July, for example, four pilots claimed a total of 13 enemy aircraft, while the following night a further eight were destroyed. By the end of July RAF nightfighters – which included some Mosquitos – had claimed 68 aerial kills; 25 of these by 600 Squadron crews. Among several outstanding crews from 600 Squadron at this time was the duo Desmond Hughes/Laurie Dixon, who claimed three Ju88s on the night of 11 August, followed by a Ju87 on the 17th. Hughes' own account of these victories was:*

> On the night of 11 August a determined enemy attack, mainly with incendiaries, was made on the day fighter airfield at Gerbini near Catania. I was on patrol at the right time and, with very accurate GCI control, was put in AI contact with four Ju88s – which obligingly flew in nicely-spaced intervals. With three of these masterly directions from my navigator, Flying Officer Laurie Dixon, brought visual contact and one bomber after another fell to the devastating punch of the Beaufighter's four cannons and six machine guns. The fourth Ju88 we followed into the AA fire zone and, as we closed in, I found we were collecting all the unpleasantness intended for the enemy bombers. When I started to *hear* the shell-bursts and some fragments rattled off us,

* Correspondence with author, 1979

I decided that discretion was the far better part of valour and broke away before visual contact. My aircraft was slightly damaged but how much was due to flak and how much to debris from the destroyed bombers was not clear.

Six nights later an odd incident occurred. I was on the last patrol, due to finish shortly after dawn. There had been no 'trade' and I was winging my way back to Cassibile at first light when the controller said that something had just shown up moving north off Syracuse, fairly low. He positioned me so that this target would be silhouetted against the dawn glow in the east. To my astonishment, I saw a Ju87 Stuka, not at all a target we expected to meet at that period. I swung in to intercept but the Stuka crew saw me before I could close to firing range. He immediately whipped into a steep turn to the left. I yanked the Beau – not exactly an agile aircraft – around after it, thinking to myself that this was going to be one helluva turning match, and fired a quick two-seconds' burst. This was mainly to impress the rear gunner who was already firing at us. I saw no strikes from this burst but, to my surprise and relief, the 87 came out of its steep turn. That was it – I got the gunsight firmly on him as he straightened, my cannon shells smashed home, and he went into the sea with an enormous splash. We never did work out what that Stuka had been up to, nor why the pilot had allowed himself to run out of darkness.

Desmond Hughes flew his ultimate sortie with 600 Squadron on 30 September 1943, but was then taken ill with malaria and jaundice, and was eventually repatriated to the UK – the end of continuous operational flying since June 1940 during which time he had been officially credited with a tally of 16 enemy aircraft destroyed and a share in a 17th. He was later to command No 604 Squadron and gain two more victories flying Mosquitos, and be awarded a DSO, DFC and two Bars.

Hughes' four victories were among 34 enemy night bombers shot down by RAF nightfighters during August, then in early September the first Allied invasions of the Italian homeland were launched, with a consequent increase in aerial activities by the opposing air forces. Between 8 and 18 September alone crews from

Nos 219, 255, and 600 Squadrons claimed an overall 'bag' of 19 night raiders destroyed. By late September most of southern Italy was in Allied hands and the advance northwards commenced, chasing a retreating enemy, with Naples being occupied by the Allies on 1 October. In October one Beau unit, No 89 Squadron, now commanded by Wing Commander W.D. David, DFC, AFC, was withdrawn from the Middle East and posted to the Far East; while by November other Beau squadrons had shifted bases in order to be within operational range of the Allies' frontal fighting zones, including 255 Squadron which left North Africa to move to Grottaglie from where it commenced night intruder sorties over Italian targets, commanded by Wing Commander H.W. Eliot, DFC.

The long successful record of Beau nightfighters in the autumn of 1943 was matched by the depredations of the Beau day fighter and torpedo-strike squadrons. So successful had the overall Allied air offensive against enemy shipping been during August-September that the Germans reverted mainly to the use of large formations of Luftwaffe air transports to move men and supplies between Italy and outlying enemy garrisons such as Corsica.

This increase in air traffic immediately resulted in several notable mass 'kills' by Allied fighters in late September as the enemy prepared to evacuate Corsica. In two days, 23 and 24 September, Beaufighters accounted for 38 enemy aircraft destroyed or damaged for the loss of five Beaus; prominent among the units involved being No.39 Squadron whose crews accounted for 24 of that total. The cost to 39 was three Beaus shot down (JM411, LX779, LX799) and two others (LX792, LX903) forced to ditch, or crash-land. These victories were all the more praiseworthy when it is remembered that No. 39 Squadron was officially a 'Torbeau' unit, trained primarily for anti-shipping operations, rather than pure aerial combat.

The squadron's ship-busting role was extended in December 1943 with the introduction of three-inch rocket projectiles (RP) in place of torpedoes, although the unit was not officially redesignated in role until 31 March 1944 when it became retitled No 39 (Day Fighter) Squadron. Another Beau unit to add RP to its armoury was No 603 Squadron in mid-November (initially) which withdrew from operations by December in order to train crews in the correct use of RP.

In mid-1943 four squadrons of the United States Army Air Force (USAAF) had been created in England, intended for eventual duties as nightfighters under the aegis of the USAAF's 12th Air Force in the Middle East. These were the 414th, 415th, 416th, and 417th Night Fighter Squadrons, which were equipped with Beaufighters and initially trained in England at (among other stations) Acklington. The first examples of Beaufighters officially transferred to the American air forces were X7610 on 10 October 1941, and X7718 on 2 January 1942, both (presumably, in view of the lack of confirmation in contemporary documentation) for evaluation testing. Actual issues of Beaus for the four embryo USAAF squadrons commenced during March-April 1943 and training – which produced a rather long saga of wrecked or 'bent' Beaus in the hands of the 'green' pilots assigned – eventually stretched until August overall. By then, however, the first squadrons had begun moving fully trained to the Mediterranean area, and eventually all four units were declared fully fit to start operations in the following sequence:

415th NFS	9 July 1943
414th NFS	24 July 1943
417th NFS	8 August 1943
416th NFS	4 September 1943

The first recorded victory claim by a USAAF Beau Pilot among these units came on 24 July 1943 when Captain N.H. Lindsay of the 415th NFS shot down a Heinkel He115 into the sea. All four squadrons were to continue operating nightfighter Beaus over Italy until December 1944, when the 414th NFS began exchanging these for Northrop P-61 Black Widows, while the 416th received a number of Mosquitos during late 1944 to supplement their Beaus. The 415th and 417th, however, soldiered on with rather tired Beaus until the spring of 1945. The actual gross total of Beaufighters officially transferred to the USAAF during 1941-45 is unconfirmed, although details of *at least* 104 such transfers are on record.

A second Allied air service in the Middle East which began using

Beau KV912 of the USAAF at Grottaglie, 17/11/43. Named 'Fluff' by its crew.

'Y-Yorker', a Beau X of 16 Squadron SAAF over the port of Benghazi, Libya.

(*Left*) Sqn Ldr R.M. McKenzie, DSO, DFC, AFC who served with Nos 89, 46, and 227 Squadrons on Beaus. (*Right*) Beau 'K' of 16 Squadron SAAF, Balkan Air Force carrying out an RP-attack on enemy barracks at Zuzemberk, Yogoslavia.

Beau Xs, including LZ331,'A', of 603 Squadron on the prowl.

Beaus was the South African Air Force (SAAF). No 16 Squadron SAAF, a Beaufort torpedo-bomber unit commanded by Lt-Colonel J. Lorentz and based at Berka, near Benghazi in late 1943, received its first Beaufighters – mainly Mk Is initially – on 4 November 1943 as a start to conversion. On 24 December the squadron began receiving Beau Xs, with which it was intended to operate in future, and the unit moved to Shallufa, Egypt for training in RP tactics in January 1944. Returning to Berka at the end of that month, 16 Squadron resumed operations from 5 February as a full RP-Beau anti-shipping strike unit, flying its first offensive sweep five days later. On 11 February, led by the squadron commander, 16 Squadron's Beaus proved the effectiveness of their RP missiles by sinking a 100-ton caique betwen Antiparos and Dhespotiki. Further attacks against shipping targets on 16 and 18 February, however, cost the squadron the losses of two Beaus and their crews.

By January 1944 the overwhelming numerical superiority of the Mediterranean Allied air forces over their Luftwaffe opponents – some 2500 aircraft opposing less than 300 German aircraft, most of the latter being single-seat fighters – meant that the Allied invasion at Anzio on 22 January (*behind* the Germans' so-termed Gustav frontline) was virtually untouched from the air and achieved complete surprise initially. Over the following weeks those Luftwaffe sorties able to be mounted were unfailingly met by Allied fighters who claimed 90 enemy aircraft shot down or probably destroyed during the last week of January alone. Ten of these had been destroyed at night by Beau crews of 600 Squadron, thus bringing this squadron's victory total to 101 in the Middle East zones to date, for the loss of just two crews. To this tally 600 Squadron added 20 more shortly after but lost six more crews.

In January too No 219 Squadron returned to England, while the Luqa-based No 108 Squadron began supplementing its Beaus with Mosquitos from 16 February for future night intruding sorties. These Mosquitos only equipped the unit's 'B' Flight, and the first Mosquito sortie was flown on 5 April. However, by the end of July 1944 all Mosquitos had been exchanged for more Beaufighters. At that period of early 1944 a number of Middle East squadrons were being returned to the UK as part of the build-up of the 2nd Tactical Air Force (TAF) which would provide the aerial element of the

The 2300-tons *Sabina* under RP attack by 252 Squadron Beau on 1/6/44.

STAR & CRESCENT. Beau TFX,NV215 in wartime Turkish national colours.

FISH-HEAD. Beau II of No 779 Fleet Requirements Squadron on 'HMS Cormorant II' (i.e. Gibraltar).

Beau VIF of the 417th NFS, USAAF in Italy.

projected Allied invasion of Normandy in June 1944, while a certain amount of reinforcements were also being sent to the Far East; one such Beau unit being No 47 Squadron which left the Middle East theatre en route to India in March 1944.

On 4 June 1944 Allied armies in Italy finally entered Rome, while two days later – 'D-Day' – the massive Allied invasion of Normandy commenced. This latter invasion immediately resulted in a high proportion of the already weak-strength Luftwaffe based in Italy being transferred north to Germany for defence of the Reich and to help oppose the Allied air forces over northern Europe. That withdrawal took away virtually the bulk of Luftwaffe night bombers from the Italian theatre, leaving only 'easy meat' (*sic*) modified Junkers Ju87s of *Nachtschlachtgruppe* 9 to continue pinpoint attacks by night against Allied objectives in Italy. The crews of this unit were to suffer serious losses, 13 being shot down by RAF nightfighters from 255 and 600 Squadrons in July 1944, and a further nine in August.

In June 1944, as well, the Allies decided to create a distinct air formation alongside the Mediterranean air forces specifically to operate in support of the many anti-Axis partisan forces in Yugoslavia, Albania, and Greece – in essence, a composite and strengthened formation of such air units which had spent the previous year carrying out such operations. Thus on 7 June the Balkan Air Force was officially 'born'. With six airfields in Italy, plus an advanced fighter control and landing ground at Vis, the BAF commenced operations *per se* from 1 July, and by late August the BAF comprised 14 squadrons, including three Beaufighter units, No 39 Squadron RAF and Nos 16 and 19 Squadrons, SAAF.

The creation of No 19 Squadron, SAAF, had been accomplished by attaching a steady flow of SAAF personnel to No 227 (Beau) Squadron based at Berka in mid-1944, with the official intention of eventually converting 227 Squadron to an all-SAAF unit. All three Beau squadrons (39, 16 SAAF and 19 SAAF/227) on becoming transferred to the Balkan Air Force were ordered to move to Biferno airfield in Italy. No 39 Squadron duly moved in early July, settling in at Campomarino airfield by the 13th complete with a recently appointed fresh CO, Wing Commander A.R. de Innis, DFC. Operations commenced next day when four Beaus flew an intruder patrol, attacked seven trains, but lost one Beau (LZ480, 'O'). By mid-August Nos 16 and 19 Squadrons, SAAF were based at Biferno and had also commenced operations. The latter unit was not officially retitled from 227 Squadron RAF until 15 August 1944, when its commander became Lt-Colonel G.E. Catton, SAAF.

By mid-1944 Allied air supremacy in Italian skies was virtually total and the Allied squadrons were being employed largely as flying artillery against ground targets and shipping from low level, with the heavy bomber elements penetrating deeper and deeper northwards into Europe and the German Reich. The BAF in particular was given the priority task of destroying all enemy railway systems in Axis-occupied territories outside Italy, with a 'second-string' priority for pinpoint attacks on specific important buildings and other installations such as HQs, troop barracks, power stations, *et al.* In the case of the BAF Beau squadrons their general use of rocket projectiles backed by cannon fire usually produced devastating results. Examples of the destructive power of accurately-placed RP were the sinkings of the Italian luxury liners *Guilio Cesare* (23,370 ton) and *Rex* (51,000 ton) by several RP-Beau squadrons on 28 August and 8 September 1944 respectively.

During October 1944 the three BAF Beau units maintained a very high pace of operations, often joining forces for mass attacks on certain targets, despite periods of bad weather and temporary aircraft unserviceability, and no few fatal casualties inflicted by flak. Then, on 25 November, No 39 Squadron received official orders to stand-down in order to convert to Marauder bombers. The unit's air crews began dispersing from 2 December – some going to join 272 Squadron – but on 16 December a detachment of six Beaus and their crews was sent to Athens to support the Allied-supported Greek forces against civil rebel forces engaged in a civil war for power since the German occupation troops had left. This detachment carried out a series of RP and cannon attacks against rebel strongholds over the following four weeks and were highly effective in destroying the opposition. A cease-fire agreement was signed on 12 January 1945 and two days later 39 Squadron's Beaus flew their final patrol. On the 18th these Beaus were relinquished to storage at Biferno and their crews posted either to No 108 or 272 Squadrons.

December 1944 had also witnessed the cessation of Beau operations by several others Middle East units. No 46 Squadron returned to England to change over to a transport role, while No 600 Squadron began receiving Mosquito XIXs at Cesenatico in the same month and recommenced operations as a Mosquito squadron on 22 January 1945. A third Beau unit, 603 Squadron, based at Gambut under the command of Wing Commander C. Foxley-Norris,* was disbanded in December, its personnel sailing from Port Said to England on Boxing Day. In January 1945, No 255 Squadron, based at Foggia Main with Beau VIFs, began receiving Mosquito XIXs and moved to Rosignano with these to recommence operations on Mosquitos from 26/27 February. No 108 Squadron was next to quit the scene, being declared non-operational with effect from 6 February 1945, and then being disbanded at Hassani on 28 March. In the following month, on 18 April, No 272 Squadron flew its ultimate war sorties, then moved two days later from Falconara to Catania where the squadron was disbanded on 30 April.

Thus, on 2 May 1945, when the official cessation of hositilities in Italy came into force, only three Beaufighter squadrons were still existing from the former Desert air forces, these being Nos 16 and 19 Squadrons, SAAF and No 252 Squadron RAF – the original Beau unit in the Mediterranean theatre of war. No 252 Squadron's actual final 'war' operations took place on 5 May 1945 – a strike against coastal defence gun installations on Melos – but thereafter was mainly employed on routine air-sea rescue support patrols on a diminishing scale in 1945. The squadron continued in being throughout 1946, based at Araxos, where it was eventually disbanded on 1 December 1946.

* Later Air Chief Marshal Sir, KCB, DSO, OBE, MA.

CHAPTER FIVE

Whispering Death

By May 1942 the Japanese forces in the Far Eastern theatre of war had, in little more than a hundred days, nullified American power and also occupied British and other Allied key territories and bases throughout the south-west Pacific, driving the depleted and exhausted survivors back into Burma and India. Within a week of the disaster at Pearl Harbor the Japanese had also invaded Burma with a two-fold purpose – to open the route to the prize of India, and at the same time to isolate its old enemy, China, from Indian supply routes and thereby weaken its ability to resist Japanese invasion ultimately. With the same speed and fanatical perseverance exemplified in the conquest of Malaya, the Dutch East Indies, and now Siam, Japanese forces flooded northwards through Burma attempting to destroy the retreating remnants of the Allied armies until the latter finally crossed over the Chindwin river into India mere days before the monsoon broke and effectively brought the Japanese advance to a halt.

This monsoon period was to be of almost five months duration, during which period the Allied forces now based in India began, virtually from scratch, to steadily accumulate strength for the future re-conquest of Japanese-occupied Burma. The retreat had left the RAF in particular almost bereft of suitable air strips for operations except within the Indian border, and while that monsoon period lasted Army sappers began constructing makeshift airfields along the Arakan coastal road as this was gradually developed, and by early December 1942 No 224 Group air command in Bengal was able to move from Calcutta to Chittagong with its few squadrons of veteran Blenheims and Hurricane fighters.

Meanwhile, in North Africa the turn of the tide in favour of the Allies was already sufficiently successful to allow a re-allocation of long overdue reinforcements to be sent to the 'Forgotten War' in India and Burma, including more modern aircraft types to replace the outmoded and battle-weary Blenheims, Mohawks, Buffalos, Lysanders and Mk I Hurricanes. One of the new types allotted to India was the Beaufighter, albeit in relatively small numbers over many months before its presence began to prove deadly to the Japanese. The first Beau to reach India was almost certainly the initial aircraft issued to No 27 Squadron which had reformed at Amarda Road on 19 September 1942, commanded eventually by Wing Commander Harry C. Daish; that first example arriving on 22 October.* This aircraft became the vehicle for converting 27 Squadron's air crews, and was joined by the next two Beaus to be allotted to the squadron on 18 November, and by 21 December the unit had a total of 13 Beaus on squadron charge. Harry Daish, who actually took up his appointment on 3 December, personally led 27 Squadron's first Beau operation on 24 December when he led off three Beaus for a low-level strafing attack on the Japanese-occupied airfield at Toungoo. That same day almost produced the first squadron casualties when Beau EL276 crashed at Dum Dum aerodrome, but its crew survived without serious injury.

From 8 to 10 January 1943 the squadron moved its base to Kanchrapara where operations were soon resumed. However, serviceability of the Beaus was low at this period due partly to the unfamiliarity of the Beaufighter to its ground crews, lack of spares, and especially teething troubles with the 20mm cannons which gave frequent jams or other stoppages; thus by the end of January only six aircraft were considered fit for operations. Such a situation was almost inevitable on a squadron when receiving new types of aircraft even in the best of circumstances but highly exacerbated when attempting to resolve on a bare jungle air strip with very limited technical resources and facilities. On 8 February the squadron was moved yet again, this time to Agartala where it came under the aegis of No 224 Group, RAF, with the obvious distinction of being the first Beau unit to join the Group as a fully operational

* 27 Squadron's Form 540 (Operational Record Book) states that the first Beaus to arrive came on 18 November; possibly counting these as the first *operational* aircraft.

INDIAN FIGHTER. Beau TFX NE225 in India, early 1945.

FLYING ELEPHANT. Beau RD367, 'H' of 27 Squadron ('The Flying Elephants') wearing SEAC livery over Burma.

unit. At Agartala the unit joined No 5 Squadron which was still equipped with Curtiss Mohawk single-seat fighters. On the day following its arrival 27 Squadron despatched four Beaus to strafe enemy river transports on the Irrawaddy and Chindwin rivers with visible success; it was the first of 18 similar sorties during that same month.

Agartala at that period consisted of a single concrete flying strip less than one mile long, but possessing a notorious 15-feet 'dip' in the middle. This 'dip' meant that any aircraft misjudging its landing could attempt to become airborne again after touchdown, thereby blanking out wheel brakes' effect and leading to a tendency to swing on deceleration of the engines. Once the tail was well down a Beau's rudder became for all intents ineffective for directional stability. The strip itself was in the centre of a vast forest of bamboo trees, which provided the main building material for huts, offices, billets, and workshops.

Shortly after 27 Squadron had introduced the Beaufighter to operations in India/Burma, a second Beau unit came into being in India, when No 176 Squadron was officially formed at Dum Dum on 15 January 1943, commanded by Wing Commander J.A. O'Neill, DFC. In fact, the personnel comprising the nucleus of this squadron had first gathered at West Kirby in England in the late summer of 1942, sailing to Capetown where they arrived on 25 September, and then lingered for several weeks in transit until higher authority made up its mind whether the 'squadron' was to be sent to North Africa or India. Eventually, the ground crews were shipped to Bombay at the end of November and based initially at Drigh Road depot, Karachi before finally assembling as a full squadron at Dum Dum in January 1943. On 13 January three Beaufighters arrived at Calcutta from Abu Sueir, Egypt, piloted by ex-89 Squadron men as the beginning of equipment, and two nights later all three flew 176 Squadron's first operational sorties, intercepting a force of Japanese Army 97 bombers attempting to bomb Calcutta.

The first Beau pilot to sight the enemy was Flight Sergeant Arthur M.O. Pring, a veteran fighter pilot with six combat victories already credited from previous service with Nos 604, 125 and 89 Squadrons, who on this occasion was at the helm of Beau 'M',

X7776. Pring's first sighting showed a steady formation of the Japanese bombers – 'like silver fish' (from their uncamouflaged liveries) – who had evidently not realised that any RAF aircraft were about. Taking a cautious look around for any escort fighters, and finding none, Pring fastened on the rear of the bomber formation and coolly shot down three in as many minutes before running out of ammunition. Pring's hat-trick of victories were given plentiful publicity and he was feted by the local population, then awarded a DFM, and in May 1943 was commissioned. On 5/6 December 1943, however, Pilot Officer Arthur Maurice Owen Pring, DFM, was killed while flying a Hurricane, being shot down by a Japanese 'Zero'.

Just four nights after Pring's feat another 176 Squadron pilot, Flying Officer Charles B. Crombie, an Australian, accompanied by this navigator Warrant Officer R.C. Moss, tackled a Japanese bomber force over Budge Budge, south of Calcutta on the night of 19 January. Early in the engagement Crombie's Beau was hit by return fire and set afire, but Crombie remained in his seat and shot down two bombers, then seriously damaged a third before the Beau's fuel tanks exploded forcing him to take to his parachute. Subsequently awarded a DSO for his courage on that night, Crombie rose to Squadron Leader, DSO, DFC by 1945 but was then killed in a flying accident on 26 August 1945. Pring's and Crombie's successes undoubtedly had an immediate effect on the Japanese because no more night bombing raids on Calcutta were attempted until December 1943.

Pedantically speaking, 176 Squadron was not actually the second Beau squadron to come into being in India/Burma; this distinction – at least, on paper – belonging to No 177 Squadron which was formed officially on 11 January 1943 at Amarda Road, commanded temporarily by Flying Officer A.P. Wills. Intended crews for 177 had arrived from Egypt in late 1942 but, having no aircraft of their own, were immediately 'attached' to 27 Squadron to gain operational experience. On 26 April 1943, however, 27 Squadron posted 17 air crew men to Pharpamau to become the nucleus of the new 177 Squadron, and Beaufighters began arriving for the unit within the following weeks. Initially, 177 was intended to become night-fighter defence unit, but in the event it was to undertake

Plt Off A.M.O. Pring, DFM of 89 and 176 Squadrons.

Wg Cdr J.A. O'Neill, DFC, OC 176 Squadron (L) talking to Flg Off C.B. Crombie (later, Sqn Ldr, DSO, DFC).

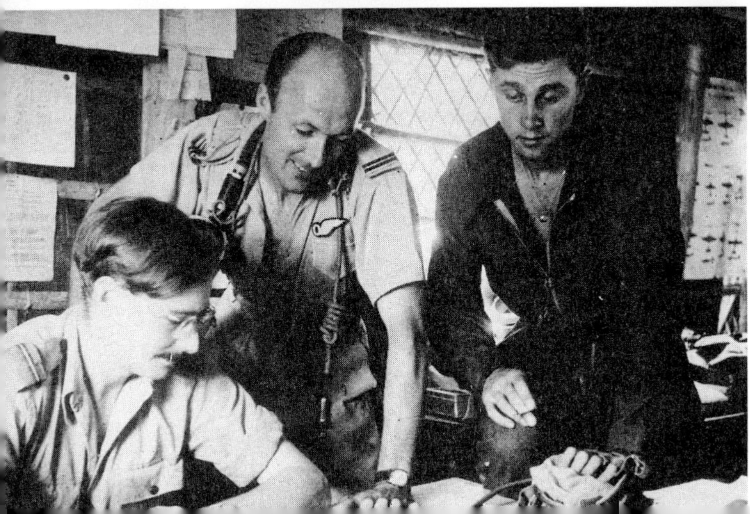

Warrant Officer Ron Thorogood (rt) and his navigator, Edgar Welch, of 27 Squadron debriefing with the unit Intelligence Officer, Plt Off Blackburn-Daniel on 20/10/43 after bagging the unit's 100th loco.

interdiction operations as its prime role and, after somewhat extended working-up preparation, 177 Squadron commenced full operations on 10 September 1943, by then based at Feni, when two Beaus led by the unit CO, Wing Commander P.H. Baldwin attacked enemy communication lines along the coastal areas.

Alongside its 'alma mater', 27 Squadron, 177 quickly became expert at low-level strafing of all and any forms of Japanese transport and communications – both units remaining within the aegis of operational control by 224 Group – resulting in a widely diverse variety of targets attacked. In September 1943 alone, for example, 177's crews claimed no less than 15 locomotives at least seriously damaged, 19 motor vehicles destroyed or badly damaged, and dozens of paddle steamers or other forms of river craft set on fire or thoroughly strafed. In the same month 177 incurred no casualties, although Wing Commander Baldwin experienced an engine failure – a rare occurrence – on one sortie and ended up belly-landing on the beach of the Naf Peninsula, though without injury to the crew.

A number of the early Beaus which first reached India were Mk IFs but these were soon replaced by Mk VIs. The latter, having originally been intended for coastal protection duties, were rated for best performance at low altitudes – almost ideal for the types of operations which became the hallmark of Beaufighter sorties over Burma. Strictly operational range for a Beau in Burma was around 500 miles, but this figure was 'extended' by 27 and 177 Squadrons by utilising the forward air strips at Chittagong or Ramu for topping up fuel tanks before setting out 'in earnest'.

Both squadrons tended at first to despatch formations of up to eight aircraft on operations but experience quickly proved the efficacy of sending Beaus out either singly or at most in pairs. In that manner the Beaus, usually skimming the jungle top or dusty plains at 50 feet or lower, were difficult to detect from above or from the ground, thereby achieving a modicum of safety and, importantly, surprise. Owing to the peculiar nature of its engines, a Beau's actual approach to any target was virtually silent, offering no pre-warning of the devastating impact its cannons were about to perpetrate, and this characteristic soon gave the Beaufighter the graphic nickname 'Whispering Death'; a soubriquet which though excellent propaganda at that time was invented as a whimsy in an RAF officers' Mess – *not*, as has been consistently reported in past accounts, by the Japanese ... Another little-publicised nickname was 'The Dreaded End' – the Burmese theatre's equivalent to the more familiar euphemisms 'Gone for a Burton' and 'Got the Chop' used in other war zones.

For 27 Squadron the first eight months of operations for 1943 brought a mixture of excellent results and no few casualties. The first crew to be lost in action was Pilot Officers Townsend/Wandless on 17 February during an attack on the Japanese airfield at Heho, while just four days later Squadron Leader Illingworth, DFC/Sergeant Osguthorpe were seen to dive straight into the ground during a zero-height attack on Frome town; victims of the enemy ground defences. March brought two more crew losses when Flight Lieutenant McMichael/Sergeant Dodd failed to return on 7 March – though McMichael eventually survived as a prisoner of war and was repatriated in 1945 – while the second loss of the month was one of the rare occasions when a Beau of 27 Squadron was lost to enemy aircraft, when Squadron Leader Statham, AFC in Beau EL286, 'U', was shot down by a Japanese fighter on 26 March.* April 4 brought yet another casualty in the air when Sergeants Ensor/Clough in Beau EL269, 'V' returning from a coastal patrol were seen to hit the sea, recover in an erratic climb, then dip a wing and plunge into the water, never to be seen again. Then, shortly after 2.30pm, 18 Type-97 Japanese bombers with a dozen Zero fighters as escort bombed 27's base at Agartala, doing some damage to aircraft and buildings and killing or injuring over 40 civilians and airmen in the immediate airfield area.

During the same month, April, 27's crews mounted only 22 sorties, but in May this total rose to 51, including attacks on oil plants, factories, communications, and several Japanese air bases. These operations cost two more losses. On the 17th Sergeants Norman/Perris in Beau EL342 crashed three miles short of the Agartala runway and perished in a resulting fuel tanks' explosion; while on 29 May Flying Officer Sturrock/Sergeant Heywood failed to return in Beau EL387, 'O' from an attack on a Japanese train –

* One official report gives the date of Statham's loss as 26 February.

almost certainly the latest victims of the deadly anti-aircraft fire met on all such sorties.

Early June 1943 brought bad weather conditions which restricted the month's sorties' total to 32 and one loss, of Beau EL273, 'A' (Flight Sergeant Petch/Sergeant Thomas) on 29 June, its fate unknown, but July saw the highest monthly total to date of 62 sorties. These included a somewhat spectacular result on 7 July when Sergeant C.G. Johnstone/Flying Officer A.M. Dinwoodie destroyed a 1-million gallon oil tank near the Irrawaddy; both men being later decorated for this feat. Three days prior to that sortie Flight Sergeant Ron Thorogood piloting Beau EL439 came back to base with defective brakes and his subsequent landing ended by crashing into the Agartala watch tower and disintegrating into several major sections. Astonishingly, Thorogood and his regular navigator Flying Officer Edgar Welch walked away from the debris unharmed – in itself a tribute to the Beau's reputation for toughness and ability to 'bring 'em back alive' ...

The vital necessity for teamwork between pilot and navigator in a Beaufighter was exemplified among Beau crews in Burma, particularly in view of the commonly solitary nature of operational sorties. Edgar Welch, eventually a Squadron Leader navigator with 27 Squadron, gives his experienced view of that relationship:

> God's providence and arithmetic apart, it should be appreciated that to complete 30 successful sorties together a crew of two had to be complementary and reasonably complete, and on long-range operations under no need to ask any guidance from anyone. When we met at the Catfoss OTU my pilot Ron Thorogood and I were happy to discover this firm basis in ourselves in our OTU exercises. Ron had some reassurance from my mechanical and electrical know-how, and ability to fly an aircraft (in the air). He, on the other hand, I found to be an excellent navigator with a sound instinct for direction. In Burma the navigation was mostly dead reckoning (DR), with none of the electronic aids used in Europe, and not difficult once it had been appreciated that the compasses would have considerable error after the cannons had been fired – the result of some magnetic effect. Wind and weather tended to be settled for weeks

at a time and over large areas, except during early monsoon periods when it could become quite suddenly violent with thunderous lowering clouds and air strips awash.

In our own territory there had to be radio watch and, when returning in the dark, radio checks for bearings etc. Out of our territory there had to be a non-stop look-out for strange aircraft – Japs *or* Americans. The latter became so unpredictable that eventually we had an arrangement under which they operated in the morning and we in the afternoon/evening – yet they *still* managed to shoot down two of our Beaus into the Akyab swamps ...! Approaching the target the guns and camera had to be set ready, and a check made that the right petrol tanks were in use – preferably the wing inners. In actual attacks pilots tended to become engrossed in their cannon shooting and temporarily ignored the world outside the aiming ring. In brief, pilot and navigator had non-stop activity and co-operation. The Beau was an exceptionally quiet, comfortable and reliable aircraft.*

Welch's reference to a camera related to the F.24 cine camera in the Beau's nose. On 27 Squadron, as an experiment originally, a five-inch lens F.24 camera was fitted rigidly to the nose armour plate of one squadron Beau. There was just enough room to do this without altering the nose cowling, and all that was needed then was to cut a small hole in the point of the nose, fit a circle of glass to protect the lens from grit, then arrange for a tumbler switch near the pilot. Once airborne a problem was met of condensation within the camera due to the rapid climbs and descents over mountains and into steamy-hot valleys – indeed, one could actually pour water out of a camera after a sortie. Contravening all contemporary RAF practice, the glass register plate was therefore removed, resulting in clear, sharp photos thereafter. The camera was then wired into the gun-firing circuit in such a manner that cameras automatically operated when the guns began firing.

A second experiment was to add another F.24 camera, this time with a 14-inch lens, inside the flare chute with a 45-degrees angled mirror attached to the lens facing aft to obtain post-attack shots,

* For fuller account see *Beaufighter at War* by C. Bowyer; Ian Allan, 1976

but this second camera proved not to be worth all the effort and was discarded. Nevertheless, the nose camera eventually became a normal modification on other Beau squadrons in Burma.

August 1943 brought 27 Squadron a new commanding officer, Wing Commander E.J.B. Nicolson, VC, who arrived on 4 August. Nicolson, the only RAF fighter pilot to be awarded a VC throughout 1939-45, still carried the scars and pain of the burns he had received in August 1940,* but was to lead 27, literally, on operations until being succeeded in his appointment in June 1944, and was later awarded a DFC for this latest tour of duty.

August also saw the 'birth' of a fresh Beaufighter unit when, on 14 August, No 211 Squadron was reformed at Phaphamau for long-range coastal strike operations, equipped initially with a mixture of Blenheim Vs and Beaufighter Xs. After extensive working-up training, including the use of rocket projectiles (RP), 211 eventually became based at Silchar from where it flew its first operational sorties on 8 January 1944, commanded then by Wing Commander P.E. Meagher, DFC, and completing a total of 50 sorties in that month.

Before 211 Squadron reached its full operational-ready state, No 27 Squadron began officially converting its 'A' Flight to DH Mosquitos. The squadron had, indeed, been operating a handful of Mosquitos since the arrival of its – and the Far East's – first example, DZ695, on 11 April 1943. Further Mosquitos gradually reached 27 Squadron during that summer, and by December the unit had a total of 13 on charge, thus commencing the Flight conversion from 4 December. 27 was to continue operating its Mosquitos until 9 March 1944, after which the squadron reverted to an all-Beau strength again; its 'Mozzies' being transferred to a photo-reconnaissance unit, No 681 Squadron or to RAF depots to await re-allocation. It should be added that there had been no intention of re-equipping 27 Squadron wholly with Mosquitos; these had merely been taken on strength for operational testing in Burma's tropical conditions.

Some idea of the operational effort of 27 Squadron during this late 1943 period can be judged by a tally of its claims for

* See *For Valour – The Air VCs* by C. Bowyer; William Kimber, 1978

LOCO-BUSTING. Beaus 'H' and 'G' (Flt Lt Williams and Flt Sgt Fosh), 27 Squadron attacking a Japanese rail line along the Kume Road on 23/9/43.

L-R: Naik Nand Singh, VC; Rajah of Faridkot; General Auchinleck; Wg Cdr E.J.B. Nicolson, VC, DFC; Grp Capt L. Cheshire, VC, DSO, DFC at a viceregal party in New Delhi, late 1944.

September. The month's 'Game Bag' included:

	Destroyed	*Damaged*
Locomotives	4	40
Rolling stock	7	36
Mechanical transport	20	58
River steamers	1	15
Other rivercraft	13	523
	45	672

The overall total 'bag' for the period January – September 1943 inclusive amounted to:

Locomotives destroyed or damaged	66
Steamers, Motor Launches destroyed	123
Rolling stock destroyed	409
Mechanical transport destroyed	96
Sampans & other small rivercraft	1368

All were achieved in some 400 sorties and cost the losses of eight Beaus and their crews. These totals did not include myriad opportunity targets struck by roving single Beau crews, such as Japanese infantry on the march, airfield strafes, oil tank strikes, supply depot attacks, or several highly successful individual sorties like the lone Beau which arrived over Myitkyina, the largest Japanese air-base in northern Burma, just as a ceremonial parade was assembled to honour Emperor Hirohito's birthday. Drawn up in full ranks, the Japanese were on the point of saluting their Rising Sun ensign when the Beau made the first of two passes; its cannons reducing the parade to a bloody shambles, with one shell severing the flagpole and draping the flag over the bodies of its colour guard. Or another lone sortie which strafed a training centre for officers of the traitor 'Burmese Army' at Pyinmana, slaughtering dozens of men caught on the open parade ground. 27 Squadron's particular penchant for attacking Japanese rail transport had by then earned it the unofficial title of the 'Loco-busters'.

By October 1943 No 177 Squadron was well into its operational stride with a normal daily commitment of either two or four aircraft, and with a stand-down every third day for training and maintenance. On 10 October, however, came the unit's first operational losses when Flying Officer Bayard/Pilot Officer Seary failed to return, having last been seen heading over the Chin Hills; while a Beau flown by Warrant Officer Crossing/Flight Sergeant Hall was seen to be hit by groundfire and 'disappeared' (*sic*). In addition on that same date two Beaus crashlanded on return; one at Cox's Bazaar due to flak damage, and the other at squadron base having hit a tree during a low-level attack. Tangible results for 177's crews in that month included 19 locomotives thoroughly strafed apart from a wide variety of road and river transports.

For 27 Squadron October brought the loss of Beau EL345, 'F' (Sergeants Humphries/Bainton) after a train strafe on the 16th, but two days later the redoubtable duo of Ron Thorogood/Edgar Welch, flying Beau JL762, 'X', 'bagged' four locomotives destroyed and three others badly damaged in a single sortie – one train being the squadron's 100th loco destroyed to date and therefore a success duly feted and well publicised.

By this time the Japanese had become extremely reluctant to expose their various means of transport to movements by day and began to use the hours of darkness instead. As soon as the Allied forces realised this the Beau squadrons (among others) adopted a different operational 'routine' by despatching patrols in the very early hours of the morning and/or at dusk, and by the close of the year had instituted regular night patrols too. As one Beau pilot put it:

> It meant getting up at two in the morning, taking off before three, but being back to base by dawn with breakfast waiting and the rest of the day off. However, it also meant that those bods on the 'Dawn Patrol' couldn't have any late drinking sessions! One 'bonus' of being on the early sorties, for me at least, was the sight of those glorious sunrises as we made tracks for base – golden sun melting the valley mists away before us.

The pace of operations, by day and by night, for both 27 and 177 Squadrons steadily increased during the last two months of 1943.

In November 177's crews had their first encounters with Japanese fighters, though initially the Beaus took evasive action and avoided actual combat, but during a strafe of the enemy airfield at Heho one of the unit's Beaus (Flying Officers Street/Logan) was intercepted by fighters and failed to return. A second 177 crew lost that month were Flying Officer Roberts/Flight Lieutenant Hickie whose aircraft crashed only minutes before getting airborne from base and killed both men in the resultant fire.

No 27 Squadron also suffered casualties in November. During an early morning strafe in the Ywataung South area on 14 November, Flying Officer 'Ginger' Hassell/Flight Sergeant Thomas in Beau JL535 were shot down by anti-aircraft guns; four days later Flight Lieutenant Williams/Flying Officer Herbert in JL590 were forced down to crashland south of Gyodaung; while on 21 November Sergeants Plummer/Collingwood in Beau 'J' were shot down during an attack on a railway south of Thazi and the Beau exploded into the ground.

December brought yet more casualties, although it also found 177 Squadron increasing its sorties' total for the month to 92, with a parallel increase in the squadron's 'Game Bag' of trains, river craft, motor vehicles *et al*, at a 'price' of three crews reported 'Missing'. 27 Squadron incurred one loss on 16 December when Beau SL534 (Flight Sergeant Vincent/Sergeant Mathewson) failed to return, being last seen flying north from Padau. Both squadrons were witnesses to several examples of individual crews returning with badly damaged aircraft, yet achieving safe and skilled crashlandings. In 177 Squadron Flying Officer Lottimer's Beau had its starboard wing severely damaged but he brought off a successful landing back at base and was awarded a 'Command mention' for his action.

On 27 Squadron, Ron Thorogood and his 'fortune-teller'* Edgar Welch set out on 16 December for a roving recce sortie and over Gwa their Beau was hit by flak which ruined the port hydraulics, rendering the undercarriage mechanism unfit. Thorogood continued his recce, securing photos of Japanese defence units, then set course for base. On approaching Agartala the two men reasoned

* The common nickname for navigators in Burma/India air crews.

that it would save the squadron's already hard-pressed ground crews time and labour if they took the damaged Beau direct to the nearest Maintenance Unit at Kanchrapara. Accordingly, Thorogood overflew base and eventually 'greased in' his Beau in a neat wheels-up landing at the MU without causing any further injury to crew or aircraft, an example of airmanship which deservedly earned Ron Thorogood a Green Endorsement.

The new year 1944 was ushered in by deteriorating weather which reduced the number of sorties flown by both squadrons through much of January; in 177's case giving a monthly total of 67 sorties, with 17 of those being night patrols, or 'Rhubarbs' as such sorties were known. Various experimental extra warloads were tried by 177 Squadron during that month, including carriage of 30lb incendiary bombs, training flares, and crowfoot spikes for distribution on enemy airfields and main roads. In attempts to seek out even more targets, patrols were now being extended north to Mogaung, south of Bassein, with the landing grounds at Ramu and Imphal being used as advanced fuelling stations for such sorties. An overall increase in the intensity of groundfire opposition was reported generally, resulting in more aircraft returning with varying degrees of damage, but throughout the month each squadron only suffered the loss of one crew apiece.

On 7 February, No 27 Squadron commenced a move of base to Parashuram, some 50 miles south of Agartala and close to 177's base at Feni. This move took four days to complete, but operations continued without halt during the upheaval. This month saw 177 Squadron tot up a total of 85 sorties against an ever-increasing variety of targets which, apart from the now customary strafes of enemy airfields and lines of communication, included such diverse duties as anti-submarine patrols, escort sorties, searches for missing Allied aircraft, short-range 'flying artillery' strikes against Japanese troop locations by special requests from the army, and attacks on oil installations, pipelines, and storage tanks. On 27 February two Beaus from 177, led by Wing Commander J.E.S. Hill, operating from an advanced landing ground, flew a particularly long-range sortie attacking the Japanese-run railway south of Moulmein and following the new Burma-Siam rail line as far as Lutshan, making successful strafes of four trains en route. For this operation the Beaus' wing machine guns had been removed and long-range fuel tanks attached.

The numerous hazards inherent with the type of ultra-low level operations undertaken by Beau crews in Burma often resulted in aircraft returning bearing damage that might easily have destroyed any other type of aircraft, and therefore exemplifying the sheer strength of a Beau. Examples of that toughness among Beaus of 27 Squadron included collisions with tree stumps, buildings, and severe flak damage. Brian Hartness, a senior NCO (later commissioned) pilot with 27 describes one such example:

> There was the case of Johnny Britter who attacked a pagoda for the simple reason that there was a Jap machine gun nest in it. These pagodas were 'forbidden fruit', for obvious political reasons, and were always referred to in reports as 'Special buildings'. Determined to put an end to this little coterie of Jap gunners, Johnny approached them very low, at eye level you might say. He blasted them and pulled away over the pagoda missing the top by inches – but *not* quite. The thing Johnny didn't know was that on top of the pagoda a long thin steel spike was protruding. The Beau's wing hit it, uprooted it from its moorings. It was fortunate that Johnny was flying straight and level with no bank on. The steel spike wrapped itself round the wing, locking the ailerons solid. Johnny flew back to Agartala, keeping the old kite level with coarse use of the rudder. His rather dicey-looking approach and landing evoked pithy comment from the spectators who were unaware that anything was wrong. The spike had penetrated the leading edge of the wing and come up against the main spar which had then bent the spike round the wing.*

March 1944 proved to be 177 Squadron's busiest month of operations to date, with a total of 102 sorties completed, including 27 night 'Rhubarbs' and three very long-range attacks. Two of the latter were against the Burma-Siam rail line, with 14 locomotives at least badly damaged apart from further damage to rolling stock,

* From an unpublished account by B. Hartness. Flight Sergeant J. Britter and his navigator Flight Sergeant Payne were lost in Beau LX926 on 11 January 1944.

installations and motor transport. The third long-range strike was undertaken by four Beaus against the Japanese airfield at Chiengmai, some 60 miles inside the Thailand border, resulting in at least seven enemy aircraft being strafed on the ground and various buildings being riddled with cannon shells.

One Beau, skippered by Squadron Leader H.B. Hunt, DFC, was hit in the port engine by flak and Hunt, after climbing to 5000 feet, feathered that engine and set course for the coast. With his remaining engine faltering occasionally en route, Hunt eventually achieved his goal, landing safely at Hove, where his starboard motor finally gave up the ghost during the landing. Hunt was awarded a DSO and his navigator, 'Clark a DFC for that 500-miles' flight on 'half an engine' (*sic*).

Another 177 pilot, Flying Officer Lottimer, was wounded in an arm but, with the aid of his navigator Flying Officer Watson, made a successful return to Chittagong; while Flight Sergeant Forbes/Flight Sergeant Reynolds' Beau was hit while attacking the Burma-Siam rail and had their cannon ammunition set alight – the fire being extinguished by Reynolds' flask of tea!

During March 177 had thus completed its first six months of 'ops', and now had a 'Game Bag' of:

Locomotives damaged	104
MT destroyed/damaged	128
River craft (all types)	317
Enemy aircraft destroyed/damaged	8
Photo-recce sorties (10,000 prints)	198

All this was achieved in a total of 538 sorties, for the overall loss of ten Beau air crews.

In the same month 27 Squadron relinquished its Mosquitos – the ultimate Mosquito sortie being flown on 9 March by Wing Commander Nicolson/Flight Lieutenant Franklin – and two days later Pilot Officer Trudgeon claimed the unit's 198-201st locomotives wrecked. Tragically, four days after that sortie Trudgeon and his navigator, Flying Officer Dobson, in Beau EL453 were hit by flak at 600 feet over some hills south-east of Taungup and lost. The rare award of a DSO was notified on 15

March for Squadron Leader E.B. Horn, and next day the squadron bade a sad farewell to its two bear mascots, Elsie and Rupert, the latter being 'posted' to 194 Squadron, based at Agartala.

On 25 March came another base move, this time to Cholavarum, near Madras where the unit came under the control of No 225 Group, and was intended to 'pair up' with No 47 Squadron to form an anti-shipping Strike Wing. No 47 Squadron, a veteran Beaufighter unit based, in March 1944, at Amriya, Egypt under the command of Wing Commander W.D.L. Filson-Young, DFC, began its move to the Far East in that month, becoming based initially at Cholavarum. The squadron was equipped with Beaufighter Mk Xs already, while 27 Squadron was still mainly flying Mk VIs at that stage. However, Mk Xs were soon beginning to replace 27's Mk VIs at that stage. However, Mk Xs were soon beginning to replace 27's Mk VIs, and by August 1944 the last Mk VI had left the squadron.*

The change to Mk Xs did not meet with unanimous approval from the air crews. For one thing a Mk X, despite its increased engine power, was some 30 mph slower than a Mk VI on operations. As Brian Hartness of 27 Squadron recorded:

> Of all the Marks of Beaufighter which saw operational service – and I flew them all – the Mark VI was undoubtedly the best. She had none of the odd tricks of the Merlin-engined Mk II, and none of the performance-spoiling appendages of the Mk X. I think I preferred the fore and aft instability of the straight tailplane Mk VI which could be pulled round in a steep turn rather tighter than a Mk VI with the dihedral tailplane, though the latter was more stable in level flight. The service ceiling for the Mk VI is quted as 16,000 feet or so, but I took one to over 20,000 feet on several occasions. The best features was her low level maximum speed. Most of these (Mk VIs) could exceed 270 knots which meant we could outdistance an Oscar 'on the deck'. Our CO, Harry Daish, with me as passenger, ran away from a Hurricane at Amarda Road. Harry had persuaded the Hurricane pilot to do this test and we landed highly elated. There was one Mk VI on 27 Squadron towards the end of my

* 27 Squadron had received and flown a number of Mk Xs during the nine months previous to this final changeover.

(*Left*) Sqn Ldr Hunt of 177 Squadron strafing Lashio airfield, 1944 (*Right*) Wg Cdr Henry G. Goddard, DSO, DFC, AFC, a near-legendary name in the Burma aerial conflict.

Beau X7898 of 89 Squadron on a forward landing ground, Mandalay Road, 1943.

tour that could outfly the lot, JL567, 'K',* which was a real lady. She could be trimmed 'hands off', and at normal cruising power was 20 knots faster than any of them, while at full power she exceeded 300 knots. She was allotted to me as 'my' aircraft and I kept *very* quiet about her when I discovered this remarkable performance – in case some 'senior' officer took her off me!

While 27 and 177 Squadrons were engaged in their day and night offensive against Japanese 'communications' throughout 1943-early 1944, No 176 Squadron had moved its based from Dum Dum to Baigachi by the end of February 1943, situated some 40 miles from Calcutta on the Jessore road. It was to remain nominally based at Baigachi until August 1944, but in practice provided a number of small detachments of Beaus to various advanced airstrips at Feni, Vavuyina, Kangla and Ratmalana; a dispersion of aircraft and personnel which tended to diminish the normal cohesive operations and maintenance customary on most firstline units.

Command of 176 from June 1943 until February 1944 was in the very capable hands of Wing Commander Henry G. Goddard, DFC, AFC (later Group Captain, DSO, DFC, AFC), a pilot whose skills and 'individualism' made him almost a legend in the Burma air forces. During 1943 the squadron flew not only Beaus but also a Flight of Hurricane IICs, fitted with pilot-operated AI Mk VI radar, for its continuing commitment for night defence of Calcutta. These Hurricanes were replaced by Beaufighters in early 1944 and during that period squadron activity became primarily training and familiarisation flying, although some patrols were carried out off the Andamans and in the Chittagong area. In late March 1944, however, 176 Squadron was called on to provide a detachment of Beaus to support the Allied defences at Imphal,† by which time command of the squadron had passed to Wing Commander G.R. Nottage, AFC, because Henry Goddard had left the unit to take up command of No 170 Wing; this latter comprising three Hurricane squadrons (Nos 11, 42, 113) and now the 176 Squadron detachment of Beaus, with whom Goddard often flew sorties.

* Ex-ND-R, 236 Squadron, Coastal Command.

† Readers are commended to *The Air Battle of Imphal* by N.L.R. Franks; Wm Kimber, 1985 for a complete account of that vital struggle.

One member of 176 Squadron's Imphal detachment was Ray Aveyard:

> The detachment's mandate at Imphal was to fly 'Rhubarbs' (low-level sweeps) into Burma at night looking for targets such as water craft moving on the Chindwin river, or for any road and rail traffic. *Any*thing seen was to be attacked. At this time we had Indian Army or West African troops looking after the perimeter patrols, and our domestic site was what was known as a 'box', meaning that earth had been piled up on four sides of a square with only one opening to enter and leave by. We lived in tents within the box and foxholes were dug adjacent to each tent. Occasionally the Japs would infiltrate during the night and send mortar bombs in our general direction, until the army rushed up with Jeep-drawn 40-pounder guns or mortars to return the fire. When such attacks were known to be a possibility we frequently had to move at half an hour's notice to another strip, Kangla, a few miles north and just south of the famous Kohima box. Whilst at Imphal we were attacked by Japanese aircraft, and one memorable daylight strafing attack by Tulihal caught several chaps unawares who at the time were perched precariously on a single bamboo pole over the ditch which served as our communal latrine. It needs little imagination to know where they ended up. They all emerged safely – but were without friends for several days afterwards! During this period a Beau from Chittagong* shot down an American B-17 Flying Fortress which failed to answer a Very Light challenge. Fortunately all the American crew were able to bail out and returned safely to their unit. However, on hearing that the Beau had used only *four* rounds from each gun, they insisted on giving a party for the Beau crew – they just didn't believe that one of their Fortresses *could* be shot down so easily! Later we returned to Baigachi base and our only casualties for the long detachment were one Beau, and its crew, which flew into a hill side near Kangla and killed both men. (*Beau X8002, 'Z', crew Flight Sergeant Lawrie/H.S. Taylor on 17 March 1944 – Author*).

* From 89 Sqn, crewed by Flight Lieutenant R.B. Morison, DFC/Flight Sergeant Powell. In 89 Sqn's unofficial history, reported as B-29 Superfortress.

In August 1944 No.176 Squadron moved to Ceylon and became semi-operational in a general sense, although its Beau crews now assisted the navy in anti-submarine patrols and air-sea rescue searches. By December, nevertheless, two separate detachments – one to Chittagong and the other to St Thomas Mount – were tasked with night fighting/intrusion roles again. In the event these proved mostly unproductive and by July 1945 the unit as a whole was non-operational as it began converting to De Havilland Mosquitos from July 14; these being Mk XIXs intended for night fighting. By 1 August 1945 the squadron had eight Mosquitos on strength but did not resume operations. Finally, commanded then by Squadron Leader L.W.H. Welch, DFC, 176 Squadron was officially disbanded at Baigachi on 1 June 1946. In the interim the middle months of 1944 had also seen 27 and 177 Squadrons withdrawn temporarily from the 'sharp end' of operations. No 27 Squadron, as previously mentioned, had been moved to join up with 47 Squadron for an anti-shipping role; while 177 flew a total of 105 operational sorties in April, adding substantially to its 'Game Bag' of enemy transports either destroyed or badly damaged, but losing three Beaus to enemy action and two crews.

In May 177's crews flew 126 sorties, operating every day without a stand-down, although several had to be aborted due to weather conditions and two Beaus and their crews were lost. Of the latter, a Beau piloted by Flight Sergeant Beanlands was hit over its target and the pilot wounded. He turned for base and had his navigator, Flying Officer Crebbin, send off a radio message to say he would try to land at Ramu. When within sight of Ramu Crebbin was at the controls and the Beau crashlanded, then erupted in flames. Though both men were still alive when rescued from the inferno, Beanlands died soon after, while Crebbins lingered for a further 24 hours before succumbing. The second Beau (Flying Officers Peever/Watson) crashed into a hill side and the Beau disintegrated in flames. By 26 May the squadron had totted up a gross total of 769 sorties in its nine months of operations, and on that date moved to Ranchi for training in the use of rocket projectiles on a course lasting until August 1944, when the squadron returned to full operations, based at Chiringa and commanded by Wing Commander J.E.S. Hill who was succeeded in command in

September by Wing Commander H.B. Hunt, DSO, DFC, a former Flight commander with 177.

As 177 returned to the 'sharp end', the Chindwin river had become the main centre of tactical interest for the Allied forces, and the Beaus were involved in attacking the riverine transports so vital to the Japanese for supplies and reinforcements, and of some 500 river craft destroyed in the month of August alone, Beaus were responsible for more than half the total. 177 Squadron detached eight air crews and ground crews to Tulihal on 4 August and in the following 12 days, prior to rejoining the rest of the unit at base, these crews flew 57 sorties – 12 by night – and lost one crew, Flying Officers Platt/Kidd, who survived their 'landing' but were handed over to the Japanese by local villagers and suffered an unknown fate.

Among many successful operations flown by 177 crews from Chiringa was a long-range attack by four Beaus on August 27. Their brief was to strafe any targets along the Burma-Siam rail line, but on this occasion the results hardly justified the cost. Although two locomotives were badly damaged, three of the Beaus received severe flak damage. Two of these achieved safe, forced landings, but the third, crewed by Pilot Officer Horwood/Warrant Officer Bateman, had one engine put out of action and failed to return. It was not until September that the news was received of this crew's subsequent 'adventures'. After flying for some 500 miles on one engine, the Beau made a safe ditching with the crew taking to their dinghy. They remained in the dinghy for 70 hours before making landfall in the Mayu Peninsula where, after an 'eventful' (*sic*) further 24 hours on land, they were led *through* enemy lines to the nearest Allied forces and safety.

In August 1944 yet another Beaufighter unit became directly involved in the Burma operational scene, when No 89 Squadron left its long stay in Ceylon to move to Baigachi as its latest base, commanded by Wing Commander (later, Group Captain) W.D. David, DFC, AFC. No 89 had a long record already of excellent operational service in Egypt and North Africa on night fighter defence and intrusion sorties, before moving to Ceylon in October 1943 for similar duties. No 89 Squadron was to remain in Burma until the end of the Japanese conflict flying Beaus and specialising in night intrusion 'Rhubarbs' until February 1945 when the unit began exchanging its Beaus for Mosquito FBVIs, and completed this conversion by July.

By the time of 89's arrival on the Burma front Japanese troops were beginning a retreat which was to escalate steadily during the following 12 months southwards through the jungles. This retreat was, as expected, bitterly, even fanatically contested mile by mile of jungle and plain, and the Allied aerial offensive against Japanese supply and communication lines was intensified. Among the desperate measures taken by the Japanese to thwart the low-level strafing attacks by Allied airmen was an increasing use of tripwires suspended between trees above railway lines, with land mines laid nearby, remotely detonated.

From 14-23 September No 27 Squadron was withdrawn from operations and moved to Ranchi to train on rocket projectiles, but this course was relatively brief, and the squadron was declared fit for operations again in mid-October. Accordingly, the unit moved back to its old base at Agartala between 18 and 21 October, then despatched a small detachment to Dohazari on 28 October. Operations recommenced on 10 November, but six days later 27 Squadron suffered the losses of two Beaus in particularly tragic circumstances. Beaus KW416 (Pilot Officers Trigwell/Chippendale) and NE641 (Flight Sergeant McDowall/Sergeant Cooper) were hunting through the Taungup Pass when they were 'bounced' by a formation of Lockheed P-38 Lightnings of the USAAF, and both Beaus were shot down killing their crews – victims of poor aircraft recognition and over-eager 'green' pilots in the American fighters.

Next day the squadron lost another Beau, NE420 (Warrant Officers Alexander/Miller) which crashed during an attack on a Japanese armoured vehicle. Two days after that loss the squadron shifted base to Chiringa, some 30 miles away from Agartala, and operations were resumed on 23 November when six Beaus strafed objectives in the Taungup-Prome area; then next day set out on the squadron's first RP sortie 'in anger' by attacking Wetwun with 25lb AP-headed rockets. Although crews from both 27 and 177 Squadrons acknowledged the potency of RP when attacking such targets as armoured vehicles, large river craft, or 'solid' buildings, the general consensus preferred the battery of four 20mm cannons for such work as equally effective, without the drag-inducing effect of carrying a load of eight RP externally below a Beau's wings.

While September 1944 had seen 27 Squadron 'on the move' several times, it was another notable period of success for 177 Squadron whose crews ran up a total of 103 sorties completed and added 30 trains and almost 60 road transports to the unit's 'Game' tally; all despite a noticeable increase in flak opposition which caused a large percentage of Beaus to return bearing livid battle scars with, in some cases, resultant landing crashes.

T.J. Denny, a pilot on 177 Squadron then, who had previously completed a very full tour of operations with 42 Squadron (Blenheim Vs and Hurricane IIs), made his first operational sortie with 177 on 10 September 1944, but less than two weeks later, on 22 September was badly wounded. An extract from his personal account of this sortie* gives an intimate glimpse of a Beau crew's reactions to such a not uncommon event:

> Joe and I had been detailed to make a low-level patrol down the Japanese-held Arakan coast road, skirting heavily-defended Taungup, and then cover the Taungup-Padang road, including the Taungup Pass over the Yomas. Joe – Flight Sergeant J. Yates – was my navigator. Accurate navigation was vital at these tree-top height patrols in order to avoid known Japanese defended positions, and Joe had little experience (then) of this type of flying. This was my fourth mission of my second tour of ops, and our first three together had been quite exciting and we had already collected several bullet holes in our Beaufighter.
>
> Take-off time was 10 am and we got off without mishap. It was the tail-end of the monsoon period and was still very hot and humid – overheating engines necessitated fast taxying to the end of the strip and quick take-off, but in spite of this we were, as usual, completely sweat-soaked by the time we were airborne, and as the whole trip was to be low-level, we'd remain in this uncomfortable state for the whole of the six to seven hours. We headed out over the Indian Ocean and then followed the

* Correspondence with author, 1986.

coastline south, cruising at 220 mph at 20 feet above the waves.

Denny next described his flying at tree-top height, trying to follow the myriad detours of the coastal road for some 30 minutes, by which time his navigator was not entirely sure of their location due to the many rapid changes of direction involved. Suddenly a large village loomed up ahead and as the Beau crossed over it all hell was let loose and the Beau was the focal point for a near-barrage of machine gun and small arms' fire – it was Taungup which they'd been briefed to avoid! Passing over at full throttle Denny got clear, though not before one Japanese gun had given the Beau a line of ragged holes in its port wing, close to the wing fuel tank. Carrying on, Denny climbed over the Yomas then nosed down steeply to continue following the road and its numerous S-bends and twists.

His final task was to be photographing a bridge at Padang where the coast road crossed a tributary of the Irrawaddy, a bridge known to have machine gun posts at both ends. This was accomplished without incident apart from a few inaccurate tracers coming his way, after which he raked some junk-type boats on the Irrawaddy nearby, then stayed low and turned north-west for his return to base. Denny picks up the account again:

> Soon I could see the Taungup-Prome road again, white in amongst the trees. At that moment there was a tremendous bang in the cockpit, a harsh brittle sound accompanied by smoke and dust. I felt strangely numb for a second or two, then my brain started working again and my first thought was that a cannon shell had exploded right in the cockpit, yet there seemed to be no obvious damage done. Then I felt a numbness in my right forearm and, on raising my arm, I saw three blackened holes in the fleshy part which at that instant started bleeding heavily.
>
> I called Joe on the intercom and as I did I noticed I was heading straight for a cluster of tall palm trees. Just in time I pulled hard on the control column with my left hand and cleared them with little to spare. Realising I was in no condition for a low-level return to base, I trimmed the Beau in a steady climb and headed in the general direction of Bengal. By that time Joe had come up front and had the first aid box out. I held my arm up for him to bandage and a stream of blood ran off my elbow

onto the instruments on the right side of the cockpit. Joe made a sound job of bandaging and then I noticed blood soaking through the left leg of my flying suit and found several slight wounds there. The pain from my arm was intense now and I felt faint and sick from the heat and loss of blood. I had a drink of water and splashed some on my face, then held my head down as far as I could and the faintness eased off. I turned in my seat and looked at Joe standing behind me – he looked white and anxious. If I'd passed out, even if he had managed to drag me out of my seat and get to the controls he had never handled a plane in his life and could never have got the Beau down in one piece.

I pulled myself together and started taking a more intelligent interest in our return trip. Looking round the cockpit I eventually found the cause of all the trouble. It wasn't a cannon shell but a rifle bullet which had entered through the bottom left-hand side of the nose section, smashed the top of the undercarriage lever, then passed out through a neat hole in the perspex at the top right-hand side of the cockpit close to my right ear. Evidently the bullet had passed between my outstretched arms as I held the 'spectacle' control wheel, and my wounds had been caused by splinters of metal.

We were now at 10,000 feet and almost over the centre of the mountains, at which height I was within radio range of base at Chiringa and therefore called them up, reporting our position (still about 100 miles inside Jap territory) and giving a rough ETA [Estimated Time of Arrival]. Time dragged interminably and my right arm was throbbing painfully. My hand was numb and I found I could only use my forefinger and thumb – I began worrying how I was going to land this ten-ton aircraft without writing us both off.

At long last the strip came in sight and after a short call to the control tower I lowered the wheels and made a hasty pre-landing cockpit check. I made the final approach fairly low and fast in order to do a wheel landing rather than a three-pointer. This would put less strain on my right hand and meant that I would fly the plane under low power until the front wheels touched, then whip the throttles shut and wind back the trim tabs with my left hand.

Everything went smoothly until the wheels touched and began to take the full weight of the aircraft, then the left wing started to drop and we began a dangerous swing to the left towards trees lining the strip. I had a flat tyre on the port wheel, no doubt punctured by a bullet. There was nothing I could do but apply full right brake. The brake lever was on the control column and designed to be operated by the right thumb, but I managed to get my left hand on it and applied it has hard as I could. The swing checked and our speed of about 80 mph began to drop. The good old Beau kept amazingly straight until about the last quarter of the landing run, then swung off the runway, shot between two lorries full of ground crews waiting to cross, then skidded to a stop in a cloud of dust.

I switched off and clambered wearily out. The MO was there in his Jeep and he took me straight away into a nearby West African Rifles field hospital. Next day I was transferred back to the RAF hospital at Chittagong where I spent the next six weeks having successful operations on my right arm to remove the worst of the splinters.

Denny returned to 177 and recommenced operations in mid December and made his last operational sortie on 11 May 1945 – his 35th Beaufighter sortie and his 141st sortie overall.; though he was to continue flying Beaus with 22 Squadron until September 1945, and was eventually repatriated to England two months later.

In October 1944 No 177 Squadron flew its 1000th operational sortie and claimed its 200th locomotive destroyed or damaged, the latter honour going to Warrant Officer Wiscombe on 5 October; but on the same sortie the squadron commander, Wing Commander Hill, and his navigator, Flying Officer Broughton failed to return. In the event Hill survived his landing in Japanese territory and became a prisoner of war until his ultimate release after the Japanese surrender in August 1945. Hill's Beau was one of three Beaus (and crews) lost by 177 in that month. On 18 October six of 177's Beaus joined in a large strike by some 200 Allied aircraft against Mingaladon airfield, north of Rangoon. Though 177's crews all returned, No 211 Squadron lost one Beau (Flight Lieutenant R. Coles/Flying Officer Painter) which was shot down by intercepting Japanese fighters. The fierce opposition of Japanese ground defences continued to mount in intensity and was responsible for a host of badly hit Beaus returning for shaky landings or others who simply 'failed to return' during the final months of 1944 and early 1945.

In November 177 Squadron lost only one Beau and its crew when Flight Sergeants J. Hudson/J. Smith in KW403, 'Y' set out to patrol roads north of Chiengmai, some 60 miles inside the Thai border on 24 November but did not return. In the same month the acting CO, H.B. Hunt, DSO, DFC – known as 'Mike' to his men – completed 300 hours of operational flying – 50 per cent more hours than the 'statutory' 200 hours laid down as the length of a tour – and was posted; command of 177 now being taken up by the veteran fighter Wing Commander George R. Nottage, DFC.

For 27 Squadron, however, November 1944 proved a costly month extending into December. Having recommenced operations on 23 November, the unit then lost five Beaus and three crews during the following three weeks, the latter three losses being in Beaus NV329 (Warrant Officer Buchanan/Flying Officer Stockwell) on 26 November; NV357 (Flying Officers White/Cross; on 29 November; and NV365, 'Y' (Pilot Officer Osbaldstone) on 14 December. In all three cases the fates of the crews remained unknown. The other pair of Beaus 'lost' resulted from somewhat horrendous take-off crashes but both crews emerged safely.

The last month of 1944 brought further casualties for 177 Squadron, with the loss of three Beaus, including its recently appointed CO. Of these, two were never seen again (Warrant Officer R. Hawkins/Hollay and Flying Officer Jacobsen/Sergeant Buckman), but George Nottage, who was shot down near Moulmein promptly enlisted local native help to hack out a crude landing strip, then through Allied agents, got word back to the Allied authorities who sent a Sentinel light aircraft to retrieve him. Flying a total of 115 sorties throughout December, 177 Squadron was able to add yet more victims to its 'Game Bag' which, at 31 December, stood at:

Locomotives destroyed/damaged	223
MT destroyed/damaged	501
Rivercraft (all types)	1553

Oil targets/installations	16
Enemy aircraft (on ground)	9

In December 1944 another, Ceylon-based, Beau unit became directly involved in the Burma battles, No 22 Squadron, commanded by Wing Commander John M. Lander, DFC. A squadron with a long, successful operational record already, No 22 had arrived in Ceylon in April-May 1942, equipped with Beaufort torpedo-strike bombers. After exactly two years of virtual non-operational duties, beyond assisting the navy and plentiful training exercises, the squadron received its first Beaufighter on 12 May 1944 at Ratmalana, and by 23 June had completely re-equipped with Beaus. These Beaus were TFXs with the intention of continuing 22's torpedo role, but by August 1944 the unit ceased to be a torpedo-bomber squadron and instead concentrated on coastal patrols, armed with RP in addition to cannon armament. Then, on 23 December 1944, John Lander led the squadron to Kumbhirgram in Burma, and four days later mounted its first operational sortie in the new area.

Shortly after, the squadron moved base to Dohazari to become a unit within No 901 Wing, and on 18 January six Beaus flew the squadron's first 'Rhubarb' sorties. Two days later, however, Wing Commander Lander was killed when his Jeep fell into a stream near the airfield, and command passed to Squadron Leader R. Gee, DFC, the 'A' Flight boss (later promoted to Wing Commander). In February 1945 the squadron suffered the losses of four Beaus and their crews, and was destined to lose five more by 4 May. On 15 May 1945 the last wartime operational sortie was flown, and 22 Squadron was then officially disbanded at Gannavarum on 30 September 1945.

The year of victory for the Allies, 1945, commenced with yet another loss for 27 Squadron when Sergeants Merritt/Culley in Beau NV367, 'K' set off at dawn on 9 January and failed to return; the burning wreckage of the aircraft was seen later near Pynshe but with no sign of its crew. In that month, nevertheless, 27 Squadron flew 160 sorties and a breakdown of the month's 'Bag' illustrates only too well the wide variety of targets attacked:

Beau X,NE478,'V' of 22 Squadron RAF from Ratmalana, June 1944.

NV551,'X' of 27 Squadron at Meiktila, 1945.

	Destroyed	*Damaged*
Locomotives	–	1
Rolling stock	–	4
MT	5	18
Bullock carts	–	18
Sampans	17	632
Barges	–	13
Large sea craft	–	24
Small sea craft	1	2
Installations	–	36
Armoured vehicles	–	1

By then the Japanese had ceased to rely on the vulnerable railway system as a means of transportation and preferred river and sea craft; a change reflected in 27 Squadron's claims. February 1945, however, brought a reduction in operations due partly to a shortage of technical spares for maintenance, despite all the trojan efforts of the indefatigable ground crew 'Erks', but also because the squadron was detached briefly to Ranchi again for a 'refresher' course on RP, moving to Ranchi on 10 February and returning to Chiringa on the 21st. This detachment cost 27 Squadron two Beaus.

On the 14th Warrant Officer G.P. Brown's Beau struck the ground as he broke away after firing on the Random RP range, and the Beau cartwheeled to destruction killing Brown and his passenger, Warrant Officer J. McGowan; five days later a Canadian pilot, Flight Sergeant R. Buck, in Beau KW329, 'V', crashed near the Mander range, causing fatal injuries. On 3 February Flying Officer A. Stephens/Flight Sergeant Butler in Beau RD275 crashed on take-off and the aircraft exploded into flames, killing the navigator Butler. Stephens, unaware of his companion's fate, sustained a dislocated shoulder and second and third-degree burns to his face, neck, and arms attempting valiantly to rescue Butler from the flaming wreckage. In spite of all its vicissitudes in February, 27 Squadron still mounted a total of 315 operational flying hours and accounted for 280 enemy rivercraft destroyed or damaged, apart from a healthy score of other forms of transport.

Nos 27 and 177 and 211 Squadrons continued their unceasing assaults against the retreating Japanese in March and April 1945, but by then targets were becoming more difficult to find. Moreover, the conquest of Burma by the Allies was seen to be certain now – it was simply a matter of time before that campaign would reach a successful conclusion as far as most men were concerned.

In the meantime the pressure on the squadrons was little relaxed in March. Casualties were still incurred, as on 3 March when a fresh 27 Squadron crew, Flying Officer R. Mackenzie/B. Tallerman failed to return in Beau NV256, 'U', from strafing road traffic in the Toungoo-Kempayu-Loikan districts. No trace of their aircraft was ever discovered in subsequent searches.

On 20 March, 27 said farewell to its commander, Wing Commander J.H. McMichael on the expiration of his tour of duty – he had commanded the 'Flying Elephants' since 6 June 1944 – and in his place came Wing Commander T.P.A. Bradley, DSO, DFC. Within days of Bradley's arrival 27 Squadron began hearing rumours of a complete change of role for the unit whereby (the grapevine had it) at least half the crews would soon be switched to Air Jungle Search and Rescue operations (AJSR). The need for such duties was grimly illustrated by statistics for the period September 1944 to March 1945 inclusive, during which time a total of 176 RAF air crew men had been shot or forced down in enemy-held jungle territories. Of those, 166 were never heard of again, meeting an unrecorded fate.

In defiance of Service tradition, these rumours proved to be true, and March 1945 became 27 Squadron's last full month of operations in their low-level interdiction role, during which month its crews totted up 438 flying hours on 101 operational sorties, destroying or damaging a gross total of 573 targets.

At Kumbhirgram No 47 Squadron began exchanging its Beaufighters for Mosquito FB VIs from 18 February 1945 and was fully re-equipped by April, in which month 27 Squadron began its change to the AJSR role. While still using Chiringa as its main base for maintenance *et al*, 27 virtually split into three smaller formations. One detachment of three Beaus, four crews and 20 'Erks' were sent to Akyab on 5 April, and a second detachment comprising five crews, three Beaus and 40 'Erks' were despatched to Monywa six days later; the remainder of the squadron stayed at Chiringa.

During this dispersal the squadron suffered the loss of its CO, Wing Commander Bradley who, with his navigator Pilot Officer C.C. Holmes, was killed in action on 10 April. In his place Lt-Colonel E.T. Strever, DFC, SAAF was appointed. For their AJSR duties all Beaus were modified to be capable of dropping emergency containers from torpedo slings under the fuselage, while a few Stinson Sentinel light aircraft – nicknamed 'Jungle Clippers' by 27's crews – were brought on strength to undertake communication duties in liaison. On 26 April the Monywa detachment moved to Meiktila Main airstrip where it was to remain until June 1.

The arrival of the monsoon rains in May 1945 naturally reduced aerial activity to some degree, but in that month two Beau squadron flew their final war operations. 177 Squadron flew its ultimate Beau sortie on 13 May and was soon disbanded at Hathazari on 5 July 1945; while 211 flew its last sortie on 8 May and then stood down to convert to Mosquito aircraft. For 27 Squadron the month of May was one of upheaval and the final weeks were spent preparing a move of base to Akyab, this move being completed by 20 June. At Akyab the squadron recommenced its daily AJSR sorties when requested, but also undertook numerous sorties to drop supplies of arms, food, and gold to various clandestine Allied formations such as V-Force, E-Force, and Force 136, located deep in Japanese-occupied territories; actual drops being made on pre-arranged Dropping Zones (DZs) on receipt of a particular signal from the ground troops.

This combination of operations was to be 27 Squadron's main work up until VJ Day (15 August 1945) and for several weeks thereafter. The remaining Beau units, Nos 89 and 176 Squadrons, remained in the Far East theatre after Japan's surrender until eventually being disbanded or retitled. No 89 Squadron was ultimately renumbered as No 22 Squadron at Seletar on 1 May 1946, having in the interim exchanged its Beaus for Mosquitos, thereby bringing to a close some four and a half years of successful operations during which its crews had claimed totals of 131 enemy aircraft destroyed, nine others probably destroyed, and a further 31 at least badly damaged.

No 176 Squadron also re-equipped with Mosquitos, commencing

TFX NE815,'H', 217 Squadron over Ceylon.

NE807,'F' of 27 Squadron, 1945 bearing, appropriately, a Walt Disney *Dumbo* insigne on its nose section.

on 14 July 1945, but remained non-operational until its disbandment at Baigachi on 1 June 1946. By then 27 Squadron – the pioneer Beau squadron in the India/Burma campaign – had also been disbanded at Mingaladon on 1 February 1946 officially, although a small detachment based in Batavia returned after that date and was not finally 'dispersed' (*sic*) until 28 February (See Chapter VII, 'Peace Years', for post-VJ-Day operations). From its reformation in 1942 until February 1945, No. 27 Squadron had lost 24 aircraft and their crews on actual operations while at least 13 other members had been killed in action or accidents.

Thus the wartime career of the Beaufighter over India and Burma came to a close. Flying in the worst climatic conditions in the world against a fanatical enemy who gave neither quarter or mercy, over areas of impenetrable jungle where any forced landing meant almost inevitable death in a variety of horrifying circumstances, the Beau crews had contributed, at no small sacrifice, an incalculably vital part to the Allies' ultimate triumph over the forces of the Rising Sun. Of those many Beaufighter crews who were lost, almost all disappearing from the sight of man, their epitaph might readily be that engraved on the Jail Hill monument to the men of the 2nd Division who died at Kohima – 'For your tomorrow, they gave their today'.

CHAPTER SIX

Down Under

In the context of media publicity and public awareness, the Allied forces who fought the Japanese in India and Burma during the years 1941 – 1945 soon came to regard their prolonged and bloody struggle as the 'Forgotten War' – with, it could be said, no small justification. Yet even their endeavours and sacrifices were – relatively – well reported when compared with the contemporary lack of public information about the concomitant unceasing campaigns against the Japanese by Allied services in what was designated the South-West Pacific Area.*

Here the forces of Nippon had advanced southwards in late 1941 and early 1942, invading the Dutch East Indies and a host of other islands stretching almost to the northern coastline of Australia with rapid success. Thus, by mid-1942, the Australian continent was under immediate jeopardy of possible Japanese invasion, even eventual occupation. Defence of Australian home territory at that stage was, to a great extent, problematical. No small proportion of Australian servicemen then were already serving under the aegis of Allied forces in Europe and the Middle East zones, apart from elements in India. Moreover, Australia was in effect the general 'base' for American forces attempting to stem and (hopefully) repulse the Japanese conquest in the south-west Pacific; a situation which quickly resulted in the American General Douglas MacArthur being appointed Supreme Commander of all Allied Forces in the South-West Pacific (SWPA).

MacArthur's overall command was vast in geographic terms, including the Philippines, the South China Sea to Indo-China, Thailand, the Malay Peninsula, all of Borneo and the Netherland

* By early March 1942 the Joint Chiefs of Staff had divided the whole of the Pacific area into the South-West Pacific Area and the Pacific Ocean Area for future operational planning.

East Indies, New Guinea, New Britain, the western half of the Solomon Islands group, Australia as a whole and the waters directly south of the continent; his appointment as supremo of the SWPA becoming effective from 18 April 1942. Two days later the Allied Air Forces HQ for the SWPA was established in Melbourne, and had under its operational control all USAAC tactical units and all RAAF service squadrons, excluding pure training units. The overall air commander appointed was Lieutenant-General George H. Brett, USA.* Administrative control of the RAAF remained with RAAF Headquarters, a division of control of the RAAF which was to remain a source of problems until the end of the war, including personality clashes among the most senior RAAF commanders at various periods.

Apart from myriad organisational problems inherent with the newly-established joint American-Australian air effort, there was an immediate need for vast expansion of available strength in firstline aircraft. Exemplifying the lack of such aircraft in the RAAF based in Australia was the firstline strength as at 12 December 1941, which comprised a total of just 177 aircraft (Wirraways, Hudsons, Catalinas, and Seagulls), with a further 306 Wirraways, Battles and Ansons designated as 'Reserve Strength'. The only other RAAF units in the Pacific zone were Nos 1, 8, 21, and 453 Squadrons, all in Malaya under RAF control.

Although a home-based aircraft production industry existed in virtual embryo in Australia by 1940, the crucial need for modern designs had been recognised in the previous year, when on 1 July 1939 an order for 180 Bristol Beaufort airframes (with spares) was placed with the Commonwealth Aircraft Corporation factory at Fisherman's Bend, Melbourne. To help in speeding production, the Bristol company despatched jigs, tools, and drawings, followed by Taurus engines and complete components to help complete an initial batch of six Beauforts. In October 1939 there followed a 'sample' complete aircraft (Beaufort L4448), but in May 1940 the British government, due to the fall of France and the immediate consequences thereof, was forced to place an embargo on exporting

* Replaced, at MacArthur's instigation, by Maj-Gen George C Kenney in July 1942, who brought into being the USAAF's 5th Air Force with effect from 3 September.

'war materials', thereby stopping further supplies to Australia of the Taurus engines for the Beaufort production order. Happily, the RAAF by then had begun receiving Lockheed Hudsons from America, and decided to re-engine the Beauforts with Pratt & Whitney Wasp engines, readily available from the USA supply. In the event, the first Australian-assembled Beaufort made its first flight on 5 May 1941, while the first fully Australian-*built* Beaufort was completed in the following August.

The order (initially) for Beauforts was propitious in that the development design, Bristol Type 156 – named Beaufighter on 2 June 1939 – was about to merge in prototype form, and the RAAF Air Board recommended the adoption of the Type 156 (then titled Beaufort Type Fighter) for RAAF equipment, conditional upon successful test results when the design's prototype completed its trials; this recommendations being dated 29 May 1939. On 19 June, accordingly, an initial order for 18 Beaufighters was placed, to be imported from Britain, with the long-term intention of manufacturing the type in Australia once Beaufort production was complete; thereby utilising the high proportion of common components of both designs. Delivery of these initial Beaufighters was delayed after the outbreak of war in Europe, followed by the embargo on exporting war materials in early 1940, and it was not until 20 May 1941 that the Australian War Cabinet was in a position to authorise the purchase of 54 Beaufighters; 12 of these were to be delivered by the end of 1941 and the remainder by stages by March 1942, by which time it was hoped to have a production line established in Australia for the type.

The proposed Australian-manufacture of Beaufighters was then temporarily shelved until late 1942, but in the interim deliveries of UK-manufactured aircraft commenced; the first pair (RAF serials T4926 & T4927) being officially taken on RAAF charge on 26 March 1942, followed by T4931 on 13 April, and a further 18 Beaus by the close of April 1942. An increase over the original order resulted in a total of at least 87 Beaufighters from the UK arriving in Australia by the end of 1942, with an ultimate gross total of 217 UK-built Beaus reaching the RAAF by the end of the war; all of which were re-serialled in the RAAF's A19-series.*

* See Appendix 3 for full serial details.

Beau A19-1 (ex-RAF,T4920) pictured at Laverton, Victoria. Issued to 30 Squadron RAAF on 27/6/42, it was lost over Buna on 23/9/42; the squadron's first loss.

A19-2 (ex-T4921) fitted with Wright Cyclone engines, at Fishermans Bend, alongside Beau LX815 (A19-218) in August 1944.

A19-3 (ex-T4922) on arrival from the UK at Wagga, NSW, 1942, still in RAF livery.

A19-15,'O' of 30 Squadron (Flg Off R.J. Brazenor/Sgt F.B. Anderson) over the Owen Stanley ranges as it returns from a strike on Salamaua, early 1943. Photo taken by Sgt W.B. Ball in an accompanying Beau.

Production in Australia of the Beaufort finally ceased in August 1944, but co-production of Beaufighters had commenced long before. The necessary engineering drawings for the Australian-manufactured Beaus – basically RAF Mk Xs with Hercules XVIII powerplants which became redesignated Mk 21 by the RAAF – began arriving in March 1943, and on 26 May 1944 the initial Australian-built Beaufighter, serialled A8-1, made its first test flight, skippered by Flight Lieutenant John Miles, commander of the Test Flight attached to No 1 Aircraft Depot, Laverton. Production was to continue until 10 January 1946, on which date the last Beau, A8-363, was officially delivered to and taken on charge by the RAAF. In fact, total Australian-built Beaufighters numbered 365, although one, A8-172, was wrecked prior to delivery and therefore not taken on RAAF charge.

Manufacture of the Beaufighter in Australia was sub-contracted among more than 600 plants for components, these being 'fed' to seven factories for sub-assembly, which in turn were passed to final assembly shops at Fisherman's Bend and Mascot, prior to initial test flying. To meet RAAF operational needs, a variety of modifications to the UK-standard equipment was incorporated in many aircraft, including replacing the normal 0.303-inch calibre Browning guns in each wing with two 0.50-inch calibre Brownings, and the UK belly torpedo gear with either a bomb carrier or a 91-litre drop-tank. Other innovations included wing bomb carriers, a rearward-firing machine gun, Australian-made radio sets, an extensively modified fuel system (for greater range), and a non-locking tail wheel (which created a few problems later in squadron use ...!).

The Beaufighter first entered service with the RAAF in Australia in June 1942 when No 30 Squadron received its first example to commence crew familiarisation. No 30 Squadron RAAF had originally formed at Richmond, New South Wales on 9 March 1942, commanded initially by Squadron Leader Charles F. Read* until the arrival on 4 June of the officially appointed commander, Wing Commander Brian Walker (later DSO). Air crew training occupied the next two months and by mid-August the squadron

* Later (1972) Air Marshal, CBE, DFC, AFC, Chief of Air Staff, RAAF.

was prepared for a move to Port Moresby as its initial base for actual operations; finally arriving on Ward's Strip, north-east of Port Moresby on 12 September, where it was to come under the operational control of Kenney's 5th Air Force, USAAF.

By that date, however, some of the Beau crews had already been 'blooded' on operations, when three aircraft (A19-13, A19-49, and A19-53), which had been temporarily detached to Milne Bay on 6 September, escorted some Beauforts of 100 Squadron on an anti-shipping strike off Normanby Island on 7 September. Beau A19-13 wrecked itself on take-off but the other two Beaus completed their sorties without incident – 30 Squadron's first official operational sorties. The unit's prime role was to be low-level strafing – a form of operations particularly suited to the aircraft's performance rating – and it was on one such strafe of anti-aircraft guns' locations at Buna on 23 September that the squadron suffered its first operational loss, when Beau A19-1 (Flight Sergeant G.W. Sayer/Sergeant A.S. Mairet) became a victim of the enemy guns, crashing and killing its crew.

The RAAF's second Beaufighter unit to be formed was No 31 Squadron, which came into official existence at No 5 Aircraft Depot (AD), Forest Hill (near Wagga Wagga, NSW) with effect from 14 August 1942. The unit's initial, albeit temporary 'boss' was one of the Flight commanders, Squadron Leader Bruce F. Rose, DFC, who duly handed over the reins to Squadron Leader Charles Read (ex-30 Squadron) on 1 September. Beaufighter allotments to the squadron commenced on August 20 (A19-40) and three days later A19-21. By the end of September a further 15 Beaus had been allotted i.e. A19-61, -52, -71, -20, -46, -64('F'), -72, -31,* -59, -62, -63, -66, -67, -69, -57 in that sequence.

Declared operational from 13 November 1942, the squadron by then was based at Coomalie Creek airstrip, south of Darwin, and flew its first operational sorties on 17 November when six Beaus set out to attack targets on Timor. Tragically this initial operation also brought the unit's first *operational* casualties,† when Squadron Leader D.C. Riding/Warrant Officer R.D. Clarke in Beau A19-46

* Named '*Feaubighter*', but destroyed 2/3/43 by enemy bombing raid.
† First actual *casualties* were Flight Sergeant J.E. Jenkins/Sergeant V. Sutherest in Beau A19-61, who were killed on 21/8/42 in a training flight crash.

were chased by a Japanese fighter at wave-level over the sea and the Beau's wing-tip hit the water while attempting a turn, then cartwheeled to destruction. On the last day of November came the squadron's second losses, when Flight Sergeant M.J. Morrison/ Sergeant A.F. Forrest in A19-69 'disappeared' during a shipping escort sortie over the coast of Timor; the only evidence of their fate was a main wheel from their Beau washed up on the coast later.

The squadron gained a modicum of 'revenge' for these losses on 2 December when six Beaus, led by Flying Officer J.E.S. Dennett (later, Squadron Leader) in A19-59, were detailed to strafe a Japanese air base at Penfoei (Penfui) at the south-west tip of Timor. Staging from Coomalie to Drysdale airstrip first, to top up fuel tanks, the sextet of Beaus, in three pairs, achieved complete surprise on reaching their objective. Below them were an estimated 40 enemy fighters and bombers undergoing early morning preparations, and the Beaus shallow-dived from some 400 feet down to ten feet as they passed across the grounded aircraft. Cannons and machine guns blasted at least 18 of the enemy aircraft, apart from destroying a fuel dump, then all Beaus returned safely to Drysdale.

As mentioned previously, both squadrons were initially equipped with ex-RAF Beaufighter Mk 1cs (in the main), which were rated for best performance at low altitudes and thus near-ideal for the role of the RAAF crews. In any air-to-air combat situation Japanese fighters (in particular) could usually out-manoeuvre any Beau if it came to a pure dogfight, but at very low heights it was soon realised that a well-handled Beau could out-run most Japanese pursuers. By early 1943 fresh Beaufighters arriving on the squadrons were ex-RAF Mk VIcs, which proved to be generally slower than the ex-Mk 1cs by up to 20 knots.

With operational experience under their belts, most Beau crews quickly gave thought to possible improvements for their aircraft, particularly in respect of increasing the operational range and thereby endurance, and the basic armament. Whilst retaining the four-cannons' belly battery, the six wing machine guns were occasionally removed and in their place extra fuel tanks installed, thus giving up to 400 km additional range (some seven hours' endurance). Other local modifications incorporated included

Tight trio of 31 Squadron Beaus on route to Timor from Coomalie, 23/12/42.

A19-118,EH-W of 31 Squadron outward bound from Coomalie, 1943. It was lost on 24/7/43 in a raid on Taberfane.

fitting a 0.303-inch calibre machine gun in the rear cupola position, primarily for defence in the event of aerial attack; while at least one Beau of 31 Squadron (A19-78), having replaced its wing guns with fuel tanks, had two of the machine guns mounted between the cannons to beef up the forward armament.

A number of other measures employed by some Beau crews when about to be engaged by Japanese aircraft amounted to sheer bluff. Among the various ploys 'operated' by the rear crew member when any enemy aircraft tried a tail attack were a bag of shredded paper sent out into the slipstream via the flare chute, which the Japanese (presumably) mistook for some new form of missile; firing pyrotechnic cartridges of multi-colours in rapid succession; 'flicking' an Aldis Lamp quickly to (hopefully) simulate gun flashes; and, once rear guns were available, firing a hail of (mainly) day tracer and incendiary bullets – all towards preventing too close attentions by enemy pilots. At least one 'Oppo' (as RAAF navigators were often nicknamed by their skippers) managed to 'acquire' (as only an Aussie could 'scrounge' ...) a Thompson sub-machine gun from a USAAF friend and duly carried this 'gangster' gun in his rear cockpit for several sorties before being supplied with an 'official' weapon! Nevertheless, when 'proper' guns were carried in the rear cupola these were awkward to operate due to the severely restricted space available. Thus aerial defence of a Beau was dependent primarily upon its pilot's skill (and muscle-power ...) in taking effective evasive manoeuvring while any Japanese opponent was within firing range of the Beau's *derrière* – at least until the full-boost urge of the Beau's engines enabled it to show an opponent a clean pair of heels.

From a pilot's viewpoint, the Beaufighter as flown in the SWPA theatre of operations received a consensus of general, enthusiastic approval, albeit without glossing over the design's inherent defects. It was heavy to handle for any necessary quick manoeuvres in air combat but was not, after all, intended for such a form of aerial warfare. The controls were likened by one pilot to 'the gentle touch of a Tiger Moth', though even he acknowledged the need for 'well-developed arm and leg muscles when things got a bit hairy'. As with all Beaus, the RAAF pilots always had to counter the aircraft's strong tendency to veer from a straight line take-off, although the sheer strength of its construction allied to its powerful engines normally ensured eventual success. Once airborne a Beau continued to require a pilot's full attention – 'hands-off' flying was not one of the Beau's virtues.

On the credit side, Beau crews knew they possessed an immensely strong, very fast, dependable weapon of war, with an unequalled battery of offensive armament. The pilot's cockpit gave him a splendid view of whatever lay ahead or above, although the actual instrument and controls layout surrounding him seemed at times to have been designed as a deliberate confusion! Minor irritations for the pilot also included the discomfort of having to remain seated for long hours over the dinghy air bottle, according to Flying Officer Jack 'Mugs' Muggleton, a pilot with 31 Squadron in 1943.

The prolonged operations over trackless sea to targets placed a special responsibility upon the broad shoulders of Beau navigators who, with astro compass and drift recorder, stop-watch, and no little ingrained know-how, maintained a constant flow of information to their skippers both on the outward and return legs of every sortie. In addition to such onerous labours navigators, in particular the 'oppo' in the leading Beau, were expected to maintain a reasonably constant look-out for enemy aircraft, and keep their pilots informed on the progress of other Beaus in the formation. Not surprisingly, many Beau crews eventually achieved a form of mental telepathy in understanding of each other's thoughts and likely reaction.

The primary role of RAAF Beaufighters in the SWPA theatre was virtually the same as that of the RAF's Beaus further north in India and Burma, i.e. ultra low-level strikes against Japanese bases, troops, and communications. In the SWPA however, the Beau crews were forced to fly a high proportion of operations over lengthy stretches of sea, and therefore were called upon for a greater effort against Japanese shipping targets than the RAF Beaus scouring Burma. Moreover, Japanese air opposition was more frequently encountered in the SWPA than over Burma, leading to a higher proportion of air-to-air combats. One facet common to both RAF and RAAF Beau operations was the constant hazard from Japanese ground defence guns – always intense and usually accurate.

Another peril shared commonly by all Allied crews in the Pacific area was the chilling prospect of capture by the Japanese in the event of being forced down within enemy-occupied territories. Japan had never ratified the 1929 Geneva Prisoner of War Convention, and continued to adhere to the precepts of its military code of *Bushido* which regarded *any* prisoner of war as a contemptible coward, bereft of honour, who had immediately forfeited all 'rights' to humane consideration. Thus every downed crew, even assuming they had survived their landing without injury, not only faced myriad forms of unpleasant death from the natural antagonism of the jungle environment itself, but also the certainty of torture, deprivation, debilitation, and all too often summary, barbaric execution if they fell into the hands of unfriendly natives and were betrayed to the nearest Japanese forces. It remains a grim fact that, relative to most other theatres of war against the Axis Powers, of the many Allied airmen forced down in Japanese-held areas of the Far East operational zones, merely a tiny handful ever managed to evade capture and return to Allied protection. The great majority either suffered cruelly at the hands of their captors and/or simply disappeared without trace or evidence of their ultimate fate.

Nos 30 and 31 Squadrons were to remain the only RAAF Beau units on firstline operations in the SWPA for just over two years, 1942-44, before additional Beau squadrons came into being in support; due in the main to the lack of Australian-built Beaufighters until mid-1944, and the increasing demand for UK-manufactured Beaus by the RAF in every other theatre of war which precluded further supplies of the type to Australia from the UK. Initially, the type of sorties flown by No 30 Squadron were significantly different to those flown by crews of 31 Squadron. Whereas 30 Squadron was literally 'up at the sharp end', being based at Port Moresby; No 31 Squadron's Beaus, based on the Australian mainland, had to cover much greater distances to any Japanese target, over considerable stretches of open sea. Such extended flights meant, for example, that any intended surprise attack timed for dawn over a target entailed taking off at least two hours before sunrise, thereby throwing even more responsibility on the well-burdened shoulders of Beau navigators.

In later December 1942 and January 1943 both squadrons were heavily committed in the Allied efforts to repulse Japanese attacks in the Gona-Buna area and a little later against Wau airfield.

A8-14 which served with 31 Squadron and crashed on 3/3/45.

An Erk's work is never done ... maintenance apace on Beau 'O', 30 Squadron (A19-15?).

During these operations 31 Squadron recorded its first aerial combat victory on 23 December 1942, when Sergeants E.J.C. Barnett/P.S. Lennon attacked ground targets at Fuiloro. In Barnett's subsequent report:

> After attacking a building from the south I climbed to about 500 feet in a left-hand turn towards the strip. As I dived towards the strip a *Nate** was coming away in a climbing right-hand turn. I made a head-on attack and let go a one-second burst from about 150-200 yards closing in. I broke away in a steep right-hand turn and the *Nate* went into a left-hand turn. I made another head-on attack and gave a much longer burst, the *Nate* breaking away to my right. My observer (Lennon) reported it slipping away to the ground, belching smoke.

Barnett's claim was verified next day and he was later awarded a DFM. His victory was the first of 21 Japanese aircraft to be destroyed in air-to-air combat by 31 Squadron crews by the end of the war, apart from two more probably destroyed, with a further 18 damaged (at least). In addition a total of 86 other enemy aircraft were to be destroyed or damaged during ground-strafing operations.

One of the perils of ultra-low level strafing of Japanese ground targets was the distinct possibility of a Beau being a victim of its own successful attack from the resulting debris thrown up from exploding objectives. Two examples of this hazard occurred to individual Beaus from each squadron on the same date, 30 January 1943. Sergeants G.R. Downing/D.K. Box in Beau A19-53 of 30 Squadron, engaged in the defence of Wau airfield, were directly over an ammunition dump when this erupted, riddling the Beau with debris in its fuselage and starboard wing, but the crew returned safely.

Meanwhile on the same day Squadron Leader G.W. Savage/ Sergeant N.G. Studt in Beau A19-57 of 31 Squadron led an attack on Penfoei airfield which hit an ammunition dump which exploded violently, throwing debris as high as 1200 feet. Caught in that

* *Nate* was the Allied code-name for the Japanese Nakajima Ki-27 Army Type 97 fighter. The equivalent Allied code for Beaufighters in the SWPA was '*Williams*'.

debris was Beau A19-66 crewed by Sergeants Barnett/Lennon, which had a mainplane holed and its cockpit hatch blown off apart from a host of minor damage. Undeterred, Barnett made two strafing attacks and destroyed or damaged four aircraft, but then ran head-on into a radio mast which became embedded between the fuselage and an engine nacelle, complete with its Rising Sun ensign! Barnett eventually regained base at Coomalie, though most of the radio mast eventually fell away before then.

Despite such dangers, added to all the natural risks inherent with their style of operations, the two Beau squadrons had suffered relatively lights losses during 1942. No 30 Squadron's casualties amounted to five Beaus (A19-1, A19-24, A19-49, A19-68, A19-132) and their crews – all victims of ground defence guns; while 31 Squadron had lost four Beaus (A19-22, A19-46, A19-69, A19-79), three of which had crashed into the Timor Sea. These were aircraft and crews which 'failed to return', but many more Beaus had staggered back to base displaying battle scars of varying severity. Nevertheless, a steady flow of replacement Beaus meant that by the end of 1942 No 31 Squadron could still count a total of 24 Beaufighters on strength.

In the first few days of March 1943 Japanese forces in New Guinea began to be reinforced, with obvious increasing extensions of several air strips, and air reconnaissance soon discovered a large enemy ship convoy intended to land troops and supplies at Lae. Allied aircraft promptly attacked this heavily escorted convoy during 2-4 March in what became known as the Battle of the Bismarck Sea, including the Beaufighters of No 30 Squadron. Thirteen Beaus from the squadron formed an advance strike force by strafing the ships from low-level in order to nullify flak opposition for a following formation of Mitchell bombers of the 90th BS, USAAF. Apart from the ships' anti-aircraft fire the Beaus had to contend with a gaggle of Japanese Zero fighters acting as air cover, and one Beau, A19-53 (Sergeants Downing/Box) was jumped by a pair of Zeros whose fire wounded both men and seriously damaged the Beau, which eventually crashlanded at Poppondetta safely.* Over the following days Allied aircraft

* A19-53 was lost on 30 November 1943 (Flg Off G.A. Lucas/Sgt W.J. Yates) over the Solomon Sea.

continued the destruction of this convoy, including all rafts and landing craft seen attempting to reach shore in the Huon Gulf – the latter targets providing the Beau crews with 'a grisly job' (*sic*) – until ultimately eight transport ships and four escorting destroyers had been sunk, and nearly 3000 enemy troops estimated to have been killed. While 30 Squadron was engaged in that 'battle', 31 Squadrons base at Coomalie was attacked by Japanese bombers on 2 March, and Beau A19-31 was destroyed on the ground.

During March and April 1943 the Beau crews of 31 Squadron were partly engaged on mundane (if necessary) routine escort patrols over Allied supply convoys around the northern coast of Australia, and partly on so-termed 'armed reconnaissances' over Japanese targets; operations which were hampered by bad weather conditions and produced relatively little action for the crews, although on 26 April Beau A19-59 – one of two sent to recce Taberfane – failed to return, having been set upon by eight Jap fighters and shot down into the sea near the Aru Islands. Its pilot, Flying Officer C.A. Greenwood (later Group Captain OBE, AFC, RAAF), spent 18 hours in the water before coming ashore the following day and being captured. Greenwood was to remain a prisoner of the Japanese until the end of the war and survived despite torture and deprivations.* His navigator, Sergeant C.W. Thompson, however, was not seen again.

Greenwood's aircraft was only the second Beau lost in action by 31 Squadron since the start of the year – the first being A19-67 (Warrant Officer N.L. Thomas/Sergeant D.L. van Nooten) on 19 January – but the month of May was to see five Beaus lost, i.e. A19-60, A19-19, A19-29, A19-45, and A19-58; the last three all on the same day, 19 May, during an attack on Penfoei airfield, with all three crews being lost. Japanese air bases remained a high priority target for the Beaus, and in June the enemy floatplane base at Taberfane in particular received much attention. On 12 June, for example, four Beaus from 31 Squadron, with three more as top cover, carried out a tree-top surprise strafe and destroyed seven floatplanes, damaged two others, then shot down a biplane which appeared on the scene.

* For Greenwood's personal account of his captivity see *Whispering Death* by N. Parnell; A. & A. Reed (Australia), 1980.

LY-F of 30 Squadron on patrol, seeking Japanese sea craft off the coast of New Guinea, early 1943; a task usually flown at dawn or dusk.

A19-87,'R' of 30 Squadron, piloted by Flt Lt Ted Marron, DFC, over Gasmata, New Britain on 25/7/43, hunting for enemy transports. The Beau is painted in RAAF foliage green and earth- brown on its upper surfaces.

On 18 June 1943 command of 30 Squadron passed from Wing Commander Walker to Wing Commander C.P. – Clarrie – Glasscock, previously commander of No 12 Squadron RAAF, and by 28 July the squadron was established on Vivigani Strip, Goodenough Island off the northern coast of Papua, where its role was to be a combination of anti-shipping strikes against enemy sea supply convoys and attacks on Japanese airfields in New Britain; operations which meant that the bulk of flying would be over the sea, although the tactics employed usually comprised pairs of Beaus hugging the coastline for some 500-plus kilometres as far as Rabaul, hunting for enemy barges and other supply boats which were normally well camouflaged and moored close to shore during daylight hours. Such 'barge-hunts' were almost invariably flown at dawn after a early-hours' take-off in order to achieve surprise, and usually meant that interception by enemy fighters was minimal. Other duties included acting as both escort and 'advance' force – to smother ground defences – for bombing raids on Japanese airfields and installations by Bostons of 22 Squadron RAAF, also based at Vivigani by July, the two squadrons forming the forward headquarters of No 9 Operational Group.

August 1943 was, in effect, a final month of preparation for an intended Allied assault on Lae and airborne invasion of the Markham Valley, with the ultimate objective of expelling all Japanese forces from the entire Huon Gulf area; the initial amphibious 'invasion' being designated to commence on 4 September. As a general prelude, aerial attacks against Japanese air bases, particularly the main airfields at Rabaul, Wewak, and Gasmata, were intensified during August, apart from the unceasing offensive hunting out enemy supply barges and known dumps.

During one such strafe of Taberfane on 21 August two Beaus from 31 Squadron – A19-47 (Flight Lieutenant F.J. Gardiner/ Flying Officer L.J. Lyne) and A19-63 (Flying Officers V.C. Leithhead/R.S. Graves) – acting as air cover for four other Beaus, both attacked a Japanese floatplane and collided with each other, crashing into the sea nearby. Nine days later the squadron lost another Beau – A19-119 (Flight Lieutenant W.E. Willard/ Sergeant P.N. Butler) – in the same area. On 1 September Clarrie Glasscock led all available Beaus of his squadron – 12 aircraft – on a barge hunt with successful results, and two days later repeated the operation. On 5 September No 30 Squadron strafed the Japanese refuelling airstrip at Cape Gloucester but suffered the loss of Beau A19-33 (Flying Officer H.M. Woodroffe/Flight Sergeant J.L. Brooks) which became the latest victim of heavy flak defences and crashed into a hill side, killing both crew members.

Four days later yet another Beau from 30 Squadron, A19-132, failed to regain base. Hit by ground fire, the Beau ditched in the sea off the Palmalmal Plantation and its three crew men – Flying Officer J.R. Newman/Pilot Officer W.G.R. Binnie, plus an Army passenger, Captain T.F. Gill – were seen to take to the aircraft dinghy safely. After dropping a second dinghy, the other Beaus kept daylight surveillance over their comrades for some 48 hours, but on 11 September the two empty dinghies were seen abandoned on a beach. Their occupants were never found.

Then, on 19 September, No 30 Squadron had to mourn the loss of its commander when Wing Commander Glasscock and his navigator, Pilot Officer J.J. Cain, in Beau A19-133, led a strafe on some barges near the Cape Hoskins airstrip. The Beau received a direct hit from flak and crashed almost immediately. Glasscock's successor on 30 Squadron was Squadron Leader (later, Wing Commander) W.T.M. Boulton, DFC, with effect from 23 September. Ten days previous to Boulton's appointment, 31 Squadron also received a new CO, when Wing Commander Read handed over the reins to Wing Commander F.W.B. Mann, DFC.

It was at this period that Beaufighters of 31 Squadron began carrying bombs under their fuselages for any anti-shipping attacks (initially), then used bombs for other targets once these had proved successful. Their carriage was by local modification utilising American bomb carriers 'borrowed' from No 18 Squadron's Mitchells, and highly 'unofficial'. Both squadrons also began being engaged more frequently by Japanese fighters as enemy resistance to the advancing Allied forces stiffened.

Though not designed for pure air-to-air combat, the Beaufighters' maximum speed at low level enabled the RAAF crews to simply outfly most enemy fighter pursuers, but whenever an opportunity for a straight fight presented itself, the Beau crews were never reluctant to mix it. An example was on 2 October when

Beaus A19-142 and A19-137 came upon a Japanese *Betty* (Mitsubishi Navy Type 1 bomber) scurrying across the sea at wave-level. Coolly formating on either side of their quarry, the Beaus then proceeded to shoot it into the sea in flames. Two days later, however, the same crews were jumped by a force of enemy fighters and reverted to the 'normal' tactic of out-running their assailants at sea-level, although some Japanese bullets punctured a main tyre on Beau A19-137 causing it to crashland back at Vivigani base.

On 12 October a dozen Beaus of 30 Squadron, based temporarily at Dobodura for this specific operation, were part of an Allied air formation comprised of 308 aircraft detailed to attack Rabaul. The Beaus, through no fault of their own, were delayed in take-off, so that when they eventually reached their objective they ran head-on into the returning Mitchell bomber squadrons and their Lockheed P-38 Lightning fighter escorts – who immediately opened fire at the Beaus, thinking they were Japanese interceptors! Fortunately, their gunnery was not accurate and Wing Commander Boulton, the Beau leader, radioed his identity to prevent further onslaughts. Over Tobera the Beaus were next attacked by about 20 Japanese fighters, and the ensuing engagement lasted over half an hour before the Beaus finally out-ran their antagonists. One Beau, A19-97 (Flying Officers D.R. Stone/E.B. Morris-Hadwell) failed to return, but the other Beau crews claimed two enemy aircraft as 'probables' plus several 'damaged'.

The lost Beau crew were further avenged on 23 October when Beau A19-111 (pilot Flying Officer E.G. Drury) was one of a four-Beau patrol which trapped a lone *Jake* (Aichi E13A, Navy Type O seaplane) at low altitude, and Drury closed on its tail and shot it down in flames into a hillside near Cape Oxford. 31 Squadron was also having an occasional success in the context of aerial combat. Prominent in the 'score' chart was Squadron Leader Reginald Lloyd Gordon, a regular RAAF officer born in Sydney. On 9 October, Gordon led six Beaus on a recce of Selaru which were attacked by several Japanese aircraft, of which Gordon destroyed two *Nicks* (Kawasaki Ki-45 Army Type 2 fighters), while another Beau shot down a *Sally* (Mitsubishi Ki-21 Army Type 97 bomber). Gordon was to destroy a total of at least six enemy aircraft before his death on 27 February 1944 while test-flying Beau A19-165, and was awarded a DFC and Bar.

The closing months of 1943 were difficult ones for both Beau squadrons, due primarily to difficulties in obtaining adequate technical and other supplies, apart from deteriorating weather conditions, due to the onset of monsoon rains in November. Despite such circumstances, 31 Squadron despatched eight Beaus, led by Squadron Leader Gordon, to attack Timor on 15 December, resulting in two barges being sunk and six schooners left thoroughly riddled. Then Gordon spotted a cargo-ship convoy, escorted by a destroyer and duly led his men in a mast-level strafing attack, killing troops on the upper decks. The Beaus rounded out their sweep by sinking a 500-tons vessel and attacking Atambua airstrip.

On return to base Gordon reported the convoy off Timor, and next day, led by Wing Commander Mann, eight Beaus carrying two 250lb bombs apiece, set off in the early morning to attack the remnants of that convoy. Despite an attempt by four *Nicks* to intercept – one of which was shot down by Gordon – the Beaus had a field day of bombing and cannon-raking the hapless transport and cargo vessels, and sank the 3000-plus tons *Genmei Maru* cargo ship, causing heavy troop losses.

By the close of the year 31 Squadron's operational records showed a gross total of 1137 operational sorties, with claims for at least 18 Japanese aircraft destroyed in air combat, plus 49 destroyed on the ground, apart from no small number of sea-going vessels sunk or severely damaged. In balance, the squadron had lost 17 Beaufighters and crews to date who had failed to return from operations.

On 5 November No 30 Squadron, along with 22 Squadron, moved base forward to Kiriwina in the Trobriand islands, this move being completed by 26 November; all part of the preparation for a new air offensive over western New Britain, which commenced in December in large strength. 30 Squadron's prime role thereafter concentrated on anti-shipping patrols and sweeps, carrying bombs and usually flown by pairs of Beaus.

On 12 January 1944 the squadron welcomed a new commander with the appointment of Squadron Leader F.R. Maguire, DFC,

AFC, son of a General and a pre-war pilot with nearly 3000 hours in his log books. Maguire's 'reign' was destined to be brief, during which time he flew a number of particularly hazardous sorties, including one on which his own cannon shells exploded wounding him in a leg. His navigator, Flying Officer Lewis Turnbull, came forward and applied a tourniquet using a handkerchief and a pair of his dividers, enabling Maguire to return to base safely.

Command of the squadron then passed to Wing Commander P.L.B. Gibson with effect from 24 May 1944. Actual operations for 30 Squadron were suspended from 14 April to 16 May 1944 – the first real 'rest' for the unit since it had commenced firstline operations. Gibson's period of command was to be even briefer than Maguire's. On 11 June, with Corporal Murphine as a passenger, Gibson took Beau A19-115 for an air test but hit a bulldozer on take-off, killing himself and his passenger.

Next day his post was taken over by Squadron Leader J.T. Sandford (later DSO, DFC), a veteran Beau pilot on his second tour of operations. After its 'rest period', the unit recommenced operations on 17 May by despatching four aircraft to search for a reported submarine, in the course of which recce Beau A19-167 (Flight Lieutenant E.C. Beer/Flying Officer J.M. Fielding) ditched in the sea; its crew being spotted in their dinghy next day and eventually retrieved. By June the squadron was based at Tadji, from where it carried out many sorties against Japanese barges; destroying 18 and damaging many more during a three-weeks' period alone.

For 31 Squadron early 1944 saw a continuation of its 'normal' operations against Japanese shipping, but on 9 March there came an emergency move of base to Potshot (now named Learmonth) just south of the Exmouth Gulf, due to the presence of a large Japanese naval force in the Indian Ocean which was thought by Allied commanders to be a possible precursor of an attempted enemy invasion of Western Australia. In the event, no such move had been proposed by the Japanese and on 23 March all the squadron returned to Coomalie and quickly resumed operations.

On 23 May 31 Squadron said farewell to Wing Commander Mann and Squadron Leader G.D. Wentworth became the latest unit commander. George D'Arcy Wentworth, later Wing

Commander, DFC, had been the B Flight commander, and on 1 July led a strafe of Japanese radio installations on Babar Island. As the Beaus turned for the return flight a voice came over the radios of all Beaus saying, 'Come back here, Wentworth, you bastard!', evidently an English-speaking Japanese radio operator who had been monitoring the Beau crews' R/T transmissions. Wentworth duly accepted the invitation by mounting a repeat performance against the same targets ...

The crews of 30 Squadron, meanwhile, had been engaged in many support operations to the various Allied forces steadily pushing the Japanese out of the myriad islands in the SWPA, flying both day and night sorties to maintain their attacks on enemy barges and other craft. July 13 proved to be a day of ill-spared casualties, when the squadron lost three Beaus and their crews, all on barge-hunt sorties. Flying Officer C.A. Satchwell/Warrant Officer J.W. McNamara in Beau A19-174 were shot down in flames while strafing a barge near Muschu Island; Beau A19-185 (Flight Sergeant H.I. McK Baldock/N Abbott) failed to return from another barge attack; while Squadron Leader G.K. Fenton/Pilot Officer R.C. Nelson in Beau A19-146 during a hunt for barges along the coast to Wewak were hit by flak over Boram airstrip and crashed at the end of the airfield, killing both men.

Due to a fresh tactical reorganisation of certain Allied air units, No 30 Squadron had come under the operational control of No 77 Wing in mid-June, and on 4 August its Beaufighters were flown to a new base at Kamiri, on Noemfoor, to be joined by the Bostons of 22 Squadron by 11 August; both units being now intended to join the aerial campaign over Dutch New Guinea. With the main Japanese air strength now being withdrawn to the Phillipines, 30 Squadron (among other units) was tasked with 'mopping up' certain enemy airstrips still occupied by the remaining Japanese, and on 23 August a total of 25 individual sorties were flown to bomb and strafe the strips at Sagan and Otawiri, with tangible success.

In September-October 1944 both Beau squadrons began training in the use of rocket projectiles (RP) for future operations, such training being undertaken 'on the job' in order not to interfere with normal sorties. During this period Wing Commander Sandford completed his second tour of operations – 80 sorties which, added

Flg Off W.J. Madigan and Flt Sgt K.M. Bond watch their 30 Squadron crew load 60lb HE RP onto Beau A19-195 at Noemfoor, November 1944.

BEAU BITE. An RAAF Beau releases its RP against a jungle target early 1945.

to the 47 of his first tour (with No 25 Squadron RAF), made Sandford the top Beau sorties' pilot of the RAAF in the SWPA – and command of the squadron went now to Wing Commander C.H.C. Thompson, AFC, effective from 9 October. 31 Squadron had also seen a change of commander when Squadron Leader John A'B.P. Boyd, DFC, succeeded George Wentworth on 1 October.

By then the first examples of Australian-built (DAP) Beaufighters were beginning to trickle through to the frontline units; No 31 Squadron receiving its first two examples, A8-6 and A8-13 on 20 September, and commencing operations with these on September 26. By early October the squadron had discarded the last of its UK-built (i.e. ex-RAF) Beaus.

No 30 Squadron, however, had to wait until November before receiving its first DAP Beaus, and commenced operations with them in December. By then 30 Squadron had moved its base to Morotai, all aircraft having arrived at the new airstrip by 16 November, and the first operations from here were flown on 18 November. Japanese intelligence – as always – was quick to note the reinforcement at Morotai and duly bombed the airfield on 22 and 24 November, virtually decimating 22 Squadron's Bostons (nine destroyed) and destroying two Beaus with ten others bomb-scarred, including some of the recently arrived new DAP Beaus.

The virtual destruction of 22 Squadron was, in a sense, propitious in that supplies of fresh Bostons and necessary components were by then difficult, and in December 1944 the unit was temporarily stood down from operations to begin 'conversion' to Beaufighters. In the same month No 30 Squadron was joined at Morotai by its sister unit, 31 Squadron, which arrived from Coomalie on 7 December, via Merauke and Noemfoor. Wasting little time in adapting to its new surroundings, 31 Squadron recommenced operations from its latest base on 9 December when Squadron Leader Boyd led a long-range strike against Jolo Island in the Phillipines by 14 Beaus, strafing troops, stores and a jetty. On 26 December Boyd was succeeded in command of the squadron by Squadron Leader J.C. Black. The last Beau to be lost in action during the year 1944 was A19-149 (Flight Sergeant D.B. Benson/Sergeant R.L.F. Jones) from 30 Squadron which failed to return from a sweep along the Celebes coastline on 30 December;

A19-205,LY-P, of 30 Squadron returning from a strike, 1944.

Sanga Sanga scene in the Phillipines, late 1944, with Beaus of 22 Squadron lining the runway. Nearest, DU-H was A8-50.

the tenth Beau (and crew) lost on operations during the year by that unit, while 31 Squadron had lost seven Beaus and four crews during the same twelve months on sorties. In addition many Beaus had been written off charge due to accidents, flak damage, *et al*, and several crew members had been wounded.

January 1945 brought further heavy operational efforts by all Allied air units in the Pacific zones as pressure mounted against the slowly retreating Japanese forces. The three RAAF Beau squadrons – Nos 22, 30, and 31 – comprised No 77 Wing of the recently titled First Tactical Air Force, a combined USAAF/RAAF command, and in January both 30 and 31 Squadrons were committed to bombing and strafing Japanese objectives in the Celebes, Halmahera, and Vogelkop areas, now carrying small napalm bombs as well as normal high explosive bombs for land targets, and occasionally even 147kg naval depth charges suitably adapted to act as pure anti-personnel blast weapons.

On 1 February eight Beaus from 31 Squadron, strafing a troop area near Tomohon, employed these depth charges and some 9kg fragmentation bombs, but lost Beaus A8-10 (Flight Lieutenant D.R. Taylor/Pilot Officer K. Packham) and A8-32 (Warrant Officer W.R. McGuigan/Flight Sergeant A.E. Lewis), both victims of the particularly fierce anti-aircraft fire met over the target. On 11 February 28 Beaus joined with 59 Curtiss Kittyhawks in attacking Tondano, and this was the first Beau operation by the newly-equipped 22 Squadron, apart from being the first occasion when all three Beau squadrons operated together *per se*.

Even before that initial Beaufighter operation No 22 Squadron, commanded by Wing Commander C.E. Woodman, had lost one Beau, A8-38 (Flight Lieutenant J.T. Robert/Flying Officer A.H. Halliday) on 20 January when it ditched in the sea. On 27 February came a second loss when Beau A8-135 (Squadron leader J. Holloway/Flying Officer D.E. Genders) was one of four aircraft attacking a bridge at Isimu. The Beau hit a tree, causing the aircraft to crash, killing Holloway, and although Genders survived the crash he was to die in captivity on 10 May 1945. Holloway had indeed only recently arrived at Morotai as the next commanding officer-designate for 22 Squadron, but his death delayed the departure of Woodman until 19 March on which date his successor, Squadron Leader John D. Entwhistle, DFC, officially took over the unit.

An old Beau hand, Entwhistle had previously served with 31 and 30 Squadrons, and was flying his second tour of operations, apart from previous flying experience as a commercial skipper. He arrived on the squadron at a period when both living and operational conditions for the residents of Morotai were by no means easy. Apart from the onset of the rains in February-March which reduced ground conditions to a virtual sea of mud, flying was also restricted by shortages of bombs, ammunition, and engineering spares. Moreover, actual operations were going through a relatively quiet sequence of somewhat monotonous repetitive air patrols over Celebes, Ambon, Ceram and other areas as part of the backwater activities in support of the Allies' island-hopping advances northwards. Only occasional sorties bringing brief clashes with the enemy provided 'bright spots' (*sic*) in the otherwise seemingly dull routine.

Such 'bright spots' – if enduring intense flak, battle damage, and perhaps personal injuries can be termed 'bright' – included several particularly dicy operations for certain individual Beau crews. As on 30 March when Warrant Officer W.J. Hart of 22 Squadron took part in an attack on Liang airfield and was wounded in both legs by groundfire. His navigator, Flying Officer D.B. Wilson, bandaged Hart's legs and despite intense pain the pilot flew the Beau over 350 miles of open sea and made a perfect landing at Morotai.

Next day one of two Beaus from 31 Squadron engaged in attacking anti-aircraft gun locations around the north coast of Ambon was hit and forces to ditch off Amboin. The Beau, A8-33, sank swiftly but its crew, Warrant Officer (later Pilot Officer) R.K. Roberts and Flight Sergeant B.W. Phillips, scrambled into their dinghy safely. Remaining afloat just off the Japanese-occupied beachline, the crew became 'bait' for the Japanese as they fired at the circuiting Beaus keeping an eye on their 'cobbers', and the Catalina flying boat* which eventually landed on the sea and retrieved the Beau crew despite heavy fire from the nearby shore.

* From No 113 ASR Flight, piloted by a New Zealander, Flight Lieutenant W.R. Mills, DFC, AFC. Formed at Cairns in January 1945, 113 ASR Flight had only commenced operations on February 4.

A8-1 at Fishermans Bend on 26/5/44 about to make its first flight.

Beau of 22 Squadron with long-range fuel tank attached.

A8-164, SK-A of 93 Squadron being flown by the OC A Flight, Flt Lt F.A. McLeod and his navigator Flg Off P.D. Pickering near Kingaroy, 1945 for the benefit of the press.

A8-122,SK-R of 93 Squadron testing its cannons at a gun butt.

On 3 April No 30 Squadron flew its last operation by a UK- built Beau, A19-215, reconnoitring Amboine, but on the previous day 22 Squadron had suffered the loss of Warrant Officer H.M. Dempster/Flying Officer W.J. Liston in Beau A8-34, shot down by ground fire over Ceram. On 4 April No 31 Squadron also lost a Beau and its crew when Flight Lieutenant C.B. Arbon/Pilot Officer R.L. Wood were hit by AA fire over Amboine and their aircraft, A8-151, fell in flames.

While the three Beau squadrons of 1st TAF continued their operations in early 1945, a fourth RAAF Beaufighter unit came into existence when No 93 Squadron was officially formed at Kingaroy, Queensland on 22 January 1945, commanded by Wing Commander D.K.H. Gulliver.* Known from its unofficial unit badge as the 'Green Ghost Squadron', 93 Squadron was slowly equipped with DAP Beaufighters over the next few months and its crews worked up to operational fitness. Its introduction to the 'sharp end' of operations was equally protracted, with the initial ground crew advance party arriving at Morotai on 22 May, and eventually moving to Labuan by 13 June, while the main unit move of its Beaus came on 31 July when Gulliver led his men to Labuan, arriving there on 5 August to become a unit of No 86 Wing, 1st TAF.

The squadron's first operations, however, had already been flown on 26 July by two of the five Beaus sent to Labuan ahead of the main party; these were Beaus A8-86 and A8-123 which strafed buildings at Sibu and Bintulu with cannons and rockets. On 7 August Gulliver led eight Beaus in an attack on a ship in the South China sea, destroying this with RP and cannon, but one Beau, A8-85 (Flight Lieutenant V.J. Sims/Flying Officer R. Farrant) failed to return. This Beau, coded SK-F, was hit by flak over the target and later crashed in the jungle near KG Bliong, but both crew men survived and successfully evaded capture over the following two weeks before being rescued and returned to Labuan on 21 August.† On 13 August the squadron received a signal to suspend all operations against the Japanese, but this order was

* Killed in take-off accident, Beau A8-184, 10 December 1945

† For full account of Sims/Farrant's evasion period, see *Beaufighter at War* by C. Bowyer; Ian Allan, 1976.

(*Right*) Flt Lt Harris (rt) and Ross Shute with their Beau A8- 122, *'Drack's Daughter'* of 93 Squadron.

A8-118 of 22 Squadron hunting for 'game'.

(*Top*) Flt Lt Sims and Flg Off Farrant, 93 Squadron being welcomed 'home' by their unit commander, Wg Cdr D.K. Gulliver after 'walking back' from behind Japanese lines, 1945.

(*Bottom*) A19-26 from No 5 OTU after a forced landing at Wagga, NSW on 22/3/43.

A8-356 over Port Phillip Bay, Victoria postwar.

A8-265, the prototype target tug variant, seen here when serving with No 30 TT Squadron, circa 1950-51, in traditional black/yellow striping.

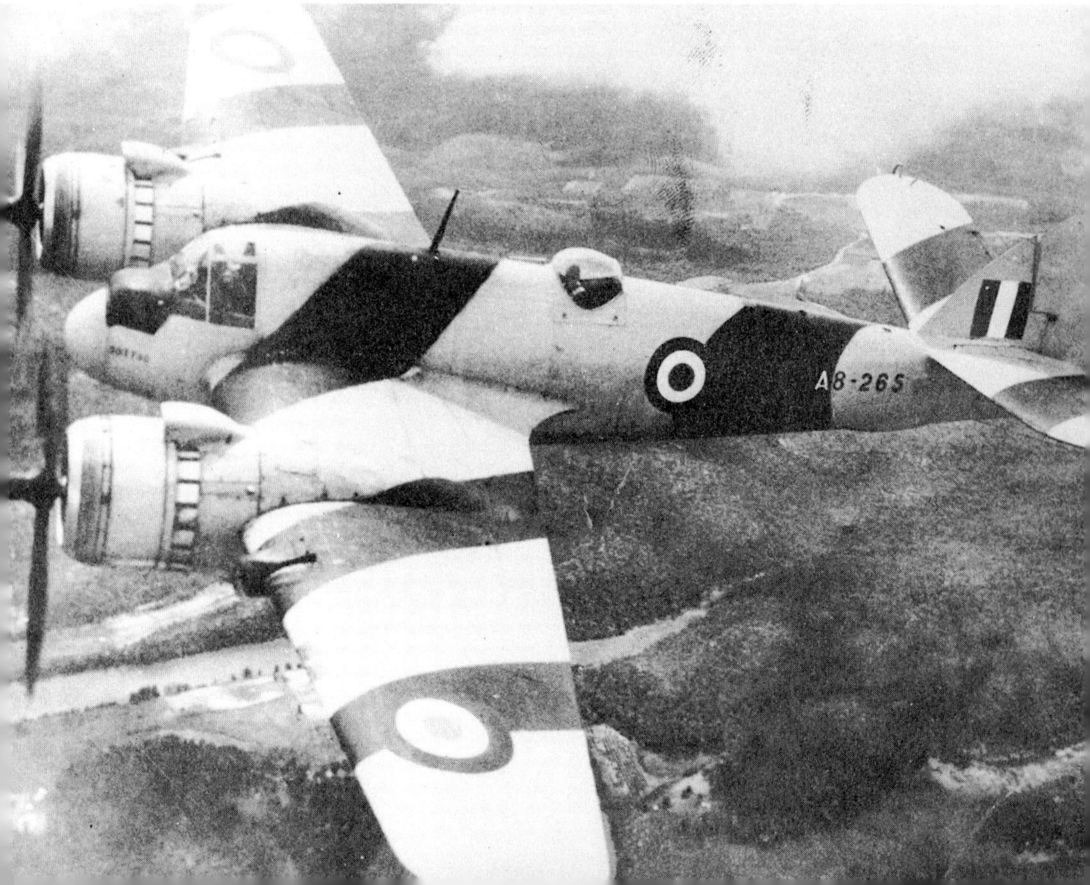

rescinded next day and 12 Beaus were despatched to attack two separate targets, Kuching and its nearby airstrip, and Trombol airfield. Using RP and cannons, the Beaus claimed successful results and all returned safely from what proved to be 93 Squadron's ultimate war sorties.

The remaining Beau units of 1st TAF gradually moved as the Allies continued capturing former Japanese-occupied territories, and on 15 May the first Beaus, from 30 Squadron, took up a new base at Sanga Sanga. By June operations were becoming slightly reduced, while another airstrip at Tarakan was considered fit for Beau operations by July, although this proposed base soon proved difficult to actually operate from, and the Beau squadrons moved either back to Morotai or Labuan. No 31 Squadron's final war sortie 'in anger' took place on 1 August 1945, an RP attack on Kuching's radio station, and thereafter the crews merely carried out general recce patrols and other mundane 'sorties'. No 30 Squadron also became mainly occupied with general recces, photographic surveys, and other routine duties by August.

In the interim just one more RAAF Beau unit was formed when No 92 Squadron came into being at Kingaroy on 25 May 1945, commanded initially by Squadron Leader H.D. Foot. The unit's first Beau, A8-245, arrived on 4 July (and eventually crashed at Narrandera, NSW on 3 September), with more Beaus following over the next few weeks. With the cessation of hostilities against Japan the need for this new squadron was considered nullified and No 92 Squadron RAAF was therefore officially disbanded on 17 September 1945 without ever having flown war operations.

By the close of 1945 the remaining Beau squadrons had (mainly) returned to Australia, and in the following year each was quietly disbanded in the following date sequence:

31 Squadron	Disbanded 9 July 1946
22 Squadron	Disbanded 15 August 1946
30 Squadron	Disbanded 15 August 1946
93 Squadron	Disbanded 22 August 1946

Although the brunt of war operations had been undertaken by just two squadrons – Nos 30 and 31 – the cost in casualties had not been light. Of a total of 137 individual crew members killed during the actual war period, No 22 Squadron had lost six; No 30 Squadron 61 men; and No 31 Squadron 70 members. It should be added that almost half the overall losses, though officially designated as 'On Active Service', were the result of a variety of flying accidents; an inevitable corollary to *any* form of operational flying when crews were commonly operating in far less than perfect conditions and circumstances in aircraft designed solely for war purposes, bereft of the much higher safety standards demanded for peacetime aircraft manufacture and employment. Whether due to an engine failure, technical defects, or enemy gunfire, *each* man had died in the pursuance of his operational duty.

Immediately after Japan's surrender, apart from a few months of 'mopping up' the debris and remnants of the conflict, the RAAF's Beaus were returned to Australia and eventually relegated to storage depots or the scrap heap. Nevertheless, the Beau was to be brought back into limited RAAF use for the next 12 years. In November 1945 Beau A8-265 was used as a 'prototype' for installation of a target-towing winch and this modification was later incorporated in several other Beaus in 1946 – almost two years before the RAF first air-tested its prototype Mk TT10 (NT913) it should be remarked – and resulting from this fresh use for Australian Beaus, on 1 August 1946 the Target Towing and Special Duties Flight was formed at Richmond, NSW, the equipment of which was a mixed bag of different aircraft types but included six Beaufighters modified for the towing role. Later expanded, this Flight eventually became retitled as No 30 (TT) Squadron with effect from 8 March 1948, which unit continued carrying out its ubiquitous duties until being finally disbanded on 21 March 1956.

The ultimate operational Beau in RAAF service was A8-357 of No 1 Air Trials Unit at Woomera, but this aircraft made what was claimed to be the last flight by a Beaufighter in the RAAF on 9 December 1957 when it was ferried from Woomera to Edinburgh, Adelaide for subsequent reduction to components. Thereafter only three RAAF Beaufighters survived – in varying states – until the present day, these being A19-43, A8-186, and A8-328; the latter pair eventually being restored by the Camden Museum of Aviation and the Moorabbin Aircraft Museum respectively. These remain as the only representatives in Australia of an aircraft which it is no exaggeration to describe as the first truly offensive aircraft to be operated by the RAAF during its struggle against Japan in the Pacific.

CHAPTER SEVEN

'Peace' Years

By 8 May 1945, when hostilities officially ceased in Europe, many of the Beaufighter squadrons operating under the aegis of RAF control had already exchanged their Beaus for other types of aircraft, notably De Havilland Mosquitos in most cases, or had fairly recently been disbanded. Nevertheless, on that date a total of 15 squadrons were still Beau-equipped, scattered across the globe in various theatres of war, albeit destined in all cases to a brief future *per se*. These were:*

Sqn No	*Base*	*Remarks*
22	Chiringa	Disbanded at Gannavarum 30 Sept 45
27	Chiringa	Disbanded at Mingaladon 1 Feb 46
89	Baigachi	Renumbered 22 Sqn at Seletar, 1 May 46
144	Dallachy	Disbanded 25 May 45
176	Baigachi	Disbanded 1 Jun 46
177	Chiringa	Disbanded at Hathazari 5 Jul 45
211	Chiringa	Disbanded 28 Feb 46
217	Vavuyina	Disbanded at Gannavarum 30 Sep 45
236	North Coates	Disbanded 25 May 45
252	Hassani	Disbanded at Araxos 1 Dec 46
254	North Coates	Renumbered 42 Sqn on 1 Oct 46
287	Hornchurch	Disbanded at West Malling 15 Jun 46
455 RAAF	Dallachy	Disbanded 25 May 45
489 RNZAF	Dallachy	Disbanded at Banff 1 Aug 45
577	Castle Bromwich	Disbanded 15 Jun 46

In addition at least eight Fleet Air Arm squadrons had some Beaus on strength, while the RAAF in the South-West Pacific Area (SWPA) of operations had four firstline Beau squadrons (Nos 22, 30, 31 & 93).

* Disbandment dates were the *official* ones, while 'bases' do not include detachment airfields at that same date.

While the Beaufighter units in India, Burma and the SWPA were to continue frontline operations until the surrender of Japan in August 1945, elsewhere the Beaufighter had ostensibly fulfilled its prime purpose as a wartime 'exigency' and appeared to have no real role in a peacetime air force beyond remaining as a stop-gap equipment until the Air Ministry hierarchy finally decided upon the postwar RAF Establishment to meet the needs of peace. In the turmoil of world events in the imediate post-bellum era, however, Beaufighters were to re-enter the lists as firstline strike aircraft in both the Middle and Far East zones; while a few 'reborn' RAF squadrons of that period were initially equipped with refurbished Beaus. In addition to the British and Commonwealth air force, several foreign air services acquired small numbers of Beaufighters in the late 1940s.

Although 15 August 1945 had been designated officially as 'VJ Day' (Victory over Japan), RAF and Commonwealth air forces' firstline operations in the Far East did not automatically cease. Fanatical Japanese army formations in distant locations either refused to obey their High Command's orders to surrender, or simply did not believe the news of their Emperor's edict that the war was over. Such men fought on against forward Allied army units detailed to mop up such outstanding pockets of continuing resistance, and the RAF was called upon to provide all forms of direct air support to those forward Allied troops.

Among the many RAF units involved in these 'peacetime' operations were several Beaufighter units, albeit briefly in most cases before disbandment. One such was 27 Squadron, the unit which had originally introduced the Beau to the Far East theatre in October 1942. By August 1945 the 'Flying Elephants' (as 27 Squadron was dubbed) was designated as an Air Jungle Search and Rescue (AJSR) unit, and during the whole month of September 1945 produced a total of 36 search sorties but also flew many contact patrols with the aforementioned Allied army forward units engaged in rounding up isolated Japanese troops.

In the same month 27's crews received news that the squadron would soon be disbanded, but shortly afterwards, due to the first murmurings of civil strife in nearby Java and the Netherlands East Indies (later to be renamed as Indonesia), the unit was granted a stay of execution. On 12 October the squadron moved base from Akyab to Mingaladon, but detached two small Flights to Kemajoram, Batavia and Bayan Lepas, Penang respectively. From Mingaladon the 'Elephants' worked up the Sittaung Valley to the Salween Valley, and north-east to the borders of Siam and China, still supply forward army elements there. Such sorties, entailing flying over mountain ranges reaching up to 13,000 ft, meant stripping the Beaus of armour and rocket installations in order to lighten them.

Another novel form of sortie undertaken by 27's crews in September-October 1945 was the disposal of some 300,000 leaflets announcing the Japanese surrender over Japanese-occupied territories – an operation which was to continue until January 1946 in the Shan States. The squadron's detachment in Batavia became involved in operations against Indonesian rebels, with the first of four recorded 'strikes' being flown on 20 November; while the squadron as a whole, from November 1945 to January 1946 inclusive, totted up a total of 327 operations, of which 104 were classified as 'war' sorties (some 300 flying hours) and the remainder 'non-operational duties'. Then, on 1 February 1946, No 27 Squadron was officially disbanded at Mingaladon, with its Batavia detachment returning to base two days later, and by 28 February all personnel repatriated to the UK or posted to other local units.

By June 1946 no Beaufighter squadrons remained in the Far East, but in November that year No 84 Squadron, based at Seletar, Singapore, began exchanging its Mosquito FBVIs for Beau Xs; while in the following month No 45 Squadron, based at Negombo, Ceylon, also commenced equipment with Beau Xs. In the interim No 42 Squadron, based at Thorney Island in the UK, was reformed on 1 October 1946 as a torpedo-bomber unit with Beau TFXs for that role – its 'reformation' resulting from a renumbering of 254 Squadron which had been disbanded at North Coates on that same date. No 42 Squadron's latest existence as a Beau unit lasted just one year, being disbanded again on 15 October 1947, during which brief span it had no less than three commanding officers appointed! In contrast, Nos 45 and 84 Squadrons were not only to retain their Beaus rather longer but also to employ them on 'war' operations in

1948-49 during the (eventual) 12-years' anti-Communist campaign in Malaya, code-named *Operation Firedog.*

Although simply a wartime 'innovation', the Beaufighter and its outstanding airborne armament capacity was considered worthy of purchase by several foreign air services in the immediate postwar era. Britain's oldest ally, Portugal, was the first to order refurbished Beaus, with 16 Beau TFXs being supplied initially in March-April 1945. These were to equip *Esquadrilha B* of the *Forcas Aereas da Armada* (later renamed *Aeronautica Naval*), based at Portela de Sacavern. In Portuguese service the Beaus were renumbered as BF.1 – BF.16 and replaced Blenheim IVFs, with some of the Beaus later being operated from a second naval air base at Averio, the *Centro de Aviaco Naval de S. Jacinto.*

On 22 October 1945 Beau BF.4 crashed at S. Jacinto, killing its pilot, 1st Lieutenant Felix F. Lobo, and a replacement Beau was bought from the RAF in 1946.* By 1950 *Esquadrilha B* was disbanded and two of its Beaus were re-assigned to the Technical High School (*Instituto Superior Tecnico*) at Lisbon as instructional airframes. This pair were to continue offering useful service in that guise until 1965 before being replaced, with one, BF.10, going to the *Oficinas Gerais de Material Aeronautica* at Alverca, a national air museum eventually founded on 1 July 1969, for full restoration and ultimate display. The other Beau, BF.13 (ex-RAF serial RD253) was presented to the RAF and eventually restored at RAF St Athan before arriving at the RAF Museum, Hendon on 15 March 1971 for permanent retention and public display.

During 1943-44 a small number of Beaus had been locally transferred to the Turkish air force – a total of nine is mentioned in one unconfirmed report – but in 1946 Turkey placed an order with Bristols for 24 Beaufighters; all of which were first refurbished at Filton in the winter months, 1946-47, then despatched in the spring of 1947. These Beaus were ex-RAF serials RD491; RD492; RD495; RD496; RD498; RD547; RD550; RD551; RD552; RD554; RD556; RD695 – RD706 inc. In May 1946 at least four other Beaus – ex-RAF serials V8569; V8608; X8027; X8204 – went

* These 17 Beaus were ex-RAF serials RD134; RD148; RD173; RD189; RD197; RD199; RD206; RD209; RD216; RD220; RD250; RD252; RD253; RD261; RD319; RD320; RD321.

to the French air service. In 1948 came further 'exports' – one official order from Dominica and one highly *un*official acquisition by the embryo Israeli air force. The Dominican order was for 10 Mk TF. X Beaus which were first to be 'converted' to Mk VI standards – by deleting all torpedo gear and installing Hercules VI engines – and which were eventually received at Ciudad Trujillo between 17 September and 1 December 1948, having been ferried by Airwork Ltd across the Atlantic via Montreal, Canada, USA, to the Dominican Republic.

The background to Israel's 'purchase' of Beaufighters was one of intrigue, deception, guile, and no little desperation. On 14 May 1948 the new state of Israel (formerly titled Palestine) was created when, on that date, British mandate control legally ceased. On 15 May Israel was immediately invaded simultaneously by forces from Syria, Iraq, Lebanon, Jordan, Egypt, with contingents in support from Saudi Arabia, Morocco and Sudan. Against greatly superior numbers in all forms of military equipment, Israel particularly lacked modern aircraaft of *any* type, having merely 28 motley types available at that date; none of which had been designed as military operational aircraft. While casting around desperately to acquire suitable aeroplanes – in the face of embargos on exporting military equipment to Israel by British and American governments – the Israel Defence Force/Air Force, or *Chel Ha'Avir* to give it its Hebrew name, was 'born' officially on 27 May.

How the new force managed to steadily gather fresh aircraaft from all over the world during the sumer of 1948 – though a saga of ingenuity and bravado – has no immediate relevance here, except that among the myriad types of aircraaft acquired were four Beaufighters. These were originally among a batch of six Beaus overhauled and converted by Fairey Aviation at Ringway and given British civil registrations G-AJMB; G-AJMC; G-AJMD; G-AJME; G-AJMF; G-AJMG. Of these, five were legally bought by 'R. Dickson & Partners', via an English-based, secret Israeli purchasing agent Emmanuel Zur, ostensibly for a projected cinematic film to feature the exploits during the late war of New Zealand Beaufighter pilots. These five were G-AJMB (ex-RD135); G-AJMC (RD448); G-AJMD (RD427); G-AJME (ND929); and G-AJMG (LZ185). The purchase was openly made for said 'filming purposes', and though the British civil servants involved gave Zur explicit warning that under no circumstances would the Beaus be permitted to be shipped or flown out of Britain, Zur received ready permission to fly the Beaus to a remote part of Scotland 'for the filming location'.

In fact, four of the Beaufighters then immediately 'disappeared en route to Scotland' – the fifth, G-AJME had crashed at Thame on 28 July 1948 and was not delivered – and were, indeed, already being flown to Ajaccio, Corsica from where they were intended to join the *Chel Ha'Avir*. However, none of the Beaus had any armament installed, while no spare parts had yet been obtained. Zur accordingly by various means managed to acquire not only the cannons, but a quantity of spares, including four spare engines, then eventually enlisted a British-born Israeli, John Harvey, who was a pilot, to charter a war-surplus Halifax bomber, civil-registered G-AJPJ (ex-RAF serial PP263), to ferry the cannons and spares to Israel. This ferry flight ultimately reached the airstrip at Lydda where, due to engine failures, the Halifax crashlanded and was wrecked, though its cargo was undamaged.

The four Beaus, which reportedly included three Mk Xs and one Mk IIF, became based at Ramat David on the strength of No. 103 Squadron, but proved difficult to maintain; one Beau became cannibalised to help keep the remaining three 'operational'. Manned by an astonishing mixture of volunteer crew men from differing nationalities and creeds, the Beaus usually carried a three-man crew, but on one occasion was piloted alone by a Canadian pilot, Len Fichert when he was engaged by an Iraqi Hawker Fury fighter. Fichert promptly put his Beau into a full-throttle dive pursued by the Fury, then pulled out of his dive at virtual deck-level and banked almost vertically away. The following Fury, attempting to emulate Fichert, spun in, killing its pilot.

Beau operations continued in October with attacks on enemy air bases and troop centres. On 20 October Len Fichert, with his crew of Stan Andrews (co-pilot) from the USA, and an Englishman, Dov Sugarman, were accompanied by a second Beau skippered by Danny Rosen in an attack with cannon and napalm 'bombs' on an Egyptian-manned police station at Iraq Suweidan. Fichert's Beau was shot down by anti-aircraft fire and the three crew men captured, then – according to Israeli reports – tortured to death. The Beaus' operational careers were, however, short-lived, due primarily to the lack of adequate spares, and they were retired from active operations in November 1948.

Even as the trio of Israeli Beaus were beginning their small but vital contribution to Israel's fight for existence, other Beaus with the RAF in the Far East were becoming involved in warlike operations on a bigger scale. Their operational area was Malaya, then a loose conglomerate of nine separate States each ruled by its own Sultan with large British help, where the predominant political party was the MCP (Malayan Communist Party). The MCP was largely comprised of dedicated Chinese communists under the leadership of Chin Peng – who, somewhat ironically, had been awarded an OBE by the British government for his services in fighting Japanese occupation forces during 1941-45. In the immediate postwar years these Chinese communists inspired a steadily swelling insurrection against all forms of European control, and by 1948 had resorted to murdering several European rubber planters, resulting in the declaration of a 'national' (*sic*) state of emergency throughout Malaya in June that year. It signalled the start of *Operation Firedog* for British and Commonwealth forces in the country, an 'emergency' destined to last for just over 12 years and thereby the longest war (for that was what it amounted to in pragmatic terms) which Britain had been involved in since the days of Napoleon. The 'enemy' were always referred to as CTs (Communist Terrorists) or simply Bandits, and initially comprised an experienced, well-trained force of at least 6000 armed men and women spread throughout the Malayan States, able to fight on totally familiar 'home' territories as veteran guerillas. The geography of Malaya – some 90 per cent covered in lush, dense, tropical jungle almost impenetrable on land and precluding virtually any observation from the air – was patently in favour of the CTs.

In the context of the RAF, its Far East strength in mid-1948 was spread thinly from Singapore to Hong Kong. It included just two Beaufighter units: No 45 Squadron based at Negombo, Ceylon (Sri Lanka), and No 84 Squadron based at Tengah, Singapore. No 45 Squadron, a former Mosquito unit, had begun receiving Beau

TFX RD819 of 84 Squadron at Kuala Lumpur on detachment, September 1948.

RD819 of 45 Squadron gets away, September 1948.

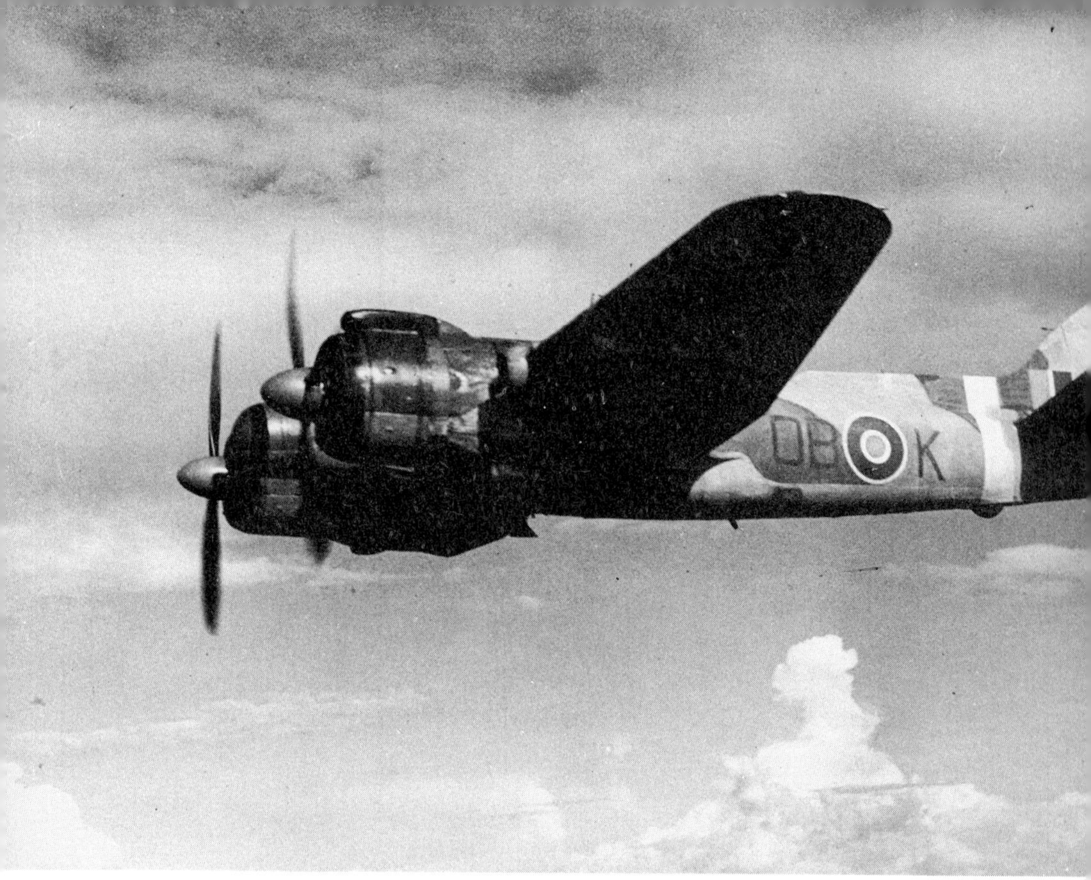

OB-K, 45 Squadron over Ceylon (Sri Lanka), February 1947.

TT.10,RD859 of the Seletar Base Flight, Singapore, 1955.

TFXs in November 1946, finally relinquishing its last Mosquito on 12 December, and was nominally a coastal-maritime unit, but in August 1948 the squadron sent a detachment of Beaus to Kuala Lumpur for *Firedog* operations and flew its first such sorties on 19 August. For the following ten months 45 Squadron remained based in Ceylon, but maintained its operational detachment in Malaya by a rotation system of crews and aircraft. Then, in June 1949, the squadron moved wholly to Kuala Lumpur, with detachments operating from Butterworth and Tengah.

In October 1949 the squadron began to convert to the Beau's stablemate design, Bristol Brigand B1, but continued flying a mixture of Beaus and Brigands until February 1950, when the last Beaufighter left the squadron, by which time the unit was based at Tengah to where it had moved base in the previous December. The squadron's contribution to *Firedog* with its Beaus had been a near-daily routine of cannon and RP strikes against reported CT centres and material dumps, carried out at tree-top height.

The other Beau unit involved in *Firedog*, No 84 Squadron, had also been equipped with Mosquitos prior to receiving Beaufighter TFXs from November 1946, at which time the unit was based at Seletar, Singapore. Moving base to Changi in October 1947, and then to Tengah in February 1948, No. 84 Squadron became involved in operations against the CTs when its detachment at Kuala Lumpur from July 1948 joined forces with 45 Squadron in attacking CT targets. 84's contribution was destined to be brief, however, while operating Beaus. By October 1948 many of its air crews had been detached to England in order to convert to and collect the squadron's initial allocation of Bristol Brigands, while in November 84 Squadron's base was moved to Habbaniya, Iraq where it completed its training and re-equipment with Brigands; eventually returning to Malaya in April 1950 to resume *Firedog* operations from Tengah.

Though no longer firstline strike aircraft thereafter, Beaus were to remain in RAF service in the Far East for a further ten years. These were a small number of Beau TT.10s based mainly at Seletar, Singapore for target-towing and other general army co-operation roles. These Beaus came under the aegis of the Seletar Base Flight, which from March 1954 to February 1956 was commanded by Flight Lieutenant R.F. Chandler, who has described the duties of the Flight:*

> The Flight with its handful of pilots flew a variety of aircraft during the mid-Fifties, and until the arrival of Meteors in 1954 the main task of providing target-towing facilities for all three Services was carried out by the ever-dependable Beaufighters. Apart from the essential towing jobs, there was also participation in defence exercises, calibration, etc, and the Beau was a most enjoyable aeroplane to fly. With its excellent all-round visibility it proved to be a most popular aircraft with all pilots and this was particularly noticeable with newcomers – young pilots with jet training and background that found themselves 'attached' to Base Flight, awaiting postings to the UK or elsewhere. It was considered a great honour to have flown the Beau and something to 'talk about'. Our flying was not restricted to just Singapore Island, and regular flights were made 'up-country' to Butterworth and long sea legs to rendezvous with the Navy. Engine performance was excellent thanks to the care and attention paid to them by the fitters, and when one considers that three Beaus were operating nearly every day it speaks volumes for the aircraft. We also flew them at night to keep our hands in and I never heard anyone complain. The only 'restriction' was no single-engine flying below 6000 feet'.

Within the United Kingdom Beaufighters were to have a brief 'reincarnation' on the strengths of RAF squadrons in 1949 when three squadrons, Nos 5, 17, and 34, were reformed for Army AAC (Anti-Aircraft Co-operation) duties. These reformations had been accomplished by the simple process of renumbering Nos. 595, 691, and 695 Squadrons respectively. No 17 Squadron, based at Chivenor, and No 34, based at Horsham St Faiths (now Norwich City Airport) were both initially equipped with mixtures of Beaufighter TT.10s and Spitfire LF16s, while No 5 Squadron at Pembrey received a few Beau TT.10s by January 1950. All three units were to have a relatively brief existence, being disbanded

* Correspondence with author, 1986. Beaus flown during Chandler's period of command included RD859, RD814, RD854, RD688.

Close stuff. Beau TT.10 of Seletar Base Flight closes up.

SWAN SONG. The ultimate RAF Beau flight on 16/5/60, from Seletar.

Beau VIF,KZ-R of 287 Squadron at Locking, September 1945.

TT.10,RD809, 8Q-A of 34 Squadron at North Weald, September 1949.

again in 1951 – 17 Squadron on 13 March, No 34 on 20 July, and No 5 on 25 September in that year. It fell to a Beaufighter TT.10, RD761, to fly the ultimate RAF Beaufighter sortie when, on 16 May 1960, Flying Officer H. Marshall took off from Seletar, Singapore for a ceremonious 'farewell' circuit of Singapore. On landing again, the Beau was relegated for scrap while Marshall was later presented with RD761's control column handgrip as a souvenir of that occasion.

It was not until the early 1960s that any firm moves were made in the UK to preserve any Beaufighters for posterity. In 1963 Beau RD867, a postwar conversion to TT.10 standard based then on Malta, was conveyed to England earmarked for full restoration and ultimate display in the RAF Museum at Hendon. At No 71 Maintenance Unit (MU), Bicester this Beau was slowly refurbished, but in July 1965 was joined at the MU by a second Beau, RD253, which had been presented to the RAF by Portugal. This second Beau, originally delivered to the RAF in November 1944, had been sold to Portugal, arriving there on 17 March 1945, where it had been

TT.10, SR914 over a Somerset vista.

renumbered as BF.13 for maritime protection duties before eventually being relegated as an instructional airframe.

About the same time it arrived in England a request was received from Canada for the 'remains' (*sic*) of Beau RD867, and accordingly this was fully restored by cannibalising RD253 components at Bicester. Then, with an all-black livery and sporting the codes BQ-I of the wartime No 600 Squadron (for unknown reasoning ...), RD867 was duly shipped to Canada in September 1969 for the National Museum of Canada. In return for this Beau the RAF Museum received the remains of Bristol Bolingbroke No.10001 for ultimate 'conversion' and restoration to a Blenheim Mk IV. The remaining structure of Beau RD253 was then transferred from Bicester to RAF St Athan where a team of enthusiasts on the staff set about full refurbishment of the aircraft. This feat of skills and lengthy labours was accomplished to such excellent effect that on 15 March 1971 a complete Beau was received by the RAF Museum, Hendon where it remains today on permanent public display – a visible 'memorial' to the many thousands of Beau crews who flew, fought – and often died – in the Mighty Beau.

CHAPTER EIGHT

From the Cockpits

Although many descriptions and opinions of the Beaufighter have been published over the past 45 years, it must be recognised that the greater proportion of these have come from writers who never actually flew, or even flew *in*, any Beaufighter in any capacity. In any field of history research and recording such a state of affairs is inevitable. It is therefore essential – at least, in this author's view – that *first*-hand esoteric experience of any facet of history be placed on record to provide *authentic* knowledge of any subject. In the context of the Beaufighter, this simply refers to the air and ground crews who flew or serviced Beaus – only they are truly qualified to judge the greatness (or otherwise) of that aircraft. Moreover – and again in this author's judgment – history is created primarily by humans, not the tools of technology as represented in any form of inanimate machine; because *any* aeroplane – despite the all-too-human leanings towards nostalgia and sentiment – remains simply a useless product until a human presses the button or switch which gives life to said aircraft. Only then can the combination of human and machine achieve any purpose. Thus, the human experience must surely claim the highest priority in the consideration of true history. The following accounts are verbatim from the experiences of various individuals who *knew* the Beau intimately, selected to illustrate many aspects of the Beaufighter's services.

Once clear of its factory assembly line, every Beaufighter was then placed in the hands of a test pilot for brief air trials prior to being ferried either to an appropriate RAF Maintenance Unit or direct to an RAF squadron or other flying unit. As men and women who were called upon to drive virtually any type of aircraft trusted to them, the crews of test pilots and Air Transport Auxiliary Ferry Services were in a better-than-average position to judge the

Beaufighter in relation to all other aircraft designs. The late H.A. Taylor was one such highly experienced test and ferry pilot whose views of the Beau were objectively critical – as his job required – but also affectionate in praise:

> Though mildly intimidating on first acquaintance because of its almost brutally powerful appearance and apparently complicated cockpit, the Beaufighter was, at least in its Hercules-engined versions, a satisfying and even delightful device when you got to know it well. The controls may have been on the heavy side; but it handled beautifully, gave its pilot a near-perfect view ahead through the flat, bullet-proof windscreen, and was surprisingly easy to fly so long as reasonable care was taken during the first part of the take-off run. In its day, a deal of near-nonsense was spoken and written about the Beaufighter's 'take-off swing'. Any aeroplane, especially one with the centre of gravity well behind the main undercarriage, will deviate from the straight and narrow if it is allowed to do so. An exaggeratedly stocky and powerful twin like the Beaufighter was no exception. Until adequate rudder control could be felt and seen, you had to keep it straight during take-off by using differential power – inching the throttles open individually while aiming at some distant object. Once there was full rudder control the throttles could be taken straight through the rated gate and the Beau accelerated along the runway like something on rails – and a very exhilarating experience it was.
>
> Its reputation for directional control peculiarities was probably partly the result of the fact that the undercarriage legs would tend to come up in an uncertain and somewhat hesitant order, causing some pronounced and not very easily controlled yawings from side to side. The Merlin-engined Beaufighter II, in particular, felt sometimes as if it was going sideways for a few seconds during the initial climb. I remember reading somewhere, long after the war, that the long dorsal fin of later Beaufighters 'cured the swing'. Of course it didn't; the extra fin area just made it more controllable during the less easy part of the take-off run and the climb out. The complication of the Beaufighter's cockpit was an initial impression rather than a

> fact. Things were placed where they could be put conveniently, rather than where they should have been placed logically. So, apart from that splendid and universally fitted invention the standard RAF instrument-flying panel, the single-seat cockpit was a fairly untidy place. However, we preferred it that way, and even liked the multifarious and independently conceived controls which were so typical of British aircraft at that time. The electro-mechanical undercarriage indicators of the Beaufighter, for instance, seemed to have been designed after a look at the drums of a fruit machine, or one-arm bandit; the engine and propeller controls were in two quite separately constructed gates, with the blower and other engine controls in a flat, horizontal panel behind them; and the fore-and-aft trimming wheel was mounted on its own little pedestal to the right of the pilot. But the Beaufighter was a satisfying aeroplane as well as an effectively functional engine of war which, in its developed Mark X version, carried, without complaint, everything but the kitchen sink. It would, no doubt, have carried that also, if required to do so for some operational purpose ...*

Another distinguished ATA pilot, the late Hugh Bergel, OBE who commanded No 9 Ferry Pool, ATA at one period, has said of the Beau:

> Captain Barnwell, head of the team which designed a long line of notable Bristol aircraft, once expressed his design philosophy in some such words as 'you can make the kitchen table fly if you put enough power on it'. Certainly the Beaufighter achieved its great success more by force than by finesse. Structurally, it was to the Mosquito as carthorse is to polo pony. It was awe-inspiring rather than difficult to fly. The forward view from the cockpit was so completely unobstructed that the pilot felt naked at first, and this feature could complicate the landing procedure. If your approach was not well-judged, and called for substantial engine power in its final stages, it was quite easy to find yourself over the start of the runway with nothing to tell you whether your tail was well up or practically in the three-point attitude. Treated with

* *Test Pilot at War* by H.A. Taylor; Ian Allan, 1970

the respect due to its power, size and weight, the Beaufighter was a safe and attractive aeroplane, but I for one never felt relaxed until I had reached 2000 feet and 200 mph.*

For wartime-trained pilots their introduction to the Beaufighter varied considerably, depending on which period of the war this occurred. Before Beaufighter-training became a norm at specific OTUs many pilots were 'converted' by the process of squatting behind a Beau pilot and watching what he did for a flight or two, then with head buzzing with a variety of 'Dos' and 'Don'ts', off he went for his first solo. Wing Commander George McLannahan was perhaps a typical example of this form of induction to the Mighty Beau:

> Having been posted to No. 604 Squadron direct from a training unit where I had been instructing, I never went to an OTU. My introduction to the Beau was in November 1941 with my Flight commander, Squadron Leader S.H. Skinner† and his observer Sergeant Larcey during a 45-minute night flying test. I remember John Cunningham a little later in order to reassure new arrivals on a Beau's single-engine performance used to give them a ride standing behind him while he cut or throttled back an engine on take-off. As a result of never having any proper instruction, and a complete lack of cockpit drills, I had many anxious moments scrambling into the air at night wondering what I had forgotten. Fortunately, however, incidents were few and far between, but the most alarming one was an apparent ASI failure on the down-wind leg on a very dark night at Middle Wallop after selecting undercarriage down. I was pushing more and more throttle on to counteract the falling airspeed when I switched on my torch for a quick look around the cockpit. I found the undercarriage was still up – but we had full flap down!
>
> As an aircraft I found the Beau Mk I a strong, powerful machine but very tiring to fly on patrol at night, or on

* *Flying Wartime Aircraft* by H. Bergel; David & Charles, 1972. Reproduced by kind permission of Mrs P. Bergel.

† Wing Commander Stanley Skinner, DFC, was later killed while acting as an observer aboard the destroyer *Berkeley* on 19 August 1942 during the Dieppe landings.

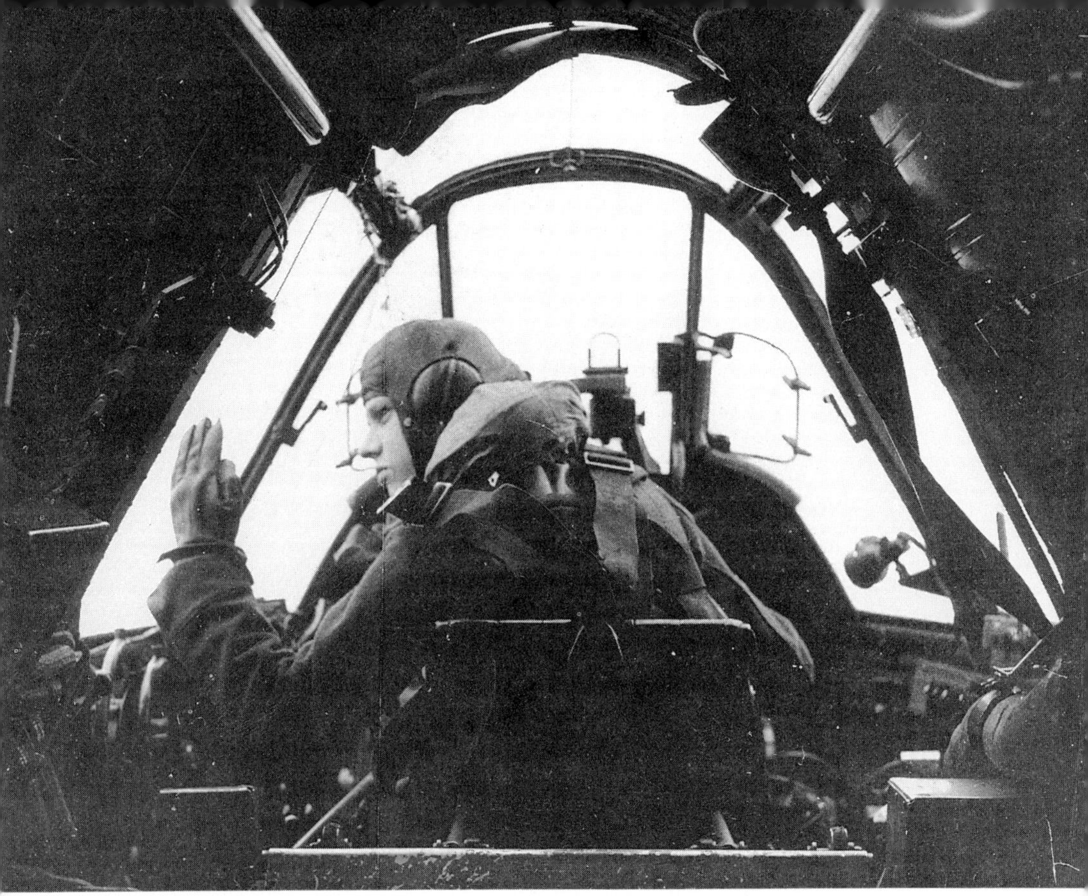

CHOCKS AWAY. An RCAF pilot about to take off in his Beau II nightfighter.

Flg Off Gonzales (L) and Flt Lt George McLannahan of 604 Squadron.

instruments, as it was completely unstable fore and aft. This was virtually cured on the Mk VI. I came onto the Mk VI after flying Mosquitos and it was like handling a battleship after being used to a destroyer. On this aspect I'll always remember an American in 153 Squadron who had joined the RCAF early on to get into the war. He commented that he felt completely at home in a Beau as he'd previously been a truck driver! Rather unfair on the Beau as it was a very fine, solid aircraft. For just one example of this, landing it in a crosswind was never a problem; once placed properly on the ground it sat there and defied any deviations.*

Another well-experienced Beau pilot was Squadron Leader J.T. Sandford, DSO, DFC, Australian-born, who saw service with 25 Squadron RAF initially, then later commanded No 30 Squadron RAAF.

The Beau was not an easy aircraft to fly, at least for the normal Empire Air Scheme pilot. The original Air Ministry Pilot's Notes contained the illuminating statement that the longitudinal stability of the Beaufighter was neutral! In the earlier models with the flat tailplane, the pilot worked constantly to maintain an even altitude; with the later dihedral tailplane it was easier, but still could not be flown 'hands off'. Taking off and landing was another story, and many were the disasters and near misses. If there was nothing in the way, a Beau would always get off, even at right angles to the strip. There was so much power that the fuselage just followed the engines. The trick was to make it go straight. Landing was easier, as the undercarriage was immensely strong, being designed for heavy landings at night. The Beau could be dropped from a considerable height without damage, except to the pilot's ego. These were small matters really; in the air and on the job, the Beau was everything a pilot wanted, a thrilling and satisfactory aircraft to fly to war'.†

Wing Commander Hugh Garlick, DFC, was another veteran Beau pilot who commanded No 235 Squadron on operations, then

* Correspondence with author, 1974-75

† *Whispering Death* by N. Parnell; A.H. & A.W. Reed Pty Ltd, 1980

became chief instructor at No 2 (C) OTU (Beaus), finally serving as Controller at No 16 Group HQ, Chatham, which included overseeing the operations of the North Coates Strike Wing.

Regarding the Beaufighter as an aircraft, those I flew were Mk I equipped with Hercules engines. This was the low-level version built for Coastal Command, initially for long-range recce, then long-range fighter cover for Beaufort torpedo attacks, Fleet operations, and combined Services' operations. Its speed at sea level was sufficient to equal, if not outpace, the current Me 109; though with increasing height the 109 gained an advantage. With its short nose and the pilot high in front it provided a magnificent forward view for low-level work. The engines were set forward so that their leading edge was in front of the cockpit. This, coupled with their weight and power, gave both advantages and disadvantages. The main disadvantage was a tendency to swing on take-off, which if not corrected immediately could become uncontrollable; and this resulted in many early Beaus wiping off their undercarriages or embedding themselves in other aircraft or in buildings. It also resulted in another trap for the unwary. If forced to abandon a landing and go round again, too sudden opening of the throttles flipped the aircraft upside down – few crews survived meeting the ground in this position.

Yet given these two traps for the unwary, the Beau was an extremely safe aircraft and one in which crew survival in a crash could be almost guaranteed *provided* the pilot cut both engines and went straight ahead, *regardless* of obstacles. The forward-placed engines battered obstructions out of the way, whilst the crew were encased in an armoured box, with the four cannons acting as skids. I have seen a Beau go through a copse of trees (scything them down), *through* the earthworks surrounding an ammunition hut, *through* the brick-built hut, and finish up literally as just an armoured box, with the pilot sustaining only a broken leg and his observer uninjured.*

* Correspondence with author

W.G. Hood, who as a navigator flew operations in Beaus with 255 Squadron for almost two years, remembers the Beau as:

> To use an engineer's expression, a real blacksmith's job. You could lose an engine and it would still fly, that is with the exception of the Beau II which was hopelessly underpowered as against the Beau I or VI. The manner in which they soldiered on with the minimum of servicing in the Middle East was amazing – when were operating from Souk el Arba we took one Beau back to Setif for servicing after two months' flying and found a cannon shell embedded in one of the wing spars! The secret of the success of the Beau – especially as a night fighter – was without doubt our ground crews; these were the boys who should have had the glory and the glamour, not us. I have seen our ground crew, when we have landed at dawn get cracking at once servicing, stopping only when the aircraft was too hot to touch with the heat of the day – then be waiting for our return with smiles all over their faces if we had the luck to hack down the odd Hun.

Hood, who with his regular skipper, Flying Officer T.A. O'Sullivan, accounted for several enemy bombers destroyed by night in North Africa, also recalls various incidents of his time with 255:*

> We worked quite an amount with searchlights as well as GCI, and one night an army officer decided to see what the effect was like from the air. As he had never flown before, he was warned against it but still decided to have a 'look-see'. He was shown how to operate his oxygen mask etc and off we went. Sure enough, a Hun came upon on the 'board' and the crew were pushed up to Angels 20 (20,000 feet). The army job was told to turn his oxygen supply to maximum, promptly turned it *off*, and passed out! The Hun turned out to be at 15,000 feet, was duly chased, and the army job came to just as a Heinkel 111 burst into flame before his eyes – so he passed out again. The aircraft was

* Correspondence with author 1975

vectored to base and by the time it was in the circuit at about 1500 feet, the army type was quite back to normal. The crew were then given permission to 'pancake' (the usual expression for landing). The army job thought this meant a crash landing – and promptly passed out yet again!

Funny things happen even in wartime. The great ambition of every night crew was to shoot down three in one night, and in North Africa one of our Wing Commanders (no name, no pack drill!) shot down a Ju88, then made a mess of his landing and finished up on top of a Hurricane – he'd got his 'three', and got a lot of leg-pulling thereafter. And when we were operating from El Aouina near Tunis we had a Norwegian crew with us who shot down an Italian aircraft one night. There was then a horrible row when it was discovered that Norway and Italy were not *officially* at war!

Of course, we had our share of line-shooters and two of the best that came to my ears were 'If the lock gates hadn't been open I'd never have got through' (this was when we were doing some intruding sorties); while on reading of some Russian who had baled out at 20,000 feet and fallen into a deep snowdrift when his parachute failed to work, we asked our champion line-shooter what he would have done. His reply, 'I'd have shot a line, greased my arse, then slid down it' ...

Tales of the legendary sheer strength of a Beau abounded in every theatre of war, and typical examples of the Beau's 'bring 'em back alive' reputation were those witnessed by one Beau pilot serving in Italy 1943-44:*

Our runway at Monte Corvino was formed of perforated metal plates placed on the grass field, but once the winter rains set in the plates floated on a quagmire. On take-off the mud spurted up through the perforations of the runway plate into the wheel-wells of the aircraft, and after a three-hour patrol at 20,000ft over the Anzio beachhead the wheels were frozen solid in the 'Up' position. Only by flying round for a time near sea level were we

* 'Flying the Whispering Death' by 'POM'; *Aircraft Illustrated*, September 1969.

able to eventually lower the thawed-out wheels. Then when we did land the mud spouted up again, fell back on top of the aeroplane and completely obscured the cockpit canopy so that it was necessary to open the small clear-view peephole for taxying.

Early in 1944 at Foggia I twice witnessed a demonstration of the strength and safety of the Beau. Coming in to land after a nightflying test I saw my Flight commander, who was landing next ahead of me, bounce in a strong cross-wind, try to 'catch' the bound with engines, and get a response only from the upwind engine. From the base leg of my approach I next saw, from underneath, a plane view of the Beau as it rolled along the runway on its wingtips and tail like a cartwheel, finally crashing down on its belly with its wheels and engines carrying on up the runway individually. As I landed I noted that the tail unit was broken clean off behind the rear cockpit, but when I taxied back I saw the crew walking over to the crash wagon for a check-up which showed only cuts and bruises.

A week or so later, during a single-engine approach, one of our pilots undershot the airfield and touched down on the wrong side of the boundary road. He then bounced over the road, but in doing so hit a telegraph pole square-on with the nose. The pole drove a trench six inches wide through the nose cone until it reached the front armoured bulkhead where it shattered, and a piece of pole about the size of a cricket ball smashed through the two-inch windshield and ended up in the tail, just missing the crew as it went. The aeroplane staggered, fell fifteen feet to the ground and disintegrated, leaving the cockpits and centre-section of the wings intact from which the pilot and navigator stepped only shaken.

For Stuart McLaren a vivid testimony to the toughness of a Beau occurred during only his second solo flight while converting at an OTU:

I was still rather intimidated by the sheer power of the Beau when I prepared for my second try at soloing and therefore, once I'd got the OK to take-off, was more than a little anxious, particular about the Beau's dreaded swing once at full bore. I pelted down the runway, all eyes and ears, and the Beau started to lift, still straight on track. Then the starboard engine coughed, grunted, and began losing power rapidly. Petrified, I found myself heading off at an angle straight towards a dispersal hangar. Instinctively I heaved back on the control column, skimmed over the hangar roof by mere inches, still crabbing sideways, then felt the Beau begin to drop a wing. I was then heading towards a pile of earthworks being dug up by the Works and Bricks people on another dispersal site. Frankly, my mind was now a blank – I simply froze at the controls and waited for the inevitable.

The Beau hit a huge pile of earth and rubble, cut *through* this like a hot knife through butter, hit the ground with a hell of a smack, bounced up, hit a stack of bricks, scattered these to the four winds, then hit the ground again and proceeded to screech along in its belly bashing anything in its way aside like some mad rhinoceros. All this time I remained 'frozen' in my seat, gripping the control column and convinced my last hour had arrived. The Beau next hit a Bedford lorry with one wing, spun in a half-circle, slid on sideways, hit some other solid object, straightened up and finally ground to a halt in a cloud of dust, smoke, and screeching noises.

Instinct then took over – I unstrapped like lightning and baled out of the cockpit and ran about a hundred yards before my knees buckled and I collapsed on the grass shaking like a jelly. It took a while before my shakes died down and I could breathe normally again. I then strolled back towards the Beau which by then was surrounded by the crash crews. Luckily there'd been no fire. The sight which greeted me left me speechless. The Beau was literally in pieces. Both wings were off, both engines had left their mountings and ploughed on ahead on their own, while the whole of the rear fuselage had snapped off just behind the main spar. Yet my cockpit was still in one piece. Obviously my guardian angel had put in some overtime that day, but it taught me a lesson. After that I always felt *safe* in any Beau.

What of the Beaufighter engaged on operations? Perhaps the 'proof of the pudding' was in the successes achieved by Beau crews in the varying types of sorties flown, exemplified by individual accounts and official combat reports. On the night of 17/18 January 1943

German bombers from KG2 and KG6 set out to bomb London – a retaliatory operation for an RAF bombing attack on Berlin – and among the Beaufighters patrolling that night was one from 29 Squadron, flown by the unit CO, Wing Commander C.M. Wight-Boycott with his observer, Flying Officer A.M. Sanders. This crew flew two patrols and claimed four enemy bombers shot down. In the pilot's own description:

> The curious thing about the first one I shot down was that although London was throwing up a terrific amount of flak and there were any number of searchlights about I don't remember seeing anything of them at all. I was looking up all the time to find the enemy silhouetted against the bright moonlit sky. We'd just popped above a thin layer of cloud and there was the Dornier, a sort of grey colour. I fired a long burst and saw an explosion behind the pilot's cockpit. It seemed to go straight down and I tried to follow, so steeply that my observer came out of his seat. When the Dornier crashed three brilliantly white blobs appeared to jump out of the ground. That was Dornier No 1.
>
> The next patrol nothing happened at all, except my observer complaining about the hardness of his seat. We got Dornier No 2 during our second alert. It must have been about four in the morning. He was travelling very fast and jinking violently. He didn't keep a straight course for more than a few seconds at a time. But there was no cloud about now; it was a good night for interception, and I managed to get in a fairly long burst. He caught fire and slowed up very quickly. I got so close to him that I was caught in his slipstream and rolled on to my back, but I managed to avoid colliding with him. By the time we were right way up again he'd hit the ground and was blazing away.
>
> Then came Dornier No 3. Again I got in a long burst amidships. There was a yellowish explosion and down he went. As he did so he fired about a second's burst, two streams of red tracer, but they went nowhere near us. Number four was a Junkers 88 and the most spectacular of the night. We found him somewhere in the Croydon area. My cannon shells set both his engines on fire and flames spread along his wing and back to the

THE OFFICE. Pilot's cockpit array of a 143 Squadron Beau.

FOUR IN ONE NIGHT. Wg Cdr C.M. Wight-Boycott (4th from rt) and his navigator Flg Off A.M. Sanders (far rt) with their ground crews, 29 Squadron, January 1943.

> fuselage. They lit up the sky so clearly that we could see his black crosses. And we saw four of the crew bale out, one after another. As it went down you could see all the streets lit up, and when it hit there was a terrific flash. Home we went; pleased but wondering what luck the rest of the squadron had had.*

Awarded an immediate DSO, Wight-Boycott was later to be credited with a total of 12 combat kills, and eventually retired from the RAF as Air Commodore, CBE, DSO, BA.

On the night of 17/18 August 1943 Bomber Command despatched an initial force of 596 bombers on a special operation to destroy the German V-2 rocket research establishment at Peenemünde, on the Baltic coast. No 141 Squadron, based at Wittering, was among several squadrons of fighters detailed to provide protection to the heavy bomber force, and prepared a total of 16 of its *Serrate*-equipped Beaus for the operation. Using the forward airfield at Coltishall, the squadron CO, Wing Commander J.R.D. Braham, DSO, DFC and his observer Flight Lieutenant H. Jacobs, DFC, took off at 2200 hrs into a full moon sky for what was technically termed an 'intruder' sortie, hoping to surprise any German nightfighters attempting to interfere with the bomber stream heading for Peenemünde.

North-east of Schiermonnikoog his Beau was one of several which suddenly encountered five Messerschmitt Bf110s from IV/NJG1. Braham's subsequent combat report read:

> We took off from Coltishall at 2200 hrs on intruder patrol to Stade. We flew to a point North of Schiermonnikoog and then turned N.E. at 2254. We continued on course for about five minutes when we sighted one Me110 flying East and jinking. We turned and followed him towards the coast, closing in on the aircraft until we were at 300 yards range, 20 degrees starboard astern, and a little below. Fire was opened with a two-second burst from all guns and strikes were seen all over the enemy aircraft. Smoke came from the port engine and the Me110 dived to port. We gave him another two-second burst from 250 yards

* That night 29 Squadron Beau crews *claimed* seven destroyed and two more damaged, but Luftwaffe losses actually amounted to five bombers lost over England.

and he caught fire and dived into the sea burning on the water. Immediately afterwards we saw a second Me110 (which had been chasing us) a little above and turning gently to starboard on to an Easterly course. We gave a one-second burst of cannon and machine gun at 50 yards in a gentle turn. The enemy aircraft appeared to blow up and we had to pull up and turn to port to avoid ramming it. At that point we saw one man bale out and his parachute open, and the enemy aircraft dived vertically into the sea in flames. We landed at Wittering at 0145. Camera gun was carried and used on both combats.

In total contrast to the silent, unseen, stab-in-the-back nature of night fighting, the types of operations flown by Beau crews of the UK-based Coastal Command units were primarily flown in broad daylight, facing the full fury of (usually) prepared enemy defences. Ray Cartwright, who flew Beaus as a Sergeant pilot with Coastal Command, described one sortie against a merchant convoy:*

I was one of four Beaus detailed to smother any flak guns from the convoy's escorts – a destroyer and two flak-ships – before the torpedo-Beaus went in at sea-level. We flew in cloud most of the way, but a few miles from the estimated convoy position we suddenly came out into clear sky with maximum visibility – ideal for our strike. Sure enough the convoy was where we expected it to be; a couple of tankers and two larger cargo-type ships with their close-flanked escorts. The leader gave a brief R/T order to 'spread out and attack', so we moved into line-abreast and dived in. Flak was already curving up at us, long lines of curving white and red beads which seemed to get thicker as we closed the range.

Being at the right-hand end of our foursome I picked a flak-ship to attack and flew at it at mast-height, opening fire with all guns when the range was about 200 yards. My shells splashed a line of spouts close to the hull then burst all over the centre superstructure, with tracers ricocheting off at all sorts of angles. As I passed over the ship I had a split-second sight of a sailor

* Correspondence with the author

standing on the open deck with his arms covering his head – I didn't blame him! Once clear of the ship I kept low but started jinking side to side in case the flak-gunners tried to follow me, then when well clear climbed and circled for a second go if needed.

My navigator, Ron, spoke, 'Christ, look at the starboard wing!' On looking out I could see a damned great hole right through the centre of the wing roundel – a bullseye by some Jerry gunner – yet I'd not felt a thing during the strike. I quickly checked out controls and instruments but all seemed well. However, not knowing what actual damage had been done I scrubbed the idea of a second attack and asked Ron for a course back to base. Once landed we inspected the damage – a ragged hole about three feet in diameter – but also found about thirty other smaller rips and slashes all around the hole. We'd been lucky. If that shell had been a foot or two further inboard it would have hit our wing tank, and I daren't think what might have happened.

Equally vulnerable when flying in the face of enemy groundfire in daylight operations were those Beau crews who carried out ground-strafing sorties along the North African coastline, or against Japanese objectives in Burma. While desert strafers at least had the advantage of being able to see their targets clearly in most cases, Beau crews operating over Burma seldom saw enemy gun positions because of the nature of the jungle terrain and the Japanese skilful use of camouflage. James Denny, a pilot with 177 Squadron in 1944-45, described one such incident.*

Most of our operations were single plane efforts and all carried out at very low level to give maximum surprise to the Japs on the ground and to escape the attentions of any Jap fighters about. There were many snags to avoid – tall thin trees, cables slung by the enemy from one tree to another on routes we were known to patrol, plus telephone and power lines. The navigator had a difficult job sitting facing backwards in the rear dome, travelling

* Correspondence with author, 1986

Beau TT.10 cockpit, Seletar Base Flight, 1955.

at 185 knots some 20 feet above the ground, and as a precaution I always carried my own map with our course heavily marked at five-minute intervals. We often saw nothing of the enemy; the Japs were masters at camouflage and moved almost entirely at night, and often the only evidence that they were there was the odd bullet hole found in the plane on return. On 12 March 1945 I wrote off my one and only aircraft in my whole flying career. I went on a patrol of the Pegu-Thawatti railway and road in the late afternoon and I heard something hit the aircraft somewhere behind me when we were flying low alongside the railway. We arrived back at Chiringa after dark and while doing my pre-landing checks I found to my alarm that I had no air pressure for the brakes! I was horrified!

Landing a Beaufighter at night on a narrow strip with large trees on either side was tricky enough with all systems working, but with no brakes I did not fancy my chances at all. However, there was nothing else for it – I had to try and get down in one piece. I made my normal approach under power and touched down as nearly as possible on the runway, cut the throttles and let the tail come down. Immediately she started to swing off to the right and as full left rudder wouldn't hold it I had to put on some starboard engine. This kept me on the runway but we weren't slowing down very much and were rapidly running out of runway. When we were about 50 yards from the last pair of paraffin flares, still doing about 60 knots, I whipped up the undercarriage lever, switched off both engines – and prayed!

The wheels did not come up until we hit a slight ridge at the end of the runway, then the plane went grinding along on its belly until we hit something with an almighty crash. The undercarriage warning horn was blaring out – I called Andy [WO Anderson] to get out quick and we both scrambled out of our top emergency hatches. We had gone into a pile of large drums of tar – there was tar everywhere and smoke rising from the engines, so we didn't linger on the scene. We were both unhurt apart from a slight bruise on Andy's head from contact with his dome when we hit. I learnt later that a bullet had penetrated the compressed air reservoir cylinder quite near the navigator's seat. The aircraft was a write-off; the engines had taken the brunt of the collision and both wing spars had been twisted back.

The preceding opinions and experiences of individuals who flew in Beaufighters could readily be multiplied a thousand times were space available. Yet, with rare exception, all such views would still be unanimous in praise, respect, even affection for the Mighty Beau. Not only was the Beau a highly satisfactory weapon of war – which, pragmatically speaking, was any operational air crew member's *raison d'être* – but it was also an aircraft in which crews had complete confidence from any pure flying viewpoint. Moreover, many hundreds of Beau men had particular reasons for blessing the sheer strength and endurability of the design; inherent qualities which had literally saved them from death or mutilation in normally fatal circumstances. Conceived solely as a wartime hybrid exigency, the Beaufighter emerged as one of the few truly outstanding operational RAF aircraft of the 1939-45 conflict.

CHAPTER NINE

They Also Serve

Histories of any aircraft used by military air services necessarily give prominence to the men and women who actually flew such aircraft in whatever guise or role. Such a priority is logical – the whole purpose of any air force is to support and sustain its 'sharp end'; the crews and aircraft carrying out firstline operational tasks. Nevertheless, it is too often forgotten that in the shadow behind the fulsome media publicity given to air crews is a virtual army of non-flying personnel – the ground crews of more than a hundred skilled or semi-skilled trades. In the Royal Air Force these wingless airmen and airwomen – universally dubbed 'Erks' – have always been the base rock foundation of every flying unit. Whether skilled fitters working on aircraft, equipment clerk, administrative orderly, cook, MT driver, or any other ground trade, *all* provided an essential service in ultimately ensuring that the aircraft and their air crews are fit, fully prepared, and able to perform their operational tasks. Put at its simplest perhaps, without the labours of that vast host of unhonoured, rarely publicised Erks, all air crews would be redundant.

On every frontline operational flying unit the air and ground crews were always merged into a single fighting team, each respecting the other's professionalism and varied skills. That mutual regard led to high morale and often outstanding achievements; moreover it also resulted in the highest form of true discipline. A clear example of such a situation is recorded by Reg Loffill, a navigator who flew Beaufighter ops with No 177 Squadron over Burma:*

* Extract from an unpublished account, *View from the Cupola* by R. Loffill.

The relationship between air crews and ground staff on the squadron was a very close one. They *cared* about 'their' air crews and 'their' aircraft. They worked all hours and fingers almost literally to the bone. When we landed they wanted to know immediately how we'd fared. It was obvious to the armourers from the state of the gun-port fabric whether or not cannon and wing guns had been fired, and from the rocket rails if these had been used. For our part our very lives depended on the quality of the work carried out by fitters and riggers, and the smooth operation of weaponry by the labours of the armourers. To be far away over enemy territory, subconsciously listening to the sound of the engines, we valued our groundstaff colleagues inestimably; they never let us down. On occasions when things did go wrong diagnosis of faults could rarely be attributed to faulty workmanship by 'the lads'.

So we mixed with 'the lads' socially, they to our messes and we to theirs, regularly and often. These contacts were very important and strengthened the bonds between us. Consciousness of rank so ingrained into members of any armed forces was at its lowest threshold here – and paradoxically efficiency was probably at its best. First-names and nicknames were in common use but no advantage was taken. I would pay a separate tribute to the wireless mechanics and radio operators who served us well. As a general rule we maintained W/T silence for this use of Morse telegraphy could be picked up many hundreds of miles away and was important information to listening Japanese. Radio Telephony (R/T) involved only short-range equipment. We used this mode within the last 100 miles to confirm our presence and be given a final course to steer. The obvious joy and relief in the operators' voices as they acknowledged our signals was evident. They knew we were safe.

How did the Erks themselves view their times on Beau units? Fred Pedgeon was a Flight Mechanic, Airframe when he first joined the ground staff of No 29 Squadron at Digby in 1940, and remained with the squadron when it moved to West Malling the following year:

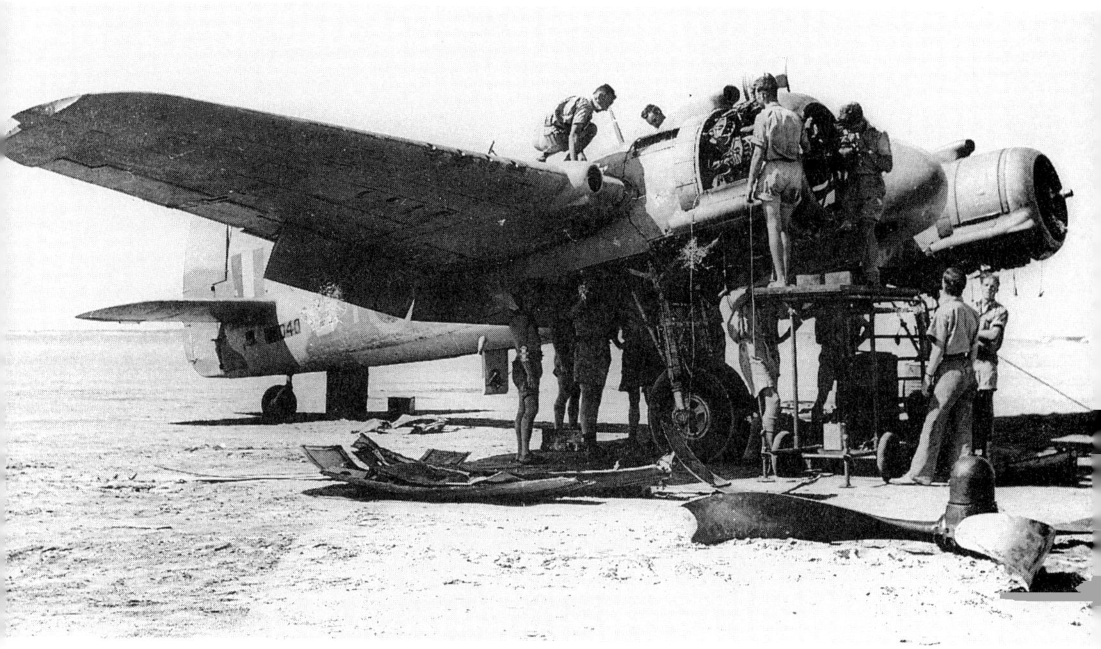

SAND BOYS. Erks of 252 Squadron overhauling Beau T5040 at Edku, mid-1942.

Major inspection at Edku, March 1943.

CANNON-FODDER. Armourers of 96 Squadron 'feeding' the 20mm Hispano cannons of Beau V8748, ZJ-R at Drem, October 1943. A posed scene purely for benefit of the media, since such a task was normally a two-man job at most ...!

Armourers loading a 3-inch RP with a 60lb HE head onto Beau TFX NE646, 'V' of an unidentified unit, Burma, 1944.

As an airframe mech, I felt very much part of a team, comprising the air crew and three flight mechanics. Though we recognised the importance of the other vital trades – armourers and fitters etc – we did not consider them to be actually part of *the* ground crew, as we were. The engine mech serviced and ran the engines, tested for mag drops, etc. The airframe mechs serviced all hydraulic and pneumatic systems, checked aircraft controls, and carried out undercarriage retraction tests. All three refuelled, locked and covered the aircraft against bad weather. They 'scrambled' with the air crew, secured them in their seats, often started the engines beforehand. They saw the aircraft in and out of dispersal, and worried about the air crew and 'their' aircraft's return. And when the aircraft did return they fought to get the engine bowser first. There were huge, heavy asbestos covers which had to be wrapped around the Beau's engines and heaters to be placed underneath – the English winters during the war were really something ...

Of course, just caring for the engines was not sufficient; the cockpit and rear cupola required covers, plus interior heaters to protect instruments against condensation, not forgetting the precious radar sets. It was often quite a game on a winter's night, lighting the internal heaters in an underground dispersal shelter and then staggering out into an icy howling wind – only to have the flame blow out again and again ... At a place like West Malling – a permanent station – life was busy but fairly comfortable. At a satellite 'drome, with the odd hut and hangar and thick mud, with no facilities, however, things could be *very* uncomfortable indeed ... yet despite the cold, skinned knuckles, and mud, servicing the Beau did in all honesty give us some sense of purpose and the feeling of a job well done.*

The foregoing comment about Erks' living and working conditions in the UK were borne out by Roy Spicer, an airframe mechanic who joined his first unit, No 255 Squadron in late 1940.†

After completing my airframes' course at Blackpool, I was posted to 255 at Kirton-in-Lindsey, Lincolnshire and duly attached to B

* See *Beaufighter at War* by C. Bowyer; Ian Allan, 1976
† Correspondence with author, 1975

> Flight. Although being allocated to a proper billet up on the main camp, most of that 1940-41 winter I spent at night trying to cat-nap in the dispersal hut, well away from the main camp areas, when our aircraft were 'up', which meant day and night flying and servicing. The weather was very wet with plenty of mud, and I recall having plenty of sticking controls and oil leaks to rectify on the Defiants with which the squadron was equipped until Beaus began arriving.
>
> During that inclement period I began to wonder what I'd let myself in for as a volunteer – almost three weeks at a stretch without getting into a proper bath or bed, and living in gum boots, sea socks, and a Balaclava headdress. As for the main camp, I saw very little of it or even managed to get far out of camp as most places were too far or too difficult to get to on a cold wet night. As the spring came and weather improved, the squadron was flying organised patrols which made life a little easier, although it was still almost a 24-hours working day. Then the squadron claimed their first night successes destroying night raiders, and it was truly a proud day when I had the honour of painting a swastika on my own aircraft.

The ever-present need for self-help and improvisation which was always the prime theme of every Erk's existence on any firstline squadron is perhaps part-exemplified by a few of the experiences of 'Bert' Chantrey, a sergeant who served with No. 600 Squadron Auxiliary Air Force – 'The Gallant 600' – from 1927-1945. Based at Cassibile, Sicily when the Allied forces invaded and occupied that island in late 1943, 600 Squadron was soon on the move again as the Allies prepared to continue their advance onto the Italian mainland, *Operation Avalanche* – the invasion of Italy at Salerno – taking place on 9 September 1943:

> Under the very noses of the enemy our advance forces had landed on the shallow beaches at points from Sorrento to beyond Salerno and had made a great clearance of the mines and other obstructions, laying out well-defined landing strips which were colour-coded to facilitate landing organisation. I seem to remember that we disembarked on 'Blue' strip in the vicinity of

(*Left*) Engine change for a 600 Squadron Beau in Italy, 1944 (*Right*) Sgt Wheeley and Cpl Haresign and unidentified Erk do a 'running repair' on a 600 Squadron Beau, Italy, 1944.

Australian erks giving an RAAF Beau a 'major', 1943.

Sorrento and men and vehicles proceeded at all speed up the beach, taking such cover as was afforded by shrubbery and other vegetation while the army and navy were weeding out the remaining opposition (the landing area was overlooked by a mountain range from which the Germans' observation posts had a commanding view) ...

Very slowly we pushed our way up the road in the direction of Monte Corvino to the accompaniment of spadmodic rifle fire and and occasionally something a little heavier. All went well for a time but eventually we came to a standstill, while many units had still not moved from the beaches. The Germans had mustered a little more opposition and skirmishes between the opposing forces were going on all around us so that we were not yet to get possession of our airfield (Monte Corvino). For a time things became so bad that to our own advance parties saving their own skins became a major task and RAF personnel were put directly under the control of the army.

So now at last we were to put to the test all the tricks of the trade we'd enjoyed learning during our toughening-up period of Commando training at Church Fenton preparatory to the North African landings in 1942. With some trepidation we were face to face with reality and after the initial shock which presumably all airmen experience when suddenly turned into soldiers, we convinced ourselves that, as in the air 600 had distinguished itself, now with Sten guns and extra ammunition we were about to add something new to our records as infantrymen. So, with other units, we were held in reserve to join in any last-ditch action if necessary, but at the crucial moment General Montgomery's 8th Army had fought its way up the coast and inland, cutting off the forward troops from the rest of the German army. This soon removed the pressure from our parent Command, the 34th Division, and we were able to move forward to Monte Corvino where camp was quickly established and we started to get organised. It was not an ideal spot but the orange trees gave us some cover, although the tomato plants beneath then were a real problem. In the end we lay our groundsheets on top of the plants, pitched our 'bivvys' (bivouac tents), and crawled in for a little rest. While the Sappers were busy clearing the mines on the airfield and filling in the bomb and shell holes, we set to making paths and roads and setting up larger tents for stores, messing, admin, etc. In the end our camp was so well organised and laid out that our own company of signwriters – known as 'City Signs Ltd' – had all tracks and paths signposted with names of London City roads well known at home. The airfield was now ready and safe for us to prepare for the arrival of our aircraft. The weather was miserable with the ground soft and muddy, and we had to work hard to keep to the high standard of efficiency we had up to now maintained.

One of our problems was to find enough undisturbed ground for dispersing our Beaufighters. So many bombs had landed on the airfield and it had been so plastered by shells from the Royal Navy that the filling-in process had left many soft spots. We had our work cut out debogging our aircraft. Fortunately the Germans had left behind quite a lot of valuable equipment, including huge inflatable bags which came in very useful for getting us out of our predicament. The general idea was to clear away under the wings as near the undercarriage as possible and push these bags under and inflate them; a tedious job with bicycle pumps! However, we succeeded eventually in 'acquiring' a compressor, and as the bag filled with air raising the aircraft inch by inch the ground under the undercarriage would be filled with hardcore. Also amongst the equipment captured were a number of BMW motor-cycles (promptly commandeered by members of the squadron for their personal use and pleasure ...), one or two Opel trucks, a very ingenious oil bowser fitted with a heating unit for use in cold weather and a highly efficient high-delivery pumping system – this latter much appreciated by the fitters and put to constant use for the rest of the Italian campaign. The weather was lousy; a condition which no doubt accounted for the falling off of enemy raids in the area during this period. Round about Christmas 1943 the airfield became waterlogged and some ground crews were moved to Gaudo from which our aircraft operated. Living conditions were pretty poor. We were wet through most of the time and so cold that we experimented with all sorts of devices to try to get warm at night when not on duty. The most effective method was to cut a hole in

(*Left*) Flg Off Edgar Welch (rt) and his skipper Ron Thorogood (hidden) receive the congratulations of Flt Sgt George Salter, BEM (hand on Welch's shoulder) and other ground staff of 27 Squadron at Agartala on 20/10/43 after claiming the squadron's 100th enemy locomotive destroyed that day.

(*Below*) Armourers preparing the 20mm cannons and engine mechs checking a 600 Squadron Beau prior to a night sortie, Italy, 1944.

a five- or ten-gallon oil drum and burn oil or dirty used petrol-soaked rags using shell cases (about 12 inches long), a number of which were joined together and put over the bung hole and extended up to the top of the tent and through the end flaps. It was a system *not* to be recommended for home use as the improvised flue pipe got red-hot and it was not an uncommon sight to see the tent fabric alight! After many such mishaps this form of heating was banned, and we then resorted to a more technical system using the small aircraft oxygen bottles removed from German aircraft in the 'Graveyard' – this was one corner of the airfield where many German fighters had found their last resting place – along with small-bore copper tubing and a jet made out of domed nuts with a small hole in the top through which atomised fuel passed. When assembled this lot gave us a form of pressure stove and on the whole worked well without being so dangerous.*

Les Green, who served with 89 Squadron, both in the North African campaigns and later in Ceylon, has a variety of memories of those momentous years:

In early 1943 we were stationed at Abu Sueir, an old peacetime station just west of the Suez Canal zone, but our Beau unit was under canvas on the far side of the airfield because the squadron commander, Wing Commander George Stainforth, AFC, had refused to be involved with the normal station activities. Then we were ordered to move and go up into the desert to follow the Eighth Army. All our tents, which had originally been 'camouflaged' by slopping old engine oil on them, then had sand brushed over the canopies, were dismantled from above the holes dug into the sand, folded and loaded into dozens of sand-coloured lorries specially supplied along with drivers, then the entire ground crew with all their equipment – admin and servicing – moved off following the one and only road which ran near the coast.

As the hours rolled by the heat of the sun increased and the

* *The City of London Squadron Magazine*, Summer 1965

only relief from the boredom of driving into the sun and the dust of the preceding vehicle in the convoy was a break for a meal – a hole in the sand, filled with petrol-soaked sand, with two long tyre levers acting as a grid providing a makeshift 'stove' to cook on. Fuel was taken on by all vehicles at army supply depots, issued in four-gallon 'Jerricans' which when empty could be used for other purposes such as wash-bowls or 'desert lilies' (funnel-shaped urinals). The distance covered was something just in excess of 100 miles per day, with night stops at the many army-maintained staging posts. Then bed rolls were laid out or on, or beside, the lorries, with washing limited to a quick sluice – everyone being restricted to one pint of water per day, while the tap on the water bowser had a lock and chain, removed only for issue under the eagle-eyed supervision of a senior NCO. In this way we eventually arrived at our LG, all with stubbly beards, then immediately unloaded the lorries, set up tents, domestic and operational, and within hours were ready for business, having moved something like a thousand miles in ten days non-stop apart from sleeping breaks and meals.

An example of 89 Squadron's *esprit de corps* – the spirit between air and ground crews engendered by our latest CO, Wing Commander David – occurred at Castel Benito, Tripoli. Following a minor inspection an air test was authorised for one Beau. As the tail came up on take-off and the Beau began to gain speed, it quickly left the ground with a perceptible nose-up attitude. To decrease the angle of climb the pilot put the elevator trim tab to more 'nose-down', but it soon became apparent that the angle of climb was increasing instead of decreasing and that a stall was imminent. He had already retracted the undercarriage so was left with no real alternative but to quickly close the throttles and belly-land in the overshoot area. He realised very quickly that the trim tab controls had been crossed, in spite of an independent SNCO check which was always made after any controls had been disconnected. During the ensuing court martial the pilot, a Pilot Officer and ex-Halton apprentice, refused to say that his life had been endangered, so the rigger and the SNCO were merely reprimanded. It was whilst the squadron was at Castel Benito that the CO instituted a scheme whereby the air crews had to assist the ground crews in DIs (Daily Inspections) and general maintenance of their aircraft, including cleanliness. The amount of 100-Octane fuel that was thrown into engine compartments and over mainplanes to clean off oil film does not bear thinking about!

The interior of a Beau was limited yet there was very good 'standing room only' on top of the front entrance door which was immediately behind the pilot's seat. This offered the opportunity for the ground crew to fly frequently, but led to at least two fatal accidents whilst 89 was based in Ceylon. An air test was in progress with a ground crew SNCO standing behind the pilot. A single-engine exercise had been carried out. The propeller feathering motor was electrically driven and, unfortunately, the internal accumulators were low. The generator was fitted to only one engine, and in this case it was to the engine which had been feathered, while all other electrics had been full on. When the time came to unfeather the dead engine the accumulators were by then too flat to operate the feathering motor. In the circuit red Very Lights were fired from the Beau and a single-engined landing was attempted on our very narrow jungle strip. To make this more traumatic there was a Beaufort torpedo squadron whose aircraft were being refuelled at the side of the strip. The single-engined Beau did a long flat approach but there was a cross wind and it touched down slightly off the runway, hit a refuelling bowser in front of the Beauforts and became engulfed in a ball of fire immediately. Thus died a very experienced Flight commander, his navigator, and the ground crew SNCO. From that day on all Beaufort aircraft were re-armed and refuelled much further back from the runway. Again, whilst in Ceylon, a daylight air test was being flown by another Flight commander (G. Webb) who had taken a ground crew Corporal along as well as his navigator. It would appear that one of the Hercules engine cylinders blew off and severed the cable around the engine cowling. A fire resulted and it was obvious that the aircraft would have to be abandoned quickly. The pilot gave instructions to his navigator to go out of the small back door exit, whilst the Corporal was told to open the door he'd been standing on, bale out, to be followed by the pilot. The Corporal was not

> enthusiastic about this state of affairs and, being something of a church man, began to pray out loud. The pilot by this time was very concerned that the fuel tanks would explode, and shouted at the corporal, 'Get the Hell out of here'. The outcome was that the pilot landed in a tree and broke his leg and was repatriated to the UK, but his navigator did not apparently operate his 'chute in time and was killed; it was thought he may have hit his head as he left the aircraft. The Corporal? With his parachute harness only clipped on by one strap, he spiralled down safely into a paddy field ...

For Harry Rhodes – inevitably nicknamed 'Dusty' – memories of his wartime service as an engine mechanic on various types of unit are reasonably typical of many thousands of his contemporaries, albeit somewhat fragmentary now after a lapse of some 40 years; a semi-kaleidoscope of the best – and worst – highlights of his four and a bit years in 'hairy blue' (*sic*):

> My chief memory of those times working out on dispersals is of being constantly cold and damp for most of the time. Our accommodation was a rusty Nissen hut with ten of us in beds inside. The only heating was the standard black stove halfway along the floor – the wartime version of 'central heating' – which needed an unending supply of wood, coal, coke, or anything else burnable which we could scrounge. Even then only the four beds nearest the stove gained any warmth from it. If you slept, as I did, further than four feet away from the stove you just froze in winter. Clothes – overalls, uniforms, etc – always felt damp; it's a wonder most of us didn't catch pneumonia!
>
> The only washing facilities consisted of a single tap – cold water, of course – sticking out of the ground just around the side of the Nissen. Meals were delivered to us by the cookhouse lorry twice a day, but we usually relied heavily on the Sally Army* canteen wagon which made regular calls every mid-morning and mid-afternoon at our dispersal site. The working week was, of course, seven days and seven nights if necessary – as our old sweat Chiefy (*Flight Sergeant*) was so fond of saying, 'You're paid for 24 hours every day, lad, so get on with it' ...

* i.e. Salvation Army

NOSE JOB. LAC R.L. Trusty with a Beau VIF of 406 Squadron RCAF at Valley, 22/4/43.

READY TO GO. Beaus of the Dallachy Strike Wing at Langham, 1945 ready to receive their air crews.

Working on the kites was a non-stop job. Even if there was no flying on the programme there were always dozens of little jobs to be done – checking systems, servicing components, testing engines and hydraulics, running up engines after servicing, or just cleaning the Beau inside and out. I remember one of our pilots, a pre-war type, who was really obsessed with having his Beau sparkling clean inside, especially in his front cockpit, and Lord help the erk who left any tools or rags inside when he'd finished his own job. When our Flight's Beaus were on ops we, the dispersal crew, worked like beavers to make sure 'our' kites were on top line, and when they returned every man was out on the dispersal anxiously counting the Beaus as they lobbed in again. When on one occasion one of our Beaus didn't return, I can still recall the sight of the little blonde WAAF driver who was waiting in a Bedford truck to take the air crews away crying her eyes out when she was told that the missing Beau had 'had it' (*i.e. been shot down*). As for the Beau's particular rigger and fitter, they just looked lost, as if they could not believe it.

On the other hand, life on a dispersal had plenty of lighter moments, thought the real humour of some situations would only be obvious to an ex-Erk. Like the engine fitter I worked with who sported a bloody great 'Flying Officer Kite' ginger moustache – it really was a beauty and you could see the tips of it even from behind him. One day were doing a pre-flight engine run-up and 'Bushy' was standing a bit too close to the engine cowl, perched on a big ammo box. Now Beau engines could be tricky when you first started them, and often would belch a burst of flames out of their exhaust. This happened on this occasion and 'Bushy' was blasted off his perch. When I picked him up he was scorched a bit round the edges – but his pride and joy had been frazzled down to the size of Hitler's mousy moustache!

On another occasion we had a couple of very young WAAF flight mechs foisted on us to learn a bit about their job. They were driven back and forth each day from their WAAF block miles away. Now our Beau pilots were supplied with a makeshift 'mobile urinal', commonly called a Pee-Tube, in case he was 'caught short' while flying, and it was one erk's first job to ask if the Pee-Tube had been used when his Beau landed. If it had,

FINAL CHORE. Beau of 27 Squadron gets its chocks removed for another sortie over Burma, 1944.

he'd immediately empty same, wash it out, then replace it in the cockpit. We decided to have a joke with one of the sprog WAAFs by taking a clean Pee-Tube filled with whisky out to the next Beau to arrive back at dispersal, keeping the tube well hidden from the WAAFs, of course. Well, the pilot got out, indicated that he'd used his tube, and the erk, accompanied by one WAAF nearby, took the 'specimen' out, then by sleight of hand, hid the real tube and calmly drank the whisky-filled tube! The little WAAF's eyes opened wide, then she was sick as a pig – all over the joker erk's overalls! A case of the biter being bit …

Looking back after all these years, I have some good and some not so good memories of my time as an airman. The good things were mainly the many friendships I made, many of them still very much alive even today. We all mucked in together, sharing work, clothes, even money when necessary – we looked after each other. On the bad side were such things as lousy pay – a few bob a day which went mainly on food, fags, and beer – and living conditions which at times felt like a throwback to the cave-dwellers.

On the whole, we got along well with our own air crews, who always seemed to appreciate our work and often dropped a few bottles of booze or some fags in to our Chiefy to hand around. Many of them were really only kids just out of school but they did a bloody good job, and I for one wouldn't have swapped with them. On the other hand some of the ground staff officers were real pigs to us whenever we made a rare visit to the main camp, SHQ, accounts, or wherever. A lot of these officers were first world war re-treads called up just for the war, and some of them seemed to think they were still fighting the Boer war! The biggest bane of our lives were the snoops [RAF Service Policemen]. Most I met were as thick as a NAAFI manageress's thighs and twice as nasty, and they seemed to delight in picking up erks for every possible reason and putting them on a fizzer.* I often wondered just whose side the SPs were on.'

The foregoing individual accounts from ex-Erks are patently a tiny selection from the myriad stories which could be told by that host of unpublicised airmen and airwomen whose labours and sacrifices made all air crews' tasks possible. If only to illustrate generically the massive support necessary to maintain the RAF's 'sharp end' through World War Two, perhaps a few bald statistics may provide a 'balanced' picture. As against the very small number of individual air crew categories – less than a dozen overall – there existed a total of slightly more than 350 distinct ground trades or sub-trades, ranging from skilled technical trades to the non-technical ACH/GDs (Aircraft Hand, General Duties). Of an estimated two million men and women who donned RAF or WAAF uniform throughout the war years, over 70 per cent were serving in non-flying capacities. And of *total* RAF personnel casualties incurred throughout 1939-45, air crew losses amounted to 70,253 killed, a further 22,924 wounded, and another 13,115 became prisoners of war. Ground crews of all types suffered totals of 9671 killed, and 4490 prisoners of war. A figure for ground crews

* Airmen's slang for a disciplinary charge.

wounded, injured, or otherwise incapacitated physically is impossible to collate from existing documentation. It should be added that such non-flying personnel statistics *include* both male and female personnel; WAAF recruits accepted for service during the whole war period ultimately totalling 217,249 airwomen of all ranks. To quote Milton; 'They also serve who only stand and wait' (*John Milton, 1608-1674, On His Blindness, xvi*).

Appendix 1

Squadrons equipped

NB: Squadrons listed below were the *main* units to employ Beaufighters and even these were not necessarily wholly or solely equipped with the type throughout the periods indicated. Code letters were those *officially* allocated, though a number of squadrons, particularly those based outside the UK, did not always carry such codes.

Sqn	*Periods*	*Codes*
5	Jan '50 – Sep '51	7B
17	Mar '49 – Mar '51	UT
22	Jun '44 – Sep '45	–
25	Sep '40 – Nov '42	ZK
27	Oct '42 – Feb '46	–
29	Sep '40 – May '43	RO
34	Feb '49 – Jul '51	8Q; 6J
39	Jun '43 – Jan '45	XZ
42	Oct '46 – Oct '47	QM
45	Dec '46 – Feb '50	OB
46	May '42 – Dec '44	FH
47	Jun '43 – Apr '45	KU
68	May '41 – Jul '44	WM
84	Nov '46 – Jan '49	PY
89	Oct '41 – Jul '45	–
96	May '42 – Nov '43	ZJ
108	Mar '43 – Mar '45	LD
125	Feb '42 – Mar '44	VA
141	Aug '41 – Jan '44	TW
143	Jun '41 – Apr '44	HO; NE

* Renumbered No.19 Sqn, SAAF on 15 Aug '44

Sqn	*Periods*	*Codes*
144	Jan '43 – May '45	PL
153	Jan '42 – Sep '44	TB
176	Jan '43 – Jul '45	–
177	May '43 – Jul '45	–
211	Aug '43 – May '45	UQ
217	Jul '44 – Sep '45	MW
219	Sep '40 – Jan '44	FK
227	Aug '42 – Aug '44*	–
235	Dec '40 – Jul '44	LA
236	Aug '41 – May '45	MB; ND; FA
248	Jul '41 – Jan '44	WR; DM
252	Dec '40 – Dec '46	PN; BT
254	Jun '42 – Sep '46*	QM; QY
255	Jul '41 – Feb '45	YD
256	May '42 – Apr '43	JT
272	Apr '41 – Apr '45	L7; XK
287	Nov '44 – Jun '46	KZ
307	Aug '41 – Feb '43	EW
404 RCAF	Sep '42 – Mar '45	EE; EO; 2
406 RCAF	Jun '41 – Aug '44	HU
409 RCAF	Aug '41 – Apr '44	KP
410 RCAF	Apr '42 – Jan '43	RA
455 RAAF	Dec '43 – May '45	UB
456 RAAF	Sep '41 – Jan '43	RX; PZ
488 RNZAF	Jun '42 – Sep '43	ME; NF
489 RNZAF	Nov '43 – Jun '45	P6
515	Jun '43 – Jan '44	3P
577	Nov '44 – Jul '45	3Y
600	Sep '40 – Dec '44	BQ; 6
603	Feb '43 – Dec '44	XT
604	Sep '40 – Feb '44	NG
695	Dec '48 – Feb '49	4M

* Disbanded/renumbered 42 Sqn RAF on 1 Oct '46

RAAF (SW Pacific Area)

Sqn	*Periods*	*Codes*
22	Dec '44 – Aug '46	DU
30	Mar '42 – Aug '46	LY
31	Sep '42 – Jul '46	EH
92	May '45 – Sep '45	OB
93	Jan '45 – Aug '46	SK

SAAF (Balkan Air Force)

16	Dec '43 – Jun '45	–
19	Aug '44 – Jun '45	–

Fleet Air Arm

721	Jul '45 – Nov '45
726	Jun '44 – Sep '44
728	Feb '44 – Jun '46
733	Jan '44 – Jul '45
736	Jul '45 – Sep '45
762	Mar '44 – ??? '45
770	May '45 – May '45
772	1945
775	May '44 – Nov '45
779	Jun '43 – Aug '45
781	Jun '43 – Oct '43
788	Apr '44 – Jan '45
797	Mar '44 – Aug '45
798	Oct '43 – Mar '44

USAAF

414th	Mar '43 (?) – Dec '44
415th	Mar '43 (?) – May '45
416th	Mar '43 (?) – May '45
417th	Mar '43 (?) – May '45

Misc Beaufighter user-units†

1692 Flt (later, 1692 BSTU); FIU; Nos. 2, 5, 9, 51, 54, 60, 63, 79, 132 OTUs; 1 TTU; 4 CAACU; AFDU; A&AEE; CFS; CGS; RAE; 1 BDU; 1 AAS; TFU; GRU; 301 FTU; Seletar Base Flt; 229 OCU; ASWDU; NRCU

† NB: Selected units only.

Appendix 2

Squadron and OTU bases (excluding detachments)

Squadrons	
17	Chivenor
22	Ratmalana, Vavuyina, Kumbhirgram, Dohazari, Joari, Chiringa, Ganavarum.
25	Martlesham Heath, North Weald, Debden, Wittering, Ballyhalbert, Church Fenton
27	Amarda Road, Kanchrapara, Agartala, Parashuram, Cholavarum, Ranchi, Agartala, Dohazari, Chiringa, Akyab, Mingaladon.
29	Digby, West Malling.
34	Horsham St Faiths.
39	Protville, Sidi Amor, Reghaia, Alghero, Grottaglie, Biferno.
42	Wittering, Church Fenton.
45	Thorney Island.
46	Edku, Luqa.
47	Protville, Sidi Amor, Gambut III, Amriya South, Cholavarum, Ranchi, Kumbhirgram.
68	High Ercall, Coltishall, Coleby Grange, Fairwood Common, Castle Camps
84	Seletar, Changi, Tengah, Habbaniya
89	Colerne, Abu Sueir, Bersis, Castel Benito, Bu Amud, Vavuyina, Minneriya, Vavuyina, Baigachi.
96	Wrexham, Honiley, Church Fenton, Drem, West Malling, Ford, Odiham.
108	Shandur, Luqa, Hal Far, Edku, Araxos, Kalamaki (Hassani).
125	Colerne, Fairwood Common, Exeter, Valley.
141	Ayr, Drem, Acklington, Tangmere, Ford, Predannack, Wittering, West Raynham.

143 Aldergrove, Thornaby, Dyce, Sumburgh, Dyce, Aldergrove, Limavady, Thorney Island, Docking, North Coates, St Eval, Portreath, North Coates.

144 Leuchars, Tain, Blida, Protville II, Tain, Wick, Davidstow Moor, Strubby, Banff, Dallachy.

153 Ballyhalbert, Portreath, Maison Blanche. Reghaia.

176 Dum, Dum, Baigachi, Vavuyina, Minneriya, Baigachi.

177 Phaphamau, Feni, Ranchi, Chiringa, Hathazari.

211 Phaphamau, Ranchi, Silchar, Bhatpara, Feni, Chiringa.

217 Ratmalana, Vavuyina, Gannavarum.

219 Catterick, Redhill, Tangmere, Acklington, Scorton, Catterick, Bone, La Sebala, Sidi Amor.

227 Luqa, Ta Kali, Edku, Derna, Magrun North, Gardabia West, Derna, Limassol, Nicosia, Berka III, Biferno.

235 Bircham Newton, Dyce, Sumburgh, Docking, Chivenor, Leuchars, Sumburgh, Leuchars, Portreath.

236 Carew Cheriton, Wattisham, Oulton, North Coates.

248 Bircham Newton, Dyce, Sumburgh, Gosport, Ta Kali, Dyce, Talbenny, Pembrey, Talbenny, Predannack, Portreath.

252 Chivenor, Aldergrove, Nutts Corner, Edku, Berka III, LG 91, Mersa Matruh, Gambut, Mersa Matruh, Hassani, Araxos.

254 Dyce, Docking, North Coates, Chivenor, Langham, Thorney Island.

255 Hibaldstow, Coltishall, High Ercall, Honiley, Maison Blanche Bone, Setif, La Sebala II, Bo Rizzo, Grottaglie, Foggia Main.

256 Squires Gate, Woodvale.

272 Chivenor, Abu Sueir, Edku, Khanka, Heliopolis, Edku, Ta Kali, Luqa. Bo Rizzo, Catania, Alghero, Foggia, Falconara, Catania.

287 Gatwick, Redhill, Hornchurch, Bradwell Bay, West Malling.

307 Exeter.

404 RCAF	Dyce, Chivenor, Tain, Wick, Davidstow Moor, Strubby, Banff, Dallachy.
406 RCAF	Acklington, Ayr, Scorton, Predannack, Middle Wallop, Valley, Exeter, Winkleigh.
409 RCAF	Coleby Grange, Acklington.
410 RCAF	Drem, Ayr, Scorton, Acklington.
455 RAAF	Leuchars, Langham, Dallachy.
456 RAAF	Valley.
488 RNZAF	Church Fenton, Ayr, Drem.
489 RNZAF	Leuchars, Langham, Dallachy.
515	Hunsdon, Little Snoring.
577	Castle Bromwich.
600	Catterick, Drem, Colerne, Predannack, Church Fenton, Portreath, Blida, Maison Blanche, Souk el Khemis, Luqa, Cassibile, Monte Corvino, La Banca, Voltone, Rosignano, Follonica, Falconara, Cesenatico.
603	Edku, Misurata West, Bo Rizzo, LG 91, Gambut, El Adem, Gambut.
604	Middle Wallop, Warmwell, Middle Wallop, Predannack, Ford, Scorton.
695	Horsham St Faiths.

OTUs

2(C)	Catfoss.
5(C)	Turnberry.
9(C)	Aldergrove, Crosby.
51	Debden, Cranfield.
54	Charterhall.
60	East Fortune.
63	Honiley.
79	Nicosia.
132	East Fortune.

Appendix 3

Beaufighters supplied to RAAF

(Total 218 allotted; 217 known delivered)

RAF Serial	*RAAF Serial*		
T4920	A19-1	T4993	A19-29
T4921	A19-2	T4994	A19-30
T4922	A19-3	T4995	A19-31
T4923	A19-4	T4996	A19-32
T4924	A19-5	T4997	A19-33
T4925	A19-6	T4998	A19-34
T4926	A19-7	T4999	A19-35
T4927	A19-8	T5000	A19-36
T4928	A19-9	T5001	A19-37
T4929	A19-10	T5002	A19-38
T4930	A19-11	T5003	A19-39
T4931	A19-12	T5004	A19-40
T4943	A19-13	T5047	A19-41
T4944	A19-14	T5048	A19-42
T4945	A19-15	T5049	A19-43
T4946	A19-16	T5050	A19-44
T4947	A19-17	T5051	A19-45
T4970	A19-18	T5052	A19-46
T4971	A19-19	T5053	A19-47
T4972	A19-20	T5054	A19-48
T4973	A19-21	T5055	A19-49
T4974	A19-22	T5070	A19-50
T4975	A19-23	T5071	A19-51
T4976	A19-24	T5072	A19-52
T4977	A19-25	T5073	A19-53
T4978	A19-26	T5074	A19-54
T4991	A19-27	T5076	A19-55
T4992	A19-28	T5081	A19-56

RAF Serial	*RAAF Serial*	*RAF Serial*	*RAAF Serial*
T5083	A19-57	EL244	A19-92
T5084	A19-58	EL438	A19-93
T5090	A19-59	EL241	A19-94
T5091	A19-60	EL443	A19-95
T5077	A19-61	EL435	A19-96
T5089	A19-62	T5263	A19-97
T5075	A19-63	T5295	A19-98
T5082	A19-64	T5296	A19-99
T5094	A19-65	EL413	A19-100
T5093	A19-66	EL395	A19-101
T5095	A19-67	EL396	A19-102
T5097	A19-68	JL430	A19-103
T5099	A19-69	JL429	A19-104
T5098	A19-70	EL412*	A19-105
T5086	A19-71	EL510	A19-106
T5092	A19-72	EL411	A19-107
T5200	A19-73	EL520	A19-108
T5201	A19-74	EL518	A19-109
T5205	A19-75	T5328	A19-110
T5203	A19-76	T5327	A19-111
T5202	A19-77	T5330	A19-112
T5204	A19-78	JL584	A19-113
EL243	A19-79	T5331	A19-114
EL245	A19-80	T5329	A19-115
EL246	A19-81	JL582	A19-116
EL260	A19-82	JL841	A19-117
EL261	A19-83	JL826	A19-118
EL259	A19-84	T5336	A19-119
T5262	A19-85	T5338	A19-120
T5254	A19-86	JL839	A19-121
T5264	A19-87	JL838	A19-122
T5255	A19-88	JL837	A19-123
T5257	A19-89	T5337	A19-124
T5270	A19-90	JL840	A19-125
EL436	A19-91	T5339	A19-126

* Crashed in UK; repaired; delivered to RAF in India

RAF Serial	*RAAF Serial*	*RAF Serial*	*RAAF Serial*
T5341	A19-127	LX988	A19-164
T5340	A19-128	LX989	A19-165
T5342	A19-129	LX990	A19-166
JL848	A19-130	LX991	A19-167
JL853	A19-131	LX992	A19-168
JL847	A19-132	LX993	A19-169
JL850	A19-133	LX994	A19-170
JL854	A19-134	LX995	A19-171
T5343	A19-135	LZ195	A19-172
T5344	A19-136	LZ196	A19-173
JM175	A19-137	LZ197	A19-174
JM182	A19-138	LZ198	A19-175
JM183	A19-139	LZ199	A19-176
JM184	A19-140	LZ200	A19-177
JM168	A19-141	LZ201	A19-178
JM177	A19-142	LZ215	A19-179
JM134	A19-143	LZ321	A19-180
JM135	A19-144	LZ322	A19-181
JM185	A19-145	LZ323	A19-182
JM169	A19-146	LZ324	A19-183
JM171	A19-147	LZ325	A19-184
JL946	A19-148	LZ326	A19-185
JM285	A19-149	LZ327	A19-186
JM286	A18-150	LZ328	A19-187
JM176	A19-151	NE357	A19-188
JM120	A19-152	NE229	A19-189
JM282	A18-153	NE360	A19-190
JM283	A19-154	NE231	A19-191
JM284	A19-155	NE232	A19-192
JM170	A19-156	NE245	A19-193
JM236	A19-157	NE358	A19-194
JM131	A19-158	NE359	A19-195
JM272	A19-159	NE361	A19-196
JM167	A19-160	NE230	A19-197
JM165	A19-161	NE356	A19-198
JM273	A19-162	NE482	A19-199
JM164	A19-163	NE485	A19-200

NE484	A19-201	NE697	A19-216
NE483	A19-202	NE698	A19-217
NE487	A19-203	LX815	A19-218.
NE584	A19-204		
NE585	A19-205	*NB:*	
NE573	A19-206	RAF Mks	RAAF Serials
NE574	A19-207	1c	A19-1 to A19-72 inc
NE586	A19-208	VIc	A19-73 to A19-136 inc
NE587	A19-209	X	A19-149 & -150
NE588	A19-210		A19-153 to 155 inc
NE589	A19-211		A19-159
NE693	A19-212		A19-162
NE694	A19-213		A19-164 to 218 inc
NE695	A19-214	XI	Remainder
NE696	A19-215		

Associated Literature

The following past published books *et al* have direct relevance to the Beaufighter's service, and are commended to the reader seeking further in-depth data of the overall subject.

Bristol aircraft since 1910, C.H. Barnes; Putnam, 1964
Beaufighter, R.H. Macaulay; Gale & Polden, 1944
Air Publication 1721, Air Ministry, 1940 etc.
RAF in the World War, Vols 1-4, N. Macmillan; Harrap, 1942
RAF 1939-45, Vols 1-3, H. Saunders; HMSO, 1953
RAAF Official History, Vols 1-4, AWM, 1954
RNZAF Official History, Vols 1-3, OUP, 1953
The RCAF Overseas, Vols 1-3, OUP, 1944-49
RAAF over Europe, Eyre & Spottiswoode, 1946
Desert Air Force, R. Owen; Hutchinson, 1948
Briefed to Attack, H.P. Lloyd; Hodder & Stoughton, 1948
Winged Phoenix, HMSO, 1945
The Defence of the UK, B. Collier; HMSO, 1957
Fighter Command, P. Wykeham; Putnam, 1960
The Dangerous Skies, A. Clouston; Cassell, 1954
Cover of Darkness, R. Chisholm; Chatto & Windus, 1953
Night Fighter, Rawnsley/ Wright; Collins, 1957
Night Flyer, L. Brandon; Wm Kimber, 1961
Scramble, J. Braham; Wm Kimber, 1985 (new ed)
Tumult in the clouds, A. Cunningham; P. Davies, 1953
Task for Coastal Command, H. Bolitho; Hutchinson, 1944
Coastal Command leads the invasion, Wilson/Robinson; Jarrolds, 1945
Two steps to Tokyo, G. Powell; OUP, 1945
Defence until dawn, L. Hunt; 1949
Desert Squadron, V. Houart; Souvenir Press, 1959
Four, Five, Five, J. Lawson; 1951

The Flying Elephants, C. Bowyer; Macdonalds, 1972
404 Squadron RCAF, Private, 1972
Fighter squadrons of the RAF, J. Rawlings; Macdonalds, 1969
Coastal & Support squadrons of RAF, J. Rawlings; Jane's, 1982
Twenty-One Squadrons, L. Hunt; Garnstone Press, 1972
Aircraft of the RAF since 1918, O. Thetford; Putnam, 1976
The British fighter since 1912, P. Lewis; Putnam, 1967
Test pilot at war, H. Taylor; Ian Allan, 1970
Profile No. 137, P. Moyes; Profiles Pubs.
Beaufighter at War, C. Bowyer; Ian Allan, 1976
Whispering Death, N. Parnell; A & A Reed, Australia, 1980
RCAF Squadrons & Aircraft, Kostenuk/Griffin; Canadian Museum, 1977
Coastal Command at War, C. Bowyer; Ian Allan, 1979
Men of Coastal Command, C. Bowyer; Wm Kimber, 1985
Men of the Desert Air Force, C. Bowyer; Wm Kimber, 1984
Desert Air Force at War, C. Bowyer/C. Shores; Ian Allan, 1981
Fighters over the desert, Shores/Ring; Spearman, 1969
Fighters over Tunisia, Shores/Ring/Hess; Spearman, 1975
RAF Middle East, HMSO, 1945
The Air Battle of Malta, HMSO, 1944
Camouflage & Markings, No.9, Ducimus Books, n/d.
The Winged Bomb (39 Squadron), K. Delve; MC Pubs, 1985
RAF Unit Histories, J. Halley; Air Britain, 1969 & 1973
Archive, Bristol Beaufighter, F. Mason; Container Pubs, n/d.
Blitz on Britain, A. Price; Ian Allan, 1977
The Strike Wings, R. Nesbit; Wm Kimber, 1984
Night Intruder, J. Howard-Williams; David & Charles, 1976
Beaufighters over Burma, D. Innes; Blandford, 1985
The Book of Bristol Aircraft, Ed: D. Russell; Harborough, 1946
Night Fighters, W. Gunston; PSL, 1976
Sent flying, W. Pegg; Macdonald, 1959
British Military Aircraft Serials, B. Robertson; Ian Allan, 1979
The Israeli Air Force Story, Rubenstein/Goldman; Arms & Armour, 1978
RAAF Publication No.615, RAAF HQ, 1945
These Eagles, AWM, Canberra, 1942
RAAF Log, AWM, Canberra, 1943

RAAF Saga, AWM, Canberra, 1944
Victory Roll, AWM, Canberra, 1945
Aircraft & Markings, RAAF, 1939-45, G. Pentland; Lansdowne Press, 1970
Eagles Victorious, Martin/Orpen; Purnell, 1977
The Dangerous Sky, T. Coughlin; Ryerson Press, 1968

Index

A separate index of place names follows on page 284

Index of place names

Beau squadrons (RAF unless otherwise indicated)